Hypertext and Hypermedia

Theory and Applications

Nigel Woodhead

 **SIGMA PRESS**

Wilmslow, England

 ADDISON-WESLEY PUBLISHING COMPANY

Wokingham, England · Reading, Massachusetts · Menlo Park, California
New York · Don Mills, Ontario · Amsterdam · Bonn · Sydney
Singapore · Tokyo · Madrid · San Juan

Cover designed by Crayon Design of Henley-on-Thames
Typeset in Great Britain by Manchester Free Press, Manchester
Printed in Great Britain by Dotesios Printers Ltd, Trowbridge, Wiltshire

First printed 1990

ISBN: 0-201-54442-3

British Library Cataloguing in Publication Data

A CIP catalogue record for this book is available from the British Library

Library of Congress Cataloguing in Publication Data available

Preface

This is a book about hypertext and hypermedia — an approach to linking and structuring all forms of computerized materials. I hope the book will be of interest and use to software development professionals, technical authors, electronic publishers and teachers, as well as computer science, information technology and business studies students. It assumes no great specialist knowledge of any of the areas discussed, apart from a basic familiarity with microcomputers.

The book itself is structured in a modular fashion so that not all readers will have to read or refer to all chapters — rather, each chapter examines hypermedia issues from a different perspective. Thus in the small but growing tradition of hypermedia (printed) texts, this book can be seen as a set of semi-parallel essays, or partially overlapping segments of a picture, each viewed from a different perspective. Use the book to assess the applicability of hypertext and hypermedia to new projects, and as a first filter on the selection of suitable off-the-shelf packages. Comprehensive listings detail primary sources and distributors in both Europe and the US, as well as an up-to-date bibliography.

The goals of the book are to present a rapidly expanding commercial technology and some of the theory that lies behind it. It also illustrates by example the vast potential for hypermedia use — from databases and intelligent information retrieval, to application and project management, electronic publishing and libraries, as well as the developing sub-culture of interactive media. Separate sections deal with hypermedia products in relation to all of these areas, and provide a conceptual map of how hypertext and hypermedia relate to each, as well as how hypermedia relates to the potentially even larger multimedia market.

For the first-time hypermedia user, I have attempted to define the core set of tools that constitutes a hypermedia system, and to sketch out a rough draft for a methodological approach to building standardized materials and applications. I hope that my own background experience and interests (psychology, artificial intelligence and computing, electronic publishing) have allowed me to present something lacking in the hypermedia literature; a discursive overview, and a synthesis of some of the many different disciplines which are relevant. If some of what follows appears relatively speculative for a computing text, I should perhaps ask for the reader's forbearance. Here is a potentially vast new field. Hypothesis precedes experimentation precedes theory. Hypermedia has a unique ability to impose alternative structures onto diverse materials, and in this respect it offers a paradigm that should encourage open attitudes and experimentation.

Paradoxically, there is probably no all-encompassing set of features that sets a hypermedia system or application apart from other more conventional programs. In fact, in many cases hypermedia will be the means by which it is possible to integrate the materials originated by other more specialized software. Indeed, there is an increasing trend to incorporate hypertext features in packages as diverse as spreadsheets, text processors and even expert systems shells. In the medium term future it is likely that hypermedia features will become central to common application architecture standards.

My first serious exposure to hypermedia was via Apple Computer's HyperCard, soon after its launch in 1987. I was struck by its remarkably user-friendly interface — capitalizing on the best aspects of Macintosh systems — not to mention its programming power and flexibility. The Press was divided as to what this new kind of software could be used for, and even as to whether it would ever prove to be useful for serious applications. The industry at large seems to have had fewer reservations. In the last couple of years a score of other commercial hypermedia packages has been released for desktop computers, and for the more powerful benchtop workstations. What has for over 20 years been a tool of isolated (and often outspoken) computer scientists is now out from the laboratories, and with a vengeance. It now seems timely to compile an overview of these packages. They form the forefront of a general technology that is set in the 1990s to become vital to as many commercial and academic organizations as have the imagination to make use of it.

Acknowledgements

Throughout the text references are made to specific commercial products and organizations. These names, trade marks and registered trade marks are all acknowledged to be the copyright and property of their respective owners. With thanks also to the many individuals who have helped by providing information and time, and without whom this book would not have been possible.

Contents

1 Introduction

1.1 A Brief Note About Terminology

Readers without experience of hypermedia will probably find it useful to familiarize themselves with the following terms before commencing on the rest of the book. Further jargon words can be found in the Glossary.

Media:

The most basic technologies of communicating and storing information. At their most general media include everyday human languages, music, pictures and film. They also include the formal code by which they are transcribed, the physical materials on which they are stored and the conventions by which they are organized into collections. Often these media overlap — a user may need to consult several media to solve any one problem. For instance, paper, books, and libraries are all forms of media — corresponding perhaps to operational, tactical and strategic levels of purpose. Traditionally, the boundary between individual items of storage media have proved a great hurdle. This book discusses possible ways in which these boundaries can be usefully reduced.

Browsing:

Strategy used in following or developing a path through information nodes; browsing may be with a specific or general purpose. Browsing is taken to be an activity at a relatively microscopic level. This is contrasted with navigation, which establishes the general location of information relative to the corpus in which it is stored.

Hyper-:

This prefix has a dictionary meaning of above, excessive or beyond. Its use in computing, as exemplified below, is perhaps related to analogous jargon or buzzwords coined by the science fiction community, e.g. hyperspace, a speculative extra physical dimension.

The hyper prefix now has a strong historical momentum, and seems likely to endure. However, with hindsight other prefixes such as meta- (among, about or between), or inter- might have been more accurate descriptors of the structural emphasis of hypermedia; the 'hyper-level' is strictly at a meta-level to the semantic or content level. (It may be interesting to note that in the meantime, metatext has become a favourite term of the Structuralist schools of literary criticism, and Intermedia is the proprietary name of an advanced hypermedia system.)

Hypermedia:

Taken to be a generic approach to constructing non-linear, computer-supported materials, as embodied by a number of commercial and academic program shells; the term is also used to describe the materials themselves. Hypermedia itself is a subset of the more general class of interactive multimedia — not all implementations of which support 'hyper' functionality. The term hypermedia will be used throughout this book unless the context is uniquely text-based, in which case hypertext will be preferred. Hypermedia is used here as a singular noun, as per the accepted contemporary use of the strictly plural noun data.

Hypertext:

Hypertext, and hypertext programs are a subset of hypermedia and hypermedia programs (albeit the largest, most central, and probably the most commercially significant, see Figure 1.1). Ted Nelson claims to have originally coined the term hypertext (meaning writing with and for the computer) in the early 1960s.

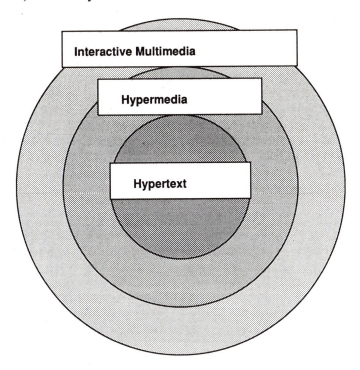

Figure 1.1 Hypertext is a subset of Hypermedia; Hypermedia is a subset of general Interactive Multimedia Technologies.

Hyperdocuments:

There is no consensus as to what the data in hypermedia applications should be called. The terms hyperbase, (hyper-)object, and (hyper-)document have been variously used by authors, and all have been used in different contexts in the present text where it is necessary to distinguish data from programs. No great significance should be attached to these terms — each implies an emphasis of the system or application rather than a large qualitative difference. The difference between byte-based and fragment-based access to information in hypermedia systems is discussed more fully in the Chapter 7 (Style, Rhetoric and Methodology).

Multimedia:

A superset of hypermedia and other interactive technology approaches.

According to this view not all multimedia approaches support the kind of referential structures sufficient to justify their being termed hypermedia.

Navigation:

Use of abstract features, structure or other cues and tools, for general orientation; directing a change of focus or movement in relation to the entire available knowledge database.

Nodes:

The microfeatures of a hypermedia system; often known as chunks. Nodes are connected by links, in a variety of possible structures such as webs and hierarchies.

Users:

The word users is preferred to readers, as implying a more active mode of interaction with the application. In hypermedia there is often a narrow distinction between users and authors.

1.2 The Structure of the Book

The present Introduction deals with the kinds of facilities which are generic to hypertext and hypermedia systems, and how these have developed historically. It is intended mainly for those with minimal knowledge of the field. The rest of the book is divided into three main sections.

A more detailed description of the hypermedia approach is given in Section I - The Potential of Hypermedia; Chapter 2 describes the formal characteristics of hypermedia and compares them with related approaches in information science, such as databases; Chapter 3 discusses the particular relevance of hypermedia and artificial intelligence to each other. Chapter 4 reviews the implications of hypermedia for the electronic publishing industry.

Section II of the book deals with hypermedia issues from the perspective of systems owners, authors and users. Package-specific information is given in Section III, and in the Appendices.

The discipline of hypermedia potentially brings with it new implications and possibilities for the structure of printed materials. In the present text it is envisaged that not every reader will wish to read every chapter — particularly of Sections II and III. In keeping with the small but growing tradition of books about hypermedia, it should be said that you do not need to read this book from front to back covers. Information has been structured therefore with a degree of overlap, so that readers will be able to pick out a customized, modular path that best suits their own interests.

1.3   History of Hypermedia — an Overview

1.3.1   The Scholar's Workstation

The concept of a mechanized support tool for thinking has a long pedigree — almost as long as those of the number-crunching and record-keeping paradigms which still dominate computing. One of the first, and to date, most articulate proponents of what we now call hypermedia, was Vannevar Bush[4], senior Science Advisor to President Roosevelt, and administrator of the wartime Manhattan Project.

Bush foresaw a time when data communications, automation and miniaturisation would combine to aid thinkers from every domain. A number of leaders in the field have acknowledged a debt of inspiration to Bush's ideas. His plan for a Memex device is designed around the concept of association — in both the traditional philosophical and more recent psychophysiological senses. He describes the Memex as "*a sort of mechanized private file and library*". This device would support selection of information by association rather than by indexing. Users would be able record and annotate items, and link them by trails which are then named and stored. He even conjectures on the possibility of direct human sensory input/output — by means of everyday media such as the voice, for instance.

The actual implementation Bush suggests is based on the technology of the day — microfilm, facsimile, photocell and telegraph, with information stored in a desk and accessed by means of levers. However, anyone reading his ideas today cannot fail to be struck by the overall accuracy of his vision. By contrast, the early pioneers of hypertext (as it was until the advent of graphics displays) were often seen as eccentrics within the computing community. Attempts to build a Memex-like machine were often hampered by lack of funding. The current wave of popular hypermedia applications had to await advances in the field of digital computing borne out of other, more mundane approaches to information.

Conventional databases, text processors and other specialist, divisive applications now all seem to be reaching a development plateau. Many now accept that the data processing approach is not sufficient to fulfill the Information Revolution proper; information is qualitatively superior to data, and a qualitative model will be needed to complement it. Only five years ago Bush's conjectures were still seen as fantastic — by those few who had heard of them. But now with the proliferation of powerful personal computers, and the advent of technologies such as natural language and virtual sensory environments, their realization seems imminent. It will also be argued in this book that a subtle change in attitude is occurring among computer users in many disciplines, and particularly in the academic humanities, leading to a rapid uptake of hypermedia.

By the early 1960s the basic computing technology was available to produce primitive prototype hypertext systems. Most of the early hypertext systems are characterized by their idiosyncratic, experimental flavor, their limitations on the size of nodes and amount of information to be displayed at any one time, and by their exclusive implementation on the predecessors of what we now know as mainframe or minicomputers. Early VDU displays could display text characters but not graphics. The QWERTY keyboard was the only available input device — a far cry from today's near-standard WIMP interfaces.

Among the pioneers of this period were Douglas Engelbart at Stanford[6,7], and the somewhat itinerant evangelist of hypermedia, Ted Nelson[9,13]. Engelbart's ideas developed into the NLS (On-line System) and later Augment systems. These are based around a hierarchical text-fragment database, mediated by selective 'view filters' and display 'views'. These filters allowed hierarchy-based operations such as level-clipping and truncation, and could be extended using the system's own high-level description language. Among the innovative features of NLS were its multi-user capability and multiple windowing, as well as two peripheral command devices to enhance the keyboard — the chord keys and the mouse. Engelbart also pioneered the use of dedicated function keys, providing access to context-sensitive Help. The Augment system is still in use with the aerospace manufacturers, McDonnell-Douglas[5].

Nelson's Project Xanadu was even more ambitious from the outset, and is only now coming to fruition[10]. Both Bush and Engelbart believed in the ability of a machine to enhance man's intelligence, and to communicate that intelligence; the emphasis, however, is on personal information, which is stored locally. For 30 years Nelson's vision has been to establish a common-access world depository of electronic literature and other materials. This database is to be accessed through a front end that automatically collects and distributes royalty payments. The actual user interface requires multi-windowing capability and a powerful but accessible query/command language; great attention continues to be given to the ideal of accessing information at the arbitrary, point-to-point byte level, rather than at the level of authors' predetermined node 'chunks' — as supported by the link structures of other hypertext implementations.

Typical of this latter, more pragmatic, chunk-based model of hyper-text was Randall Trigg's Textnet thesis[12]. Most of today's commercial hypermedia systems have also chosen this paradigm. However, few have taken up Trigg's notion of extensible typed links — i.e. that links can be defined with an associated name describing the relationship between nodes. Only the most ambitious systems now give users the ability to define their own link types. (See Sections 3.2 and 7.1 for a discussion of the role of typed links in hypermedia.) Trigg's ideas continue to be influential in the development of Xerox's NoteCards[11].

One of the best-known hypertext systems of the 1970s was ZOG, a frame-based text database developed at Carnegie-Mellon University[1]. Hierarchically linked, ZOG's screen-sized frames of information and menu options provided a consistent interface. It also offered an environment suitable for multiple users, allowing it to be applied to areas such as teleconferencing and computer-based training. In 1982, ZOG was networked on the state-of-the-art nuclear aircraft carrier USS Carl Vinson, as a ship-wide information and management system. It has since been continually extended in several versions. The commercial version, KMS (Knowledge Management System) now incorporates graphics facilities along with text. This ability to handle graphics as well as textual notes was fundamental in Vannevar Bush's model of the thinking machine, as reflecting one of the commonest everyday means which people use to store and communicate information.

1.3.2   From Hypertext to Hypermedia

Among the other early hypertext systems that have been augmented with graphics facilities are Hyperties, from the University of Maryland, and Intermedia, from Brown University's Institute for Research in Information and Scholarship. The trend was much boosted by the introduction of high-resolution screen displays, and the mass production of memory chips capable of driving them. These advances would eventually lead to practicable hypermedia packages for personal microcomputers.

So far this history of hypermedia has dealt mainly with systems implemented on early mainframes and minicomputers. The focus of attention has now shifted to the personal computing arena. One of the earliest microcomputer implementations of hypermedia was Guide. This was originally developed by Peter Brown at University of Kent[3] to run under the UNIX operating system, but was quickly ported to other environments. Although at first it was not as ambitious in its facilities as some of its predecessors, the original version supported hierarchical document struc-tures, multiple scrolling windows, and replacement buttons. Central to priorities was the maxim that there should be no difference between readers and authors, in terms of the facilities provided for their use. The much-improved commercial versions of Guide for PC-compatibles and the Apple Macintosh have a very similar feel, and are among the most successful in the field (see Chapters 9 and 10).

The most significant break-through in terms of popularizing hypermedia came with Apple Computer's decision to bundle a program called HyperCard with new Macintosh machines. HyperCard offered users the ability to link text and graphics, to multi-task between other applications, and for the first time a really user-friendly, high-level programming environment was available for the Macintosh — with HyperTalk. HyperCard combines aspects of relational database models with the ability to integrate materials from heterogeneous external sources such as digitized audio and video. It capitalizes on the graphical Macintosh interface — the use of mouse-driven menus, buttons and icons, as well as providing conceptually simple development tools.

1.3.3 Out of the Margins

It is now nearly half a century since Bush formulated his plans for the Memex. Five years ago the word hypertext was still hardly known outside of the largest US computer science laboratories. It is less than three years since Apple Computer began to bundle HyperCard with new machines. Since then, there has been a growing flood of commercial software marketed as hypertext, hypermedia, intelligent tutoring systems and interactive multimedia. Much of this software runs on personal microcomputers. Yet this software also allows users to link their computers to the hardware of other technologies — to drive CD-ROM, video players, synthesizers or editing suites — that until now have been developing in near isolation[8]. In effect, we are on the verge of the realization of Bush's vision — the individual's multimedia, desk(-top) Memex.

However, we are still some way short of being offered what Nelson calls 'co-operative' hypermedia systems — in which the file formats and interface protocols are transparent to users, and via which users can themselves collaborate. Unless developers can agree common standards of this kind hypermedia will remain a set of tools capable of taming vast forests of information, but used only to trim the scrublands.

1.3.4 The Electronic Alexandria

Modern computers provide a delivery device capable of providing the user with materials from many sources, in many formats, within a common framework. This synergistic approach means that users are no longer limited to a static view or context of information within a single document or application. It provides continuity between the means to reduce the amount of detail accessed, the means to increase it, and the means to manipulate it in a totally new way or in an arbitrary direction.

In the creative media we are seeing a move away from the traditional model in which individuals produce single (often single media) works. Instead, we are increasingly using or witnessing collaborative, process (often multimedia) models of production. This is one aspect of — or the first stage of — the Information Society, the Society of Text which commentators such as Nelson have long been proclaiming[2.9]. The other side of this commercial revolution, still to be realized, is a community of interactive information users; the social model of (hypermedia) information end-users has yet to be accepted. Furthermore, a community of users requires a community of co-operative applications, and that patently does not yet exist. Rather, we have several hundred data 'standard' formats. This diversity continues to increase.

Even within an individual library, the problems involved in providing local, online access to materials are immense. The best facility most users can expect to find at present is an online indexing system. These still tend to be primitive — based on alphabetic subject, title and author categorization — so that the only advantage over their cardfile predecessors is in terms of speed. However, the individual technologies needed to implement large-scale, distributed libraries and hypermedia databases are now available, and ambitious prototype systems are being developed[7, 8]. There is the potential to provide very real improvements in the quality of general information, as well as the efficiency with which it may be used. Perhaps most importantly, the ease with which it may be used by those without specific expertise either in the subject or in the use of computers. These issues are taken up in the following chapters. Some of the technologies and approaches to which hypermedia has particular relevance are summarized in Figure 1.2:

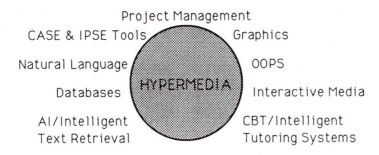

Figure 1.2 Hypermedia in relation to other computer-based technologies and disciplines.

Perhaps the most exciting of all the developments imminent in hypermedia is a new class of hybrid software. All the signs point towards a decade characterized by tools with which the flexibility of user-driven information management (the relational database, for instance) will be augmented by the inference-making and natural language techniques of artificial intelligence. These topics are given special attention in Chapter 3.

SUMMARY: HYPERMEDIA AS A UNIFYING PARADIGM

The hypermedia approach was foreseen accurately 40 years before technology had advanced sufficiently to implement it on a commercial scale.

Developments in hypermedia systems have often been closely linked with innovations which we already take for granted — such as the mouse and dedicated function keys.

The hypermedia approach is not a specific technology limited to a narrow informational domain — as epitomized by single, non-computerized media, traditional databases, or text and graphics processing software. It goes beyond the means to structure groups of documents seamlessly. In fact that is only half the story. Rather, it is potentially a unifying paradigm for the present diversity where each task or material requires a specialized and independent tool. The seamless hypermedia environment is the idealized application manager; its functionality persists between applications rather than being unique to each of them. This model provides the ability both to increase the quality of heterogeneous information, and to increase the ease with which it can be used, by making consistent the tools for its presentation and manipulation.

REFERENCES

1. Akscyn, R., McCracken, D. and Yoder, E. KMS: A distributed hypermedia system for managing knowledge in organizations. *Communications of the ACM,* **31 (7)**, July 1988, pp. 820-835.

2. Barrett, E. Textual intervention, collaboration, and the online environment. In: Barrett, E. (Ed.), *The Society of Text*. Cambridge, MA: MIT Press, 1989.

3. Brown, P. Interactive documentation. *Software — Practice and Experience,* **16 (3)**, March 1986, pp. 291-299.

4. Bush, V. As we may think. *Atlantic Monthly,* **176 (1)**, July 1945, pp. 101-108.

5. Conklin, J. Hypertext: An introduction and survey. *Computer,* **20 (9)**, September 1987, pp. 17-41.

6. Engelbart, D. A conceptual framework for the augmentation of man's intellect. In: *Vistas in Information Handling*, Vol. 1, London: Spartan Books, 1963.

7. Fiderio, J. A grand vision. *Byte,* **13 (10)**, October 1988, pp. 237-244.

8. McClelland, B. Hypertext and online... a lot that's familiar. *Online,* **13 (1)**, January 1989, pp. 20-25.

9. Nelson, T. (1981). *Literary Machines*. Swathmore, PA: Nelson.

10. Nelson, T. Managing immense storage. *Byte,* **13 (1)** January 1988, pp. 225-238.

11. Trigg, R. Guided tours and tabletops: tools for communicating in a hypertext environment. *ACM Transactions on Office Systems,* **6 (4)**, October 1988, pp. 398-414.

12.   Trigg, R. and Weiser, M. TEXTNET: a network-based approach to text handling. *ACM Transactions on Office Information Systems*, **4 (1)**, January 1986. pp. 1-23.

13.   Van Dam, A. Hypertext '87 keynote address. *Communications of the ACM*, **31 (7)**, July 1988, pp. 887-895.

Section I

The Potential of Hypermedia

Introduction

The first section of the book is aimed in particular at newcomers to hypermedia. Following on from the historical context presented in Chapter 1, it gives an overview of how hypermedia currently compares and contrasts with other computer-based fields, including traditional database models and software development. Separate chapters describe the special relevance hypermedia has for artificial intelligence and electronic publishing. It is argued that hypermedia can be used to develop stand-alone educational and reference applications, or as a complementary methodology to augment existing systems with powerful tools for online help and search.

Section I also introduces some of the ideas central to the hypermedia development issues as outlined in Section II, and to the discussion of specific packages in Section III.

2 Hypermedia and Other Software

2.1 Introduction: Genre Approaches

In this chapter, hypermedia is compared and contrasted with a number of other, more conventional genres of software. These fall broadly under the headings of database, object-oriented and text processing approaches. It is argued that the present specialization of software applications (including hypermedia itself) will be eroded by (i) integrated packages and (ii) system-level interfaces that can seamlessly integrate materials from heterogeneous sources. Hypermedia has the unique potential to provide the paradigm for this holistic approach. To say this is almost a tautology, but can hardly be overemphasized. This discussion leads directly into Chapter 3, in which it is argued that hypermedia has most to benefit from the assimilation of problem-solving techniques from artificial intelligence.

2.2 Database Approaches

2.2.1 Hierarchies

The hierarchy or file system is the oldest, and most rigid of the true database models[4,15]. Data is classified into a tree structure consisting of abstract entities or 'types'. These can be instantiated by records (the actual data) each of which in turn is composed of attributes. Records at a particular level in the hierarchy can be organized into categories. Starting at the root record type, record occurrences can have dependent or child record occurrences, linked by directed arcs or links from the parent; as no child can exist without a unique parent instance, the principle of referential integrity is upheld.

Navigation in a hierarchy is by means of the 'Parent-Child' structure itself, and is an expert task. Altering the structure once a database has been set up is also a complicated procedure; for instance, parent records are necessary to the existence of all child records, so that deleting the former entails the deletion of the latter. A particular limitation of the model is in the lack of adequate means to represent many-to-many relationships — such as those typical between teachers and students in a school (each teacher has many pupils, each of whom has many other teachers). This severely restricts the conceptual clarity with which a file-based model can represent reality. The family tree provides a fixed view of the world. Query construction may also be difficult if queries do not fall exactly within the structure of the hierarchy. Figure 2.1 shows a simple hierarchical schema for Departments, Resources and Jobs. Note that Job occurrences are assigned to an Employee; if Jobs were also to be assigned to Machines, data would need to be duplicated.

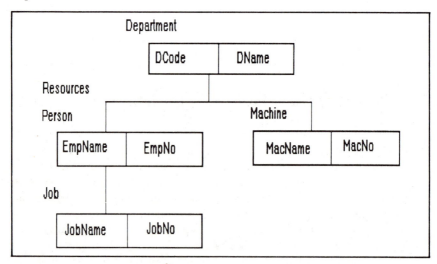

Figure 2.1   Hierarchical Schema.

2.2.2 Networks and Sets

The network model, linked closely with the programming language Cobol, overcomes the last problem mentioned above by introducing the concept of sets (co-sets of 'member' plus 'owner' record types rather than sets in the strict mathematical sense), which can intersect[13]. Networks are in fact elaborated hierarchies. Records can be members of more than one owner record set. Thus a network permits many-to-many relationships to be represented without the data duplication necessary in a strictly hierarchical implementation. For the two co-sets shown in Figure 2.2, a Machine can be a member in relationship both to Employee and Job owners.

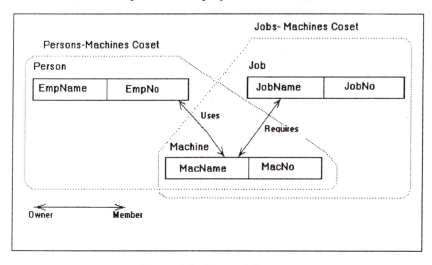

Figure 2.2 Network Co-sets.

However, navigation in the network model depends on the notion of currency indicators (current active context in relation to the overall network of sets), and as in the hierarchical database it requires skilled operators. In a network database attributes are still related to each other in terms of record instances, and entities are related strictly by explicit pointers.

2.2.3 Relational Databases

In the last couple of years relational database management systems (RDBMS) have become increasingly popular. Their advantages over the more traditional COBOL-based network model fall under two broad headings: ease of navigation or manipulation, and ease of maintenance.

The relational database model is attributed to the seminal work of Ted Codd[2]; for an excellent theoretical discussion including more recent refinements readers are referred to Chris Date[5]. The model draws heavily on mathematical Set Theory and the use of relational operators; its tabular format allows easy high-level navigation by users, via relations rather than records and explicit links. Items are represented by occurrences (or tuples) of entities. Each tuple is categorized by a number of attributes. Each attribute must be a single value, rather than a repeating group or set of values. From an attribute or combination of attribute conditions, it is possible uniquely to identify a tuple. However, the real power of the relational database is in its ability to apply queries over entire tables, and conjoined tables. For instance, in Figure 2.3, the JobNo attribute can be used to join the EmpJob and MacJob Tables, giving a view of resources — Employee and Machine — needed for a given job. There is little or no need for the user to specify how this is actually done, beyond specifying the search pattern criteria to be matched against the database. (In fact this is itself a moot point; performance of many proprietary 'relational' databases is greatly affected by the DBA's or programmer's initial choice of data structure.)

EmpJob Table

DCode	EmpName	EmpNo	JobNo
10	Smith	999	123
10	Green	234	123
10	Jones	876	125

MacJob Table

DCode	MacName	MacNo	JobNo
10	Lathe	67	123
10	Spray	1006	123
10	Cutter	45	125

Figure 2.3 Relational Tables.

Many proprietary relational database implementations include sophisticated, compiled Query Languages (also known as Fourth Generation Languages or 4GLs) with which to specify these relations of attributes to tuples. The most well-known of these is SQL (Structured Query Language), implementations of which are marketed by IBM and Oracle Corporation, amongst others. In addition, features such as Query by Example allow non-expert users to reach a dynamic 'view' of data tables without any need to learn the actual query language. Furthermore, these virtual views can be saved separately from the data they present at any one time; this is useful for regular but complex queries which cut across the actual tables in which tuples are stored. Most packages also emphasize report generation and formatting facilities.

Details of the underlying implementation of a relational database are hidden then behind its tables, which are themselves at a virtual level of abstraction. The canonical model of the real world represented by these tables may itself be overlaid at further virtual levels by 'views' of tables. Data can thus be manipulated and viewed using a variety of strategies, while the logical independence of its organizing structure is retained. This is critical to the ease with which a relational database can be restructured (often done to achieve optimal query speeds rather than because it is strictly essential to satisfy a given query). Complex relations, such as from accounts to purchase orders (many-to-many), are easily specified. Many-to-many relationships can be conceptualized graphically as combinations of vertical and horizontal subsets of tables.

The relational model has N dimensions — a feature which will become increasingly significant in the discussion of hypermedia. Furthermore, the user's conceptual, real-world model of the data can be accommodated in the virtual structure of the database, without the need to fully comprehend the storage mechanism and physical location(s). It has been suggested[1] that the relational model provides the only adequate framework for implementing distributed databases (see below).

All of this power comes at some expense; before tables can be properly designed it is necessary to perform a detailed data analysis to establish the logical relationships between occurrences and attributes. In other words, it is necessary to determine logical form before inserting contents — a top-down approach. Of course, both hierarchical and network models also require prior data analysis. But the point to be made below is that authors of hypermedia databases do not normally need to impose the same degree of structural rigour on their materials; there is less need for uniformity. By contrast, a prior requirement for (relational) database staff is that they have a thorough understanding of such areas as:

a)   Set Theory/relational algebra/first order predicate calculus (FOPL)
b)   Data normalization techniques
c)   Terminology, and functional relationships of the subject domain
d)   Terminology of the RDBMS, which may differ, for instance, from pure SQL.

Such considerations, particularly (a) and (b) are generally less important in beginning a hyperbase or hyperdocument, where structure is less vitally constrained by logic or mathematics. Consequently, hypermedia development can be incremental, aesthetic and possibly even idiosyncratic. It is possible, for instance, to prototype a subject application linking a reference document purely on major headings and sub-headings, and to do much of this via automated mark-up techniques (introduced later in this book). At further stages, a richer, micro-level linking structure can be developed within the actual body text; users with access to the development tools can then customize their own overlays, personal commentaries and so forth. This may be particularly beneficial when dealing with very large amounts of information, or information that is constantly updated or uncertain.

A number of observers have noted apparent similarities between relational database systems and hypermedia systems. The most salient of these are given below:

- Both models have a high degree of control transparency; users need to learn and employ less syntax, and fewer commands to reach their goals

- Both support ad hoc queries — use can be interactive rather than pre-specified

- Navigation is 'automatic' — users may specify (non-procedurally) what data to find, not how or where to look for it

- Both offer flexible levels of abstraction, i.e. rather than display data in full detail, it is possible to obtain an overview of the database at the top level (relational tables/sets, hypermedia documents/stacks)

- Data files can be combined dynamically with 'link' structures

- Access levels can be easily restricted according to user-name or level

- Prototyping is relatively fast and simple

- Templates for linking, retrieving and displaying data can be provided as default options for users

- Audit trails can be provided for administrative analyses or user modeling.

Indeed, in some cases these similarities are more than skin deep. A number of the commercial hypermedia packages examined in Section III have claims to being hybrids between hypermedia and relational database systems; typically a highly structured and relatively static document database is maintained. In addition hypermedia functionality is provided for navigation within documents in the database. Idex, from Office Workstations, is a good example of just such a system (see Chapter 9).

All of the above characteristics can be seen as descriptions of what the system can do, of its functionality or potential. However, it is also valid to examine what users actually wish to do with the system, and here lie the major differences between conventional databases and hyperbases. In practice, the issues are confused by the addition of auxiliary features to database and hypermedia shells: free-form (textual) databases with point-and-click navigation or hypertext-style keywords; hypermedia systems with SQL or Boolean search operators, and simple calculation facilities. However, users should bear in mind that these generic products are aimed at target audiences whose aims differ, as summarized below:

A. Relational databases are biased towards:

(1)   set-level manipulation of homogeneous data;

(2)   selection by relational operators and/or query language;

(3)   calculation of results;

(4)   generation of printed reports;

(5)   common storage mechanism for all data contents, regardless of record type (string, numerical, etc.);

(6)   priority of logical form over contents;

(7)   one-to-many reference links;

B. Hypertext/Hypermedia systems are biased towards:

(1)   non-linear reading and augmentation of heterogeneously formatted or non-tabular materials;

(2)   selection by natural language, reduced keystroke techniques and graphical overviews;

(3)   exploration/browsing;

(4)   integration of heterogeneous media (text, graphics, sound, video, executable programs, etc.) and respective storage mechanisms;

(5)   priority of content (objects) over form;

(6)   one-to-one links (lower-end commercial market).

In fact it should be emphasized that the last point is more a characteristic of present hypermedia implementations than of ideal models[7]. Indeed, having a one-to-many link structure is often very desirable in building an application; with multi-windowing systems there is no longer any good reason why a reference button should not access N examples rather than one. Yet most of the packages currently capable of this are for the more powerful and expensive workstation machines.

Note that the search terms 'depth-first' and 'breadth-first' do not have quite their usual meaning in the cyclical and non-linear structures common with hypermedia (see also sub-sections 3.2.4 and 6.6.2).

For a further discussion of the differences between hypermedia and database models, readers are referred to Franklin, who characterizes the main difference by an analogy to legal and statistical information formats, respectively[10]. In the former, records have a greater variance in size and precise structure as well as actual content than in the latter. Another way of describing the difference might be to say that the goal in searching a hypermedia database is often to match a canonical or best-fit example against criteria, and is normally reached by a series of discrete movements via single links. In a conventional database the goal of a query is more likely to be the selection of all occurrences matching the criteria exactly.

2.2.3 Query Languages

Query languages such as SQL are relatively 'high-level' representations designed for interrogation of a database. Most remain formal in structure, and they typically have small vocabularies and syntaxes. However, they also tend to be less procedural in flavor than, for instance, structured programming languages, resembling more closely some aspects of natural language (see sub-section 3.3.2). One further feature of so-called Fourth Generation query languages is that they are 'global' in so far as the scope of the query can be over all tables specified, without any need to specify how to access these tables. At the furthest extreme the Fifth Generation AI language PROLOG is increasingly used for database querying, and has a decidedly declarative emphasis (stating what information is to be found rather than how to find it). Non-procedural control makes a database considerably more powerful than network databases, for instance, which require explicit navigation by users. An example of a simple SQL-type query might be as follows:

```
SELECT Name, Salary
    FROM Sysuser
        WHERE Status = 'DBA'
        AND Registration < '01-JAN-90';
```

This query will retrieve the name and salary for all instances of users in the system user table who satisfy the double criteria of having status of database administrator and whose registration was prior to 1990. Some implementations even provide terms such as 'like' or 'soundslike', and sophisticated pattern masking facilities. As mentioned above, it is also possible to create virtual 'views' as stored templates, which do not exist in the stored data *per se*, but can be used for commonly needed queries.

How then might query languages relate to hypermedia? Firstly, a conventional query language can deal only with records that have some form of alphanumeric attribute against which a pattern or criterion may be matched. In fact there is no reason why, for instance, a musical query language should not be possible for either analogue or digital records;

although it might be difficult to implement for pieces with more than one voice. For media without a formal structural description (such as video or bit-mapped graphics) there is presently no means of automatic cataloguing and retrieval — records must somehow be manually typed and described. To be useful, most query languages need to operate on data stored in a relatively formal, homogeneous structure. Hypermedia documents are generally free form; feasible query facilities are likely to be capable of locating single pattern items, or items against a keyword index, or they may employ more complex algorithms, drawn, for instance, from natural language research[7] (see also Chapter 3).

This is not to say query languages are incompatible with hypermedia. In various forms they are fundamental to some of the more ambitious hypermedia implementations. For example, in his book, Literary Machines[12], Ted Nelson provides a detailed theoretical overview of the Xanadu query language. A similar, Commonlisp-based query/command language for the proposed LinkText electronic publishing design is given by Hanson[8]. However, query formulation has been underplayed in many commercial text retrieval and hypermedia systems[19], apparently taking a lower development priority than facilities for providing hard-wired links. The road towards consolidation of database and hypermedia features currently seems to be led by RDBMS developers such as Oracle Corporation, which is providing a HyperCard-based front end to the Oracle database in its Macintosh implementation.

2.2.5 Distributed Databases

A distributed database system or DDBS is located at two or more physical locations, and linked by data communications technology, typically a Wide Area Network or WAN. Databases at the nodes may differ in terms of the hardware and the local DBMS (database management system) that they employ. Both vertical (hierarchical or star) and horizontal (ring) networks are possible, as are hybrids (see Figure 2.4). Often DDBSs reflect corporate structure and history. Central to the ideal DDBS concept is the possibility of (seamlessly) accessing data at any or all locations; duplication of data at all sites is not called for, but in cases where copies exist, provision needs to be made for synchronized mutual revision[1]. Eventual plans for the Xanadu system are to link a multiplicity of server databases — some of which may be deeply buried or even extraterrestrial for security purposes[12].

DDBSs (often managed by relational databases) have much in common with hypermedia database management. As has already been emphasized, the hypermedia approach is geared towards the seamless integration of heterogeneous media, applications and storage devices.

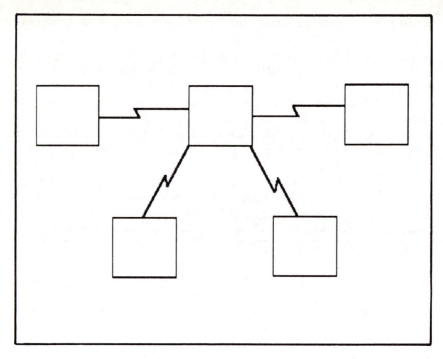

Figure 2.4   A hybrid DDBS.

2.2.6   Real-time Databases

Traditionally databases have been relatively static structures. They are still predominantly updated by 'batch' process — typically off-line, and at the record or document level. In other words, a database receives new files of material, daily, weekly or even monthly. The actual data structure is unlikely to be altered.

In contrast, real-time databases are dynamic, in the sense that information is added to them at arbitrary times, by external sources such as news services, networks and monitoring devices. As in more traditional systems, the new material may be of document type (as in electronic mail systems), but also of record/field type (data for a single cell). However, the essence of such a database system is that internal change or executable actions may be contingent on the ad hoc arrival of new information. In the most sophisticated applications this may mean that qualitative change to the actual structure of the information is initiated — by the database itself.

The term real-time is also used is a second sense, to describe systems in which queries can accommodate items which are not explicitly categorized in the database's structure — for instance, matching user-supplied terms as opposed to explicit master keywords from an inverted list. An example of this sort of real-time matching is provided by Dow Jones' DowQuest full text retrieval system — although the actual database is only updated daily[20]. Figure 2.5 shows the relationships between a hypermedia front end and other software systems for a hypothetical real-time news text system[22].

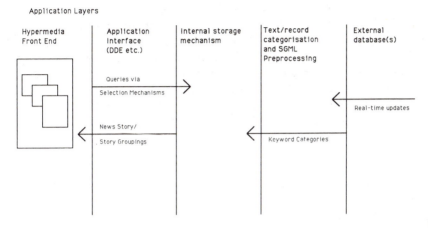

Figure 2.5   Hypermedia front end to a real-time database.

There is no inherent reason why hypermedia systems should not be used as a front end to real-time databases; their advantage is that a capacity for multiple hierarchies, non-linear structures and dynamic media such as video can be easily applied to time-stamped data as well as one-off, hermetically sealed applications. However, there are few commercial programs at the lower end of the market capable of rising even part of the way to meet this challenge. This is probably as much a result of the hardware and operating systems constraints with which these systems are designed to operate: serial processing; prohibitively low working memory for multi-tasking; unreliable or obscure protocols for implementing 'interrupts' as an analog of truly concurrent processing.

There are a few notable exceptions. A number of communications packages now allow limited transmission of real-time data values between standard MS-DOS software: for instance, Crosstalk now supports Windows DDE protocols, allowing data to be transferred to and from other Windows applications — such as Excel, and Guide[3]. However, even without the use of third-party communication utilities, there are possibilities. Guide and several other products are now committed to being ported across to the more powerful multi-tasking or 'server' architectures that characterize state-of-the-art operating systems such as OS/2. A dedicated DDE (Dynamic Data Exchange) module is also being developed by OWL for use in conjunction with Guide and other MS-Windows/Presentation Manager applications[22]. Impressive real-time hypermedia would seem to be imminent.

2.2.7 Spreadsheets

Briefly, although some hypermedia systems have auxiliary spreadsheet or calculation features, very few spreadsheets have any of the generic features characteristic of hypertext (and none works with multimedia files). To date, the nearest contender for the role of spreadsheet/hypertext hybrid appears to be Lotus Agenda. This is a free-field spreadsheet and outliner designed for personal organisation and project management. It allows users to integrate and filter text and numerical data by means of semi-intelligent matching techniques (see Chapter 9). In contrast, conventional spreadsheets are multi-cellular calculators. They are designed for batch-processing and updating of homogeneous, standard format numerical material. Their role is well circumscribed, being restricted almost exclusively to budgeting, simple accounting and forecasting.

A serious limitation of the spreadsheet is its inability to deal with inaccurate or uncertain data; any errors in one cell are rapidly multiplied when values are passed to the next function, so that resulting estimates may be quantitatively wide of the mark without any qualitative self-criticism. In practice, spreadsheets are often used with a range of starting values, to calculate a range of outcomes. However, the number-crunching is narrowly determined. Even in a spreadsheet with 'programming language features' it would be extremely difficult to set up the simplest of pattern matching algorithms.

This is in contrast to the dynamic capacity for 'fuzzy' search and discovery that the hypermedia approach offers. It is unlikely that a spreadsheet could be used effectively, if at all, for the kind of heterogeneous classificatory tasks and idea generation which are central to the role of hypermedia. The difference is as great as that between a simple electronic switching circuit and a system like the brain itself — in which feedback between the components critically moderates behaviour.

2.3 Object-oriented Approaches

2.3.1 Objects and Re-usability

True object-oriented programming systems or environments (OOPS) include Smalltalk and LOOPS. Most implementations of OOPS are still in the experimental stages, requiring large-memory workstations. However, it seems highly likely that object-oriented techniques will increasingly be available in high-level software development tools and languages for many machines[14]. A number of conventional structured programming language implementations have recently been extended with object-oriented libraries; these include C++, LPA's PROLOG++ and Turbo Pascal.

The advantage of OOPS is that program code is stored in re-usable software modules (objects), that can be cut and pasted into applications — often using a highly graphical, windowing environment. There is a narrow distinction between data and procedures in such a system. Except to design new objects, the programmer need not normally be concerned with the implementational details; the object is defined with an interface protocol that specifies possible operations, or methods that an object allows on itself or performs on others. This is known as data encapsulation.

Objects can also be organized into classes within hierarchies or lattices, and thus derive or inherit some of the characteristics of parent levels. (In fact objects are one sort of a representation known as frames, discussed in the next chapter). This organization may occur dynamically, as operations are required of an object, or during program linking, when external code is imported, as in Modula-2. (Modula-2 has facilities for data abstraction — the separation of implementation from declared properties — but is not truly object-oriented in that it is a purely procedural language i.e. data is passively passed between procedures).

Just as code can be organised into object hierarchies, so can object-oriented databases. These can be examined or manipulated via user-defined views, which can themselves be developed from template view objects. The main difference between such databases and, for instance, relational databases is that the former typically include many object types but few instances of each (in the order of dozens), the latter typically have few occurrence types but very many occurrence instances (in the order of hundreds or thousands).

Object-oriented databases can contain many types of objects. For instance, these may be purely textual objects, graphics[11], or a combination[24]. In the case of graphics or CAD systems, sophisticated vectorization techniques are often built into facilities such as Auto-trace tools. These make it possible to analyze and separate homogeneous, bit-mapped images into discrete shapes, according to relative contours and tones. Each graphic object can then be manipulated separately.

One advantage of the OOPS approach is that it facilitates collaborative software development and the management of code libraries. Teams can work in a top-down fashion from a set of parent objects with general classes and methods, to more specific objects. Development can proceed at the conceptual level, unobscured by the code of lower level objects whose implementation can be assigned to individual programmers. However, the provision of browsing facilities (for instance in Digitalk's Smalltalk/V — available for DOS, OS/2 and the Macintosh) allows users to investigate their code libraries as and when they need — either for debugging or general familiarization. The multi-window browser with Smalltalk/V allows users to examine a number of local code objects at any one time — and it is possible to draw direct parallels with multi-window hypertext browsers, e.g. HYBROW[16].

2.3.2 Overloading

Overloading in OOPS is an extension of a common programming device, whereby one operator or procedure in the source language can be applied to different arguments or data types; differentiation is often achieved by means of context, interpreted by the language compiler's parser routines. This provides a means of economizing on the number of syntactic and semantic objects within the system — although ultimately this may be at the expense of computational efficiency. In other words, code is re-usable at the statement level as well as the macro/procedural level — commands themselves are re-usable objects.

Arguably, this overloading allows some reduction of the overhead involved in learning to use a high-level environment. Typically, the number of objects in an OOPS system is so large as to require a large investment in familiarization. However, once familiar, the user can develop very rapid prototypes of application software. This process is sometimes referred to as templating; from library objects it is possible to build new, modified or extended objects with a minimum of effort. In summary, it is probably fair to say that OOPS is useful as a host environment which supports a variety of other approaches and tasks.

2.3.3 Hypermedia Objects

Object-oriented techniques such as inheritance are rapidly being incorporated into a wide variety of electronic publishing products, including hypermedia systems[6,10]. Several hypertext/hypermedia systems make explicit claims of object-oriented features. In fact, both OOPS and hypermedia owe much to frame-based systems, which will be discussed more fully in the next chapter (sub-section 3.2.1). For instance, Guide and HyperCard treat text and graphics as structural objects and allow certain legal operations on each. It is also possible for users to cut and paste active objects such as buttons and (in HyperCard) card fields into their own applications. Along with each object the underlying HyperTalk script is imported, yet this remains transparent to the user unless he or she chooses to examine the script. This in turn allows rapid prototyping of applications.

HyperTalk itself, although not a true object-oriented language, employs a relatively high degree of operator overloading — a small vocabulary permits high-level operations on objects of many underlying types. Typically, procedures and functions are represented by verbs, relatively unqualified by arguments. Variables are represented by nouns, without formal type declarations. This results in the flexibility to write scripts which have an artless resemblance to natural language, in comparison to code written in conventional structured programming languages.

HyperTalk Scripts that react to messages are known as message handlers. These are analogous to OOPS methods. Using message handlers the user can build simple context-sensitive demons, the sleeping policemen of the procedural world. These can be used, for instance, to display message-boxes, compile audit trails, or erase a shareware stack after a certain number of usages, e.g.:

```
on mouse-up
   if mouse-V > 300
      then beep(200)
      and dissolve to next card
      and show message box
   end if
end mouse-up
```

However, HyperCard does not merit true OOPS status (to date), in that there are no hierarchies and thus no inheritance of class features (see Chapter 12). Perhaps the most truly object-oriented commercial hypermedia system is Intermedia[23]. This incorporates object-oriented programming in its actual environment, and also has true hierarchical inheritance at the author/user interface level. In fact, Intermedia's developers admit that conceptually the design owes much to the Smalltalk environment.

Both OOPS and hypermedia approaches are similar in the flexibility they offer to applications developers to work top-down, bottom-up or both-ends-in. This is in contrast with the structured methodologies which have become dominant in the design of conventional software systems and databases. In fact top-down methodologies, and incremental methodologies as exemplified by OOPS and hypermedia, may have complementary roles; this is discussed further in Chapter 5. The movement towards OOPS by the microcomputing community seems likely to be boosted by the advent of Windows, OS/2 and Presentation Manager development tools, featuring both multimedia and object-oriented facilities.

2.4 Text Processing Approaches

2.4.1 Outliners and Text Processors

Simple text editors or word processors have little in common with hypermedia. Most have automated text search facilities, with wildcard filtering. A few can even import or create graphics. Sections of text can be cut and pasted or cloned to different locations, but the resulting document remains linear.

By contrast, outliners emphasize the organizational and structural aspects of writing or creating. Examples of excellent outliner packages include the high-end FrameWork from Ashton-Tate, and Brown Bag Software's PC-Outline. Versions of the latter are available from shareware distributors. Outline entries are defined at the top level, and can be expanded as vertical, linear text, or as horizontal or hierarchical structures. Entries may also be promoted or demoted in the hierarchies, and cloned to new locations. Some programs, such as Houdini and BrainStorm, allow inter-entry reference links as well as strictly hierarchical references.

Several of the more recent commercial outliner programs have adopted a card or window metaphor that gives something of the look and feel of hypertext. The present text was itself written using an outliner; the ease of cross-referencing and text location more than compensated for the slight loss in terms of advanced editing/formatting (this can be better accomplished on the finished document using other software).

The main distinctive utility of outliners is in being able to fold away lower levels of an outline, allowing a high-level view of the structural backbone of a document. The word processing facilities provided are normally sufficient to allow smooth progression from an outline of section headings to a full document. The non-linear structure facilitates production of large documents — it is quicker for the user to direct hierarchical navigation than for the program to scroll through one monolithic file. Thus a document is treated as a collection of semi-autonomous but thematically structured ideas — the structure can be made explicit or extracted at any time, and modified relatively simply.

However, what these programs typically lack is the sophisticated interface provided by hypertext; there is little attention to providing multiple types of link (as provided by a choice of hypermedia buttons perhaps). Another difference is that outliners tend to support the more primitive keyboard cursor direction keys rather than providing mouse drivers. (These last points are perhaps quite trivial criticisms in that such features could be easily bolted onto programs.) State-of-the-art outliners that can concurrently process several separate documents or even integrate suites of programs including graphics (such as Ashton-Tate's FrameWork III), are a step further towards meriting the term hypermedia. If future product versions are augmented with cross-hierarchy search and point-to-point link facilities the difference will have become more one of perceived marketing emphasis than of actual functionality.

2.4.2 Text-based Databases

There are now hundreds of public and subscription, on-line database sources in the US and Europe. Yet most are remarkably unimaginative in their organizational and referential structures; they are collections of linear documentation which has often been imported from printed, textual sources. The terminal provides a centralized delivery device, but scant attention has been given to providing readers with any extra facilities for accessing or cross-referencing data. Even the high-end databases lack the kind of overlays — orthogonal to the main data structure — that characterize a hypermedia corpus.

Furthermore, interface protocols in these systems tend to be relatively primitive, needing to cater to the lowest common denominator of machine configuration that accesses them. Much of the information is to be downloaded only, selected 'as is' at the document level; there is little or no user interaction (program and bulletin boards aside), and even less freedom of choice in the manner the user searches or filters the database. A powerful commercial example of a text database in which users can specify search terms is Dow Jones' DowQuest[20] (see sub-section 3.2.5).

2.4.3 Text Retrieval

Text retrieval software programs can typically be used to search and/or index files which could have been created with another program such as a text processor. They support such facilities as searching for alphanumeric strings and partial strings, and combinations of criteria constructed with Boolean logic (AND, OR, NOT). Figure 2.6 shows the relations of Boolean logic as functions of sets.

Full text categorization produces an inverted list, i.e. after all 'noise' words have been removed documents are categorized by each term they contain, each of which is compiled into an alphabetical list with pointers to term occurrences. More complex techniques for classifying and retrieving text involve statistical attribute clustering algorithms[9,21] and are discussed more fully in the next chapter. However, even the most basic text retrieval package may provide an easy way of obtaining limited hypertext functionality, as an extension to existing materials, without commitment to time-consuming manual linking as required by most explicitly hypertext packages.

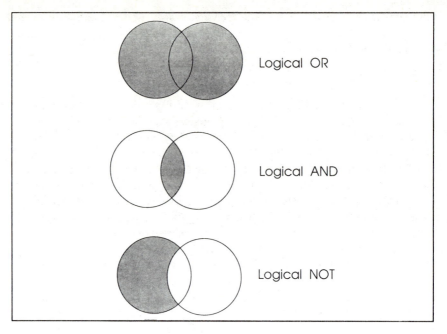

Figure 2.6   Boolean operators as functions of overlapping sets.

SUMMARY: HYPERMEDIA IS A GENERAL APPROACH

As described above, hypermedia (mainly hypertext) features have been incorporated in programs as diverse as databases, spreadsheets, text processors and outliners. Hypermedia has a particularly strong affinity with relational databases, which allow relatively heterogeneous data to be easily structured into virtual 'views'.

Another approach which is complementary with hypermedia is object-oriented programming. Both can be seen as members of the family of frame-based approaches — supporting default hierarchical structures, data abstraction and encapsulation.

Hypermedia is a more sophisticated approach than those of text processing, outlining and conventional text retrieval, in terms of the additional structural possibilities it gives to free text, and the high-level tools it provides for managing text databases.

Hypermedia is a general approach that can be applied to arbitrary knowledge domains; at this level it is perhaps best described as a medium of electronic publishing, in its widest sense. This role is examined in Chapter 4.

Hypermedia is also an approach that can be incorporated as secondary functionality in software primarily developed for tasks other than computerized referencing. Hypermedia features are beginning to appear in software as diverse as desktop publishing, electronic mail and programming packages.

So far one particular area of software development is conspicuously missing from the discussion — that of expert or knowledge-based systems. In the next chapter hypermedia's special relation with expert systems technology is examined in depth.

REFERENCES

1.   Ceri, S. and Pelagatti, G. *Distributed Databases. New York: McGraw-Hill, 1984.*

2.   Codd, E. *A relational model of data for large, shared data banks. Communications of the ACM,* **13 (6)**, June 1970, pp. 377-382.

3.   Dallas, K. Windows works it out. *PC User*, 119, 8-21 November 1989, pp. 104-113.

4.   Date, C. *An Introduction to Database Systems*, Volume 1. Reading, MA: Addison-Wesley, Fourth Edition, 1986.

5.   Date, C. *Relational Databases: selected writings*. Reading, MA: Addison-Wesley, 1986.

6.   Feiner, S. Seeing the forest for the trees: hierarchical display of hypertext structure. In: Allen, R. (Ed.) *Proceedings of the Conference on Office Information Systems*, March 23-25 1988, Palo Alto, California. *ACM SIGOIS Bulletin*, **9 (2-3)**, April and July 1988, pp. 205-212.

7.   Franklin, C. Hypertext defined and applied. *Online*, **13 (3)**, May 1989, pp. 37-49.

8.   Hahn, U. and Riemer, U. Automatic generation of hypertext knowledge bases. In: Allen, R. (Ed.) *Proceedings of the Conference on Office Information Systems*, March 23-25 1988, Palo Alto, California. *ACM SIGOIS Bulletin*, **9 (2-3)**, April and July 1988, pp. 182-188.

9.   Hainebach, R. Focus on full text. Interview. *Information World Review*, February 1990, pp. 20-21.

10. Hanson, R. Toward hypertext publishing. *Sigir Forum (ACM Press)*, **22 (1-2)**, Fall/Winter 1987-88, pp. 9-27.

11. James, G. Artificial intelligence and automated publishing systems. In: Barrett, E. (Ed.) *Text, ConText and HyperText*. Cambridge, MA: MIT Press, 1988.

12. Nelson, T. (1981). *Literary Machines*. Swathmore, PA: Nelson.

13. Oxborrow, E. *Databases and Database Systems*. Chartwell-Bratt, 1986.

14. Parsaye, K. set al. *Intelligent Databases — Object-oriented, deductive hypermedia technologies*. John Wiley and Sons, 1989.

15. Potter, W. and Trueblood, R. Traditional, semantic, and hyper-semantic approaches to data-modelling. *IEEE Computer*, **21 (6)**, June 1988, pp. 53-66.

16. Seabrook, R. and Shneiderman, B. The user interface in a hypertext multiwindow program browser. *Interacting with Computers, The Interdisciplinary Journal of Human-Computer Interaction*, **1 (3)**, December 1989, pp. 299-337.

17. Shetler, T. Birth of the BLOB. *BYTE*, **15 (2)**, February 1990, pp. 221-226.

18. Thomas, D. What's in an object. *Byte*, **14 (3)**, March 1989, pp. 231-240.

19. Thompson, R. and Croft, W. Support for browsing in an intelligent text

retrieval system. *International Journal of Man-Machine Studies*, **30 (6)**, June 1989. pp. 639-668.

20.   Weyer, S. Questing for the ''Dao'': DowQuest and intelligent text retrieval. *Online*, **13 (5)**, September 1989, pp. 39-48.

21.   Willett, P. Recent trends in hierarchic document clustering: a critical review. *Information Processing and Management*, **24 (5)**, 1988, pp. 577-597.

22.   Woodhead, N. Master's Dissertation, Polytechnic of the South Bank, London, 1989 (unpublished).

23.   Yankelovich, N., Haan, B., Meyrovitz, N. and Drucker, S. Intermedia: The concept and the construction of a seamless information environment. *IEEE Computer*, **21 (1)**, January 1988, pp. 81-96.

24.   Younggren, G. Using an object-oriented programming language to create audience-driven hypermedia environments. In: Barrett, E. (Ed.) *Text, ConText and HyperText*. Cambridge, MA: MIT Press, 1988.

③ Intelligent Hypermedia

"In many ways, hypermedia and knowledge-based systems are a natural fit."
Frank Halasz, 1988[17].

3.1 Introduction: Expert Systems, Knowledge-based Systems

In this chapter special attention is given to hypermedia in relation to artificial intelligence formalisms. AI techniques are not central to hypermedia, (which seeks to provide instead an augmented structure to information). However, it is argued that the representations commonly used in hypermedia systems and relational databases are compatible with frame-based representations, and that they may lend themselves directly to integration with the rule-based search and decision-making techniques that characterize AI[35,36].

Firstly, for readers without a background in knowledge-based systems or KBS, a quick word of definition. In KBS, as opposed to conventional programs, the onus of decision-making, in a dynamic context, is with the software rather than with the user. By analogy to hypermedia, this means an

35

emphasis on context-sensitive guidance by the system, as opposed to undirected navigation or browsing by the user.

To the casual user or observer, a high-level presentation of information and a high-level means of interaction with the system may give an impression of intelligent software; typically, both expert systems and hypermedia systems have these surface features. However, the different emphasis of decision-maker in each type of system requires a different level of rigor in the imposition of a representational formalism onto information.

Putting this the other way around, users normally have enough real-world knowledge to be able to generalize to rather loosely structured knowledge bases. Machine intelligences do not have this same real-world knowledge, so that their decisions will only be reliable for tightly circumscribed, highly structured information — governed by a set of rules that includes all permutations. However, as strategic decisions remain with the user in the hypermedia model, representations of knowledge are more important than self-determining, meta-level control mechanisms. On the other hand, as the amount of available hypermedia information grows, there will be an increasing need for auxiliary (intelligent) means to reduce the apparent complexity to manageable 'views', to orientate and to navigate; these tools might come in the form of simple, task-specific rule-bases or general heuristics that explore information and report to the user with suggestions rather than final solutions *per se*.

The representations employed by expert systems range from the syntactically oriented predicate calculus (First Order Predicate Logic), and logic-based programming languages e.g. PROLOG, to the family of semantic attribute or frame-based description models. In fact, a consensus is emerging to the effect that there is no *lingua franca* of knowledge representation. This implies that systems developers need to analyze the system domain and user requirements before opting for any one central representation[40,46].

Representations are grouped together into a knowledge base. This in turn is often manipulated by a set of appropriate rules. Rule bases are one means by which expert systems can perform automated reasoning or inference tasks. However, they are also labor intensive and costly to develop; the resulting structures tend to be relatively rigid. Moreover, monolithic rule bases are notoriously difficult to modify, because their formalisms are alien, and feedback from rules may cause the system to interact in ways that are not immediately obvious. Thus it is often preferable to develop small sets of rules as modular 'tools' which can be manipulated by users without the need to understand the intricacies of their implementation.

In discussing intelligent hypermedia, it is useful to distinguish those facilities which are primarily of use to authors of new materials, and those which are provided as aids to end users. The former will probably depend on the foresight of the designers of the hypermedia shell, although shells with an application development language may allow authors to build or customize their own tools. Only the most experienced users, and those with specialized needs are likely to build their own tools, relying instead on general-purpose pattern-matching facilities and navigational aids.

3.2 Decision-making

3.2.1 Frames

Frame-based systems in computation and Artificial Intelligence applications have developed from similar models in the psychology of memory and cognition [1,2,33,45]. The former include semantic nets[26,57], frames themselves, and other hierarchical or taxonomic structures (including object-oriented programming as discussed in the previous chapter). These are formal models of knowledge representation, which are claimed to have, if not true psychophysiological equivalents, at least a degree of psychological appeal as metaphors for reducing semantic complexity. Indeed, semantics is the key word — content nodes are the main features, and the closer the similarities between nodes, the greater the physical proximity between them in the network.

Semantic net representations are similar to the object-oriented systems introduced in the previous chapter. They are organised hierarchically — so that properties can be inherited by nodes lower in the net, thus saving storage space. Figure 3.1 shows simple semantic net inheritance from the Bird node, to Parrot via an is__a arc, and from Parrot to Wing via a has__part arc.

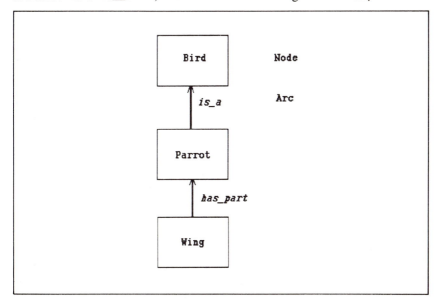

Figure 3.1   Relationships between nodes in a semantic net.

Nodes in true Frame systems are similar to those in semantic nets, and are linked together by typed arcs, but have attribute 'slots' at each node (see Figure 3.2). These hold default values at their creation, or they may be instantiated with specific occurrence values. They may also have executable procedures or methods attached to them, which are tested — and if appropriate executed — whenever a value is accessed or changed. Frame nodes are often called concepts — they are clusters of values describing an entire object, or perhaps an event. They are frequently appropriate representations for stereotyped scenarios, which can be dealt with via default values.

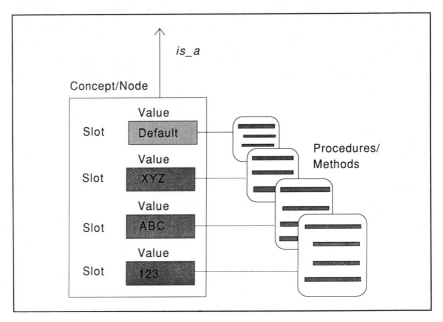

Figure 3.2   A Frame node or concept.

Thus the basic form of the frame family of Structured Object Representations (SORs) is a triple consisting of:

OBJECT x ATTRIBUTES x VALUES

Frames have been successfully employed in a number of expert systems shells and more complex AI toolkit environments; it is interesting to note that these same packages frequently feature hypertext as a tool for transcript analysis or system navigation[34,47].

However, frame-based systems in AI are formally more rigorous than the linking structures in hypertext; they are designed to be used in conjunction with automated procedures, whereas automated hypertext is still very much an area of academic speculation that has yet to make an impact in off-the-shelf software. For instance, in semantic nets the links between nodes are strongly typed. In other words, they are objects in their own right — categories defined by the system designer or user, such as: IS__A, PART__ OF, USES, OWNER, OWNEE, HAS__PROPERTY. By contrast, only the most ambitious of hypermedia systems have so far implemented typed links. Another difference between hypermedia and frame representations is in the number of links relative to the actual amount of information stored at the nodes. The following diagram, Figure 3.3 shows the relative positions of hypermedia and frame representations against the two indices of structure (link density) and semantics (node information density).

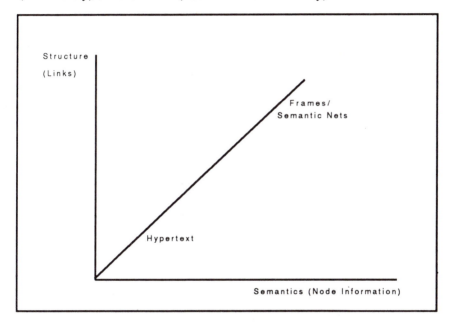

Figure 3.3 The richness of structure and content for knowledge representations.

It is important to note that these differences are basically quantitative rather than qualitative; there is no inherent reason why typed links should not be implemented in future releases of many more hypermedia products, for instance. However, frame-based systems differ from conventional programs in one fundamental way: they are said to be declarative representations, rather than procedural[55]. Declarative representations have a particularly useful property; they can be used to generate additional information by means of very general procedures, such as logical resolution and heuristics.

One other form of declarative representation, which is already in widespread use in electronic publishing, is the document template. Such tools are not normally understood to be connected with intelligent software, in that the user specifies when material should be structured with a particular template. However, by combining templates with techniques such as automated mark-up and natural language processing (see below) it seems likely that the burden of a further stage of production can be lifted from human shoulders, leaving authors free to concentrate on the more intellectual aspects of their materials. Templates are discussed more fully in sub-section 7.3.1.

3.2.2 Uncertainty

The techniques employed within expert systems to deal with uncertainty constitute a large topic in their own right which it is beyond the scope of the present text to describe. Readers are referred to Gale and Rich for comprehensive introductions[11,37]. However, these techniques can be broadly divided according to the ends sought — into those methods which seek to reduce the search space (tree/graph pruning) or direct search along a single path, and those which calculate the degree of uncertainty accompanying the eventual solution. They can also be divided by the means with which those ends are achieved — into probabilistic and heuristic methods. In fact there is often some overlap between these neat categories — probabilistic reasoning often underlies the implementation of fuzzier or more relativistic representations, for example.

With conventional databases queries tend to produce an all or nothing result — and typically selections produce a large number of data objects directly from the database; there is little or no role for uncertainty. This is in contrast to expert systems. Here raw data, and/or rules are used to compare incremental possibilities, and perhaps to generate new information. Most expert systems are structured so as to produce a single answer, or limited range of answers, to a query — a diagnosis, for instance — although a few more sophisticated environments give the user options to develop parallel models — to generate and explore alternative existential 'worlds'[35].

It may be useful here to examine what precisely is uncertain in an expert system or hypermedia system. In an expert system the goal may be to estimate the most likely outcome (the match of a result against a starting position and conditions), given uncertainty (randomness) in a world itself, a lack of sufficient information to produce an exact answer, or because testing all possibilities is infeasible.

Users of a hypermedia system are likely to encounter the following problems of uncertainty: Where am I? Where can I find something like that? Where is the best place to find something interesting? Which will be the most promising direction? As in the expert system, the user is likely to be seeking a relatively small number of possible solutions for each new situation encountered. However, these solutions are likely to exist in the database materials — the onus is not so much to predict an outcome in the real world. Rather, the problem is one of finding an acceptable solution without having to (manually) search all the available materials.

3.2.3 Control Mechanisms

So far this discussion has dealt mainly with data representation structures; this is only half the story. In addition, the kinds of control mechanism that can be employed for any one data structure can result in a variety of applications with vastly different functionality.

In fact, rule bases and knowledge bases are not mutually exclusive; there is a lesser degree of difference between them than between procedures and data in a conventional program. Rules in AI are often conditional match-execute pairs that are themselves based upon a considerable amount of knowledge. If a fact condition comprising the first half of a rule is positively matched the second half of the rule (often an action) is fired. In declarative representations such as PROLOG clauses facts and rules take broadly the same form.

Rules do not normally operate in isolation. Instead they are nested or linked together into inference chains — which are actually paths through the decision tree composed of all possible rule combinations. In some expert systems special 'meta-rules' may also be invoked. These may add new facts to the knowledge base, or modify the rule base.

In hypermedia systems the function of meta-control is normally the domain of the user. However, there are two other areas in which hypermedia may be 'intelligent': the knowledge representation itself; the interface. As Carlson points out, a loosely structured knowledge base will require greater development of interface facilities for a non-expert user to achieve an acceptable solution with the same degree of ease[5]. Methods for providing this intelligence are examined below.

3.2.4 Automated Search, Linking and Inference

"Indeed, all the available evidence with reference to both large and small collections indicates that properly designed text-based systems are preferable to manually indexed systems." Gerald Salton, 1986[42].

A problem which may not be immediately apparent from a conceptual point of view, but is familiar to anyone who has ever tried to build or maintain a large hypermedia application, is the speed with which links can be created between nodes. Although most commercial systems have relatively sophisticated text search facilities (across some or all nodes), it is still necessary for the user to initiate the linking of nodes manually, at a more or less local level. At present, off-the-shelf systems provide little or no computational power to provide new group solutions — to generate new links from a batch of dynamic data items, for instance. This is one of the main criteria for the next generation of hypermedia, as foreseen by Halasz[17].

What would reduce the expensive activity of manual linking or searching is some means by which the system could cast its net (or web!) more widely. In other words, the system would be able to anticipate the author's or user's likely requirement at run-time, from some combination of attributes of the development structure or of the search criteria so far.

The difference in navigational style between conventional databases, AI approaches and hypermedia can be understood by examining three basic categories of search strategy. These are known as breadth-first, depth-first and best-first search, and are relatively independent of the actual database model implemented. Each is a systematic method of accessing information, and they form a subset of a more general class of strategies known as heuristics (see sub-section 3.2.6).

Taking a simple hierarchical tree structure it is easy to describe breadth- and depth-first searches. Given a particular problem to solve, breadth-first search examines all information at the highest level of granularity (or proximity from starting position) before moving to lower levels in an attempt to satisfy the criteria for an acceptable solution. In relation to Figure 3.4 this corresponds to visiting nodes in the sequence (1,2,3,4,5,6,7,8,9...).

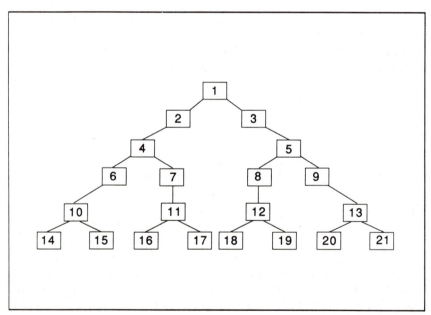

Figure 3.4 A hierarchical search tree.

By contrast, depth-first search follows a single branch of the tree through successive nodes to a leaf node (or a given depth) before returning to examine other nodes at the level above, as per the node sequence (1,2,4,6,10,14...).

Best-first search is normally a compromise between breadth-first and depth-first search; it employs general rules to determine which direction, from present position, offers the most promising chance of a solution. This may involve abandoning some branches of the tree or problem space only to return to them as other possibilities are themselves exhausted or become unlikely to yield an acceptable result.

One way in which the AI problem is likely to be different from that faced in conventional database tasks is in the degree to which the problem and solution can be specified. In the AI problem, the solution may not actually exist in the database — it may have to be generated from existing information using inference rules. The solution will be an optimal or best fit within constraints designed to limit a combinatorial explosion of possible generated solutions; i.e. it may not be a perfect match.

In contrast, the basic hypermedia approach is far simpler — the user can choose which paths to explore, to what depth, and how to backtrack. However, the issue is confused to some extent by the provision in some hypermedia systems of filtering mechanisms which combine criteria and operators in a manner similar to that employed by relational databases or expert systems. The parameters in a hypermedia system can normally be shifted to produce either a set of close-fit alternatives or a single best-fit solution.

Suggestions for increasing the generality of search and linking mechanisms have included the following:

- Synonym lists; supplied by a thesaurus and/or user

- Truncation, prefix and suffix-stripping; these reduce a term to its root, by removing verbal participles, for instance

- Wildcard matching; the characters ?, % and *, for instance are allowed to represent single or multiple characters in a term, permitting all possible matches at these points

- Semantic 'fuzzy set' filter techniques; possibly related to hierarchical inheritance of properties, which at higher levels in the hierarchy are more abstract, and thus more general (see also the Templates section below, for the relevance of declarative representation)

- Hierarchical scoping can also be used with the opposite aim, i.e. to narrow the scope of a query

- Other approaches which can be used to increase either recall or, more often, precision include:

- Proximity operators, e.g. within * words of 'term'

- Timeline operators, e.g. before/during/after 'date' / 'term'

- Term weighting approaches; in relation to term co-occurrences in and between documents (discussed in depth below).

All these techniques can be combined within a framework of natural language querying or in combination with standard Boolean criteria (use of the operators AND, OR and NOT). In some cases Boolean combinations can increase recall measure, e.g. by use of alternatives, and in other cases they can increase precision, e.g. by use of AND to conjoin restrictive criteria.

Searching and linking are very much bound up with each other in hypermedia systems. Some form of the searching (whether automated or user-driven) is necessary prior to linking. With automated term indexing of whole documents or document collections, linking results in a key index. This precedes and facilitates individual term searches. The main problem is two-edged. Firstly, a search mechanism needs to be able to access a high percentage of relevant items for any given search criterion. This is known as the recall measure. Secondly, of the items retrieved, a high percentage needs to be relevant to the search criterion. This is known as the precision measure.

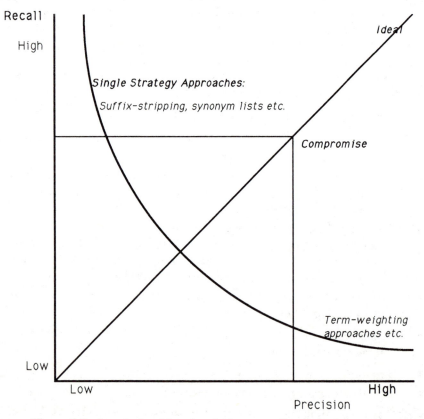

Figure 3.5 Search algorithms in relation to recall and precision measures.

Unfortunately, the two measures tend to be inversely related in automated systems (see Figure 3.5). To encompass a high percentage of relevant items, it is likely that search criteria will have to be 'fuzzy'; this in turn means that items will also be retrieved which are not themselves relevant to the search for a given term. On the other hand, approaches such as term weighting that increase the precision measure of a search also run the risk of being too specific; all items retrieved may be relevant, but they may be only a subset of relevant material[42,43]. Term weighting presupposes certain *a priori* conclusions about relevance. Combinations of these approaches may lead to a compromise, more closely approximating the ideal of retrieving all and only those items corresponding to the search criteria. Compare this with the combination of forward chaining inference and backward chaining deduction in some expert systems; the two techniques are used to converge on optimum solutions (see below).

These techniques are still very much an area of academic research — of speculation even — in relation to commercial hypermedia packages. The integral facilities for automated linking provided by the majority of commercial software in Section III are limited to finding occurrences of a term, or of a node and those nodes to which it already has hard-wired outlinks. However, in some cases it is possible to use a clipboard of button creation macros in conjunction with materials that have been somehow 'marked up' by an intermediate preprocessing module, to achieve a similar result.

In addition, several algorithms and hybrid models have been proposed and even implemented, using existing shells to demonstrate that automated inference in conjunction with hypermedia materials is at least feasible [20,28,37,53]. Similarly, Garg notes the theoretical possibility of treating hierarchical abstraction in hypermedia as a domain amenable to problem-solving via first order predicate logic (FOPL) and set theory[15].

3.2.5 Term Weighting

Other approaches to automated text retrieval include term discrimination and cluster analysis, or hybrids of the two. Willett[53] provides an excellent review. The former uses term frequency measures to differentiate between documents. The latter employs multivariate statistical techniques to define nodes' proximity to each other; content term frequencies may be involved, or more abstract properties of documents. Each variable can be seen as one dimension in the sort of n-dimensional information space described by Younggren[58]. Using attributes or properties of objects to define sets and levels of detail, the system can index and retrieve information via a single, simple conceptual framework. It is possible to compile two kinds of structure from cluster analysis:

- Term clustering, based on the documents or sections in which terms are found together
- Document clustering, based on the number of terms they share (for instance common keywords, citations or references).

One example of this sort of approach is given by Hintzman's algorithm, and adaptations of it[22,23]. These allow nodes to be accessed as a function of a weighted sum — that of attributes in a probe vector corresponding to the attributes of the node itself. Although this may result in a computational explosion in large hypermedia databases, Kibby and Mayes note that the algorithm is amenable to parallel processing[28]. Indeed, term weight propagation methods such as this are not specific to hypermedia. In various forms they are also common in Bayesian and connectionist expert systems [10,12] — for forward chaining and backward chaining substitute the terms spreading activation and feedback mechanisms.

Frisse's Hypertext Medical Handbook[11] uses two weights to determine a card's expected utility or relevance to a query: intrinsic (for terms within a card) and extrinsic (for weights propagated from neighbouring cards). More specifically, the intrinsic weight is given as:

$$\text{WEIGHT}ij = k \times \text{FREQ}ij \times (\log(n) - \log(\text{CARDFREQ}j) + 1)$$

where *WEIGHTij* is the weight of card *i* determined by term *j*, *k* is a constant value, *FREQij* is the number of times term *j* occurs in card *i*, *n* is the number of cards in the network, and *CARDFREQj* is the number of cards containing the term *j*. This allows for moderately infrequent terms to assign more weight, as a function of the number of occurrences of such terms. Very frequent terms among all documents are of little use, as are very infrequent terms, since neither is useful for discriminating groups of documents from within the collection.

Possible problems with this approach develop when a card network is cyclical as opposed to a strict, one-way hierarchy or tree. Salton and Buckley provide a review of recent research into the relative utility of these approaches, concluding that single-term indexing is generally superior to that using more complex combinations of terms[44].

On a more applied level, Nicolson has produced a HyperCard hybrid with a database implemented by means of the logic programming language, PROLOG[37]. The former provides support for browsing, whilst the latter is capable of accepting natural language queries, and has a more sophisticated database mechanism than that available within HyperCard. Similarly, Knopik and Ryser have used PROLOG both for its natural language, query-handling capabilities, and to implement a series of heuristic rules for locating new concepts in text and linking them together[29]. At present this prototype system provides elementary text parsing for (German) nouns, but the authors propose a more sophisticated semantic parsing mechanism to extend its power and accuracy.

Of course, HyperTalk itself is in some ways a compromise between structured, procedural languages and AI programming languages[9]; it supports features characteristic of the latter, such as pattern matching on text strings, list processing, and recursion (though currently recursion is seriously limited by memory requirements). However, it seems that even higher-level, more declarative representations than PROLOG will be required before such systems are sufficiently usable by non-programmers to truly merit the term hypermedia.

Using full text search and statistical comparison algorithms (matching database documents against a master list of keywords or a list of user-supplied terms) are very much brute force methods, potentially requiring vast processor power. For example, the latter approach is taken by Dow Jones' DowQuest news and text search service[52]. This employs the 32,768 Connection Machine to provide parallel text search of a one gigabyte database. Documents are categorized by their 100 most frequent words, against which a list of user's words or phrases are compared using basic proximity and frequency weighting measures. The system offers a first set of 16 ranked story headlines. Users can then select stories from this set to further refine a second search.

However, at present DowQuest does not have a timeline facility, and its interface only supports queries/commands via the alphanumeric keyboard i.e. there is no selection via cursor keys or mouse. There are no explicit hypertext-style links in the database, although the processing power makes it feasible for implicit links to be generated ad hoc. (In a large database which is regularly changing, explicit link structures would probably prove too inflexible for maintenance.)

A variety of hybrids or compromise systems seem equally feasible. For instance, it might be possible to economize on the prohibitive need for raw processing power in such a system by employing full text or master keyword categorization of new, incoming material, combined with a facility for user-defined term searches within a specified scope[56]. An initial categorization against known terms would also allow for provision of consistent presentation and navigation metaphors, which are likely to be particularly useful in the interface to very large databases.

3.2.6 Heuristics

The easy incorporation of heuristics in hypermedia is perhaps the most significant contribution of the model over the basic semantic data models described above[39]. Examples of the sort of heuristics a user could employ in browsing might include 'lateral' approaches such as searching recent editions of an interesting journal, or searching on an author's name for related material[48]. Furthermore, an automated inference approach might be able to use a user's dynamic context to augment navigation[20]. Bertino *et al.*

describe a query processor developed in conjunction with the experimental document retrieval system MULTOS, which applies three general heuristics in turn[4]. However, the study of heuristics is best developed in relation to mathematical problems; it is unclear what heuristics are best applied in 'semantic' hypermedia problems, and how to rank them. Further research into methods of evaluating search cost is needed.

3.3. The Expert System Interface

3.3.1 Cues

In contrast to expert systems then, systems with an exclusively hypermedia approach may specify default paths for navigating through information, but much of the decision making is left to the user; the representation is not structured enough to be interpreted by a machine rule-base alone. However, to say that an expert system's structure is more rigid than that of a hypermedia system is not to say that the structure is itself sufficient to support hypermedia-style interrogation of the knowledge base. One way to resolve this is to see the differences as complementary, the two approaches as symbiotic[19]. Expert systems are typically required to provide explanations of their recommendations to users — interrogation by the user is in fact quite similar to browsing. To be effective, expert system documentation must be given its own priority, and not produced as a side-effect of afterthought of system design. What expert systems technology offers is a basis with which to implement analogs of high-level 'cognitive' tasks: declarative formatting; synthetic, natural language approaches to the interface; and management of complexity[24].

It is possible to compare both expert systems and hypermedia systems with a decision tree or directed graph. However, directionality in the hypermedia system is more arbitrary. At each node in the hypermedia system information is linearly structured as flat text. The textual and graphic forms used in hypermedia are typically far more familiar to end users than the esoteric representations used by expert systems — they are based in those of printed materials. In addition, there is the non-linear structure of intra- and inter-document links. Although a number of commentators have emphasized the unfamiliarity new users have with such structures,[7] it can be argued that these techniques are in fact analogous to those familiar from film drama (discussed further in the Chapter 7).

The contrast between primary purposes of hypermedia and expert systems is summarized below:

System	Primary Purpose
Expert System	Symbolic reasoning (limited or expensive explanations)
Hypermedia	Symbolic annotation (limited or expensive calculation

3.3.2 Natural Language

We have seen how hypertext is the most central of the new hypermedia; textual information is the most crucial content matter of most applications. To be useful to the broad community of end users, information can only be represented in natural language — as spoken and written in everyday communication. AI approaches to natural language processing are attractive in that they offer a seamless transition from interface control to node content. They differ from other AI approaches in several respects. Firstly, they deal with a different level of granularity — that of microlevel structure in individual sentences, and relations between sentences. This is in contrast to techniques that deal with the structure of the system and information predominately at the node level and above. Secondly, natural language processing in all but the most limited of contexts is relatively difficult to achieve[6,54].

Many phenomena contribute to this difficulty, and are beyond the scope of the present text. However, one of the most difficult aspects of NL is ambiguity, of which there are several types. Very broadly, ambiguity can be divided into structural and referential categories. Structural ambiguity exists in the relation between words in a sentence or sentences. To resolve it is the task of a (machine) grammar, i.e. a set of grammatical rules and the means to match them with a sentence. The latter, referential ambiguity is a more difficult problem to resolve. It requires knowledge of the 'real world', of objects and their relations. An example of a simple text processing system, START, based on Chomsky's Transformational Grammar is given by Katz[27].

3.3.3 Templates

Utilities tools provided with hypermedia shells tend to be designed for relatively high-level purposes; pop-up clipboards or maps, for instance. Thus they are independent of any specific application. However, in contrast to the expert system tools, cognitive input is left to the user. At the macro level, there appears to be a move towards providing authors with 'template' hierarchies or similar structures, that experience has shown to be similar across domain-specific hypermedia applications[49,50,51]. This parallels the provision of such templates in other publishing software, and in programs such as expert systems shells. Although templates *per se* are not an 'intelligent' feature, they are included here in that they may be manipulated in a way similar to the kind of frame-based structures described in section 3.2.1. Four sorts of template can be useful:

- Style sheets for formatting raw text or other materials — according to predefined house and personal preferences
- Structural skeletons — for instance deep and shallow hierarchies
- Filtering templates — user preferences for what search attributes to emphasize, which to suppress
- User identity templates — possibly stereotyped, rigid user levels, or adaptive, personalised profiles that are updated as users' performance improves
- Object templates — code that can be re-used in different program contexts and applications

It should be noted that these templates are very much more useful with formally structured or marked-up materials than with loosely structured material or material from informal domains, where either no formal indexing vocabulary exists, or no arbitrary document structure can be imposed in a uniform manner. Where a formal vocabulary exists, such as the US MeSH (Medical subject Headings), extensive automatic 'preprocessing' can be performed on materials before a human overseer provides the finishing touches[14]. This can be accomplished using a markup language such as Scribe, Troff, TeX or SGML, which in turn is interpreted by a parser such as TOLK[36]. A parser can then assign the document to a template, and/or carry out appropriate file indexing and distribution.

A similar knowledge-based, content-analysis approach is presented by Eirund and Kreplin[8], who integrate document classification with electronic mail distribution. Donald Hawkins has developed the similar concept of 'knowledge gateways' into databases. A gateway is a guidance system that seeks to automate intellectual aspects of search rather than the mechanical aspects of conventional 'information gateways' — and provides a review of some prototype systems. It is interesting to note that several of these adopt a declarative-style implementation in dialects of the AI language PROLOG[20,21].

At a micro-level also, several commercial developers now supply a selection of default buttons, with for instance three empty link nodes attached, so that an author can begin at once to produce standardized materials. An example of use might be in educational materials. Consider a subject such as crystals. These could be illustrated by three examples of structure, or by three static stages in development, or by material from three perspectives — chemical or mathematical formulae, an animation, and a verbal explanation. Each of these tripartite structures can be implemented by one of the pre-supplied buttons, which are gradually built up into a hierarchical system. If the buttons allow multiple references to an object, the application can contain non-hierarchical or horizontal links as well as vertical links. Objects such as buttons have the further advantage that they can be treated in different ways by users with different levels of expertise — either cut and pasted as virtual objects, or used as code modules (cf HyperTalk).

Within the category of user facilities, there is another important distinction — between facilities for helping users to orient themselves in relation to the overall structure, and tools for moving most efficiently through all relevant materials. Different users require tools focusing on quite different operational levels. In particular, expert and naive users benefit from different tools — see Chapters 6 and 8. (As an aside, note that authors also become users as their applications grow, and in many cases users will have the opportunity to become authors by extending materials to suit their own needs.) The above distinctions are similar to the three-layer models described by Knopik and Ryser and by Koh and Chua[29,30]. At the most general level, developers can provide only the basic means to implement nodes and links. At the next level, authors determine the application-specific frame/net/stack layer. In turn, the author/user can overlay his or her own personal layer, which may extend or edit the structure supplied by the author.

3.3.4   Expert Help

Consider next the problems facing developers of intelligent knowledge-based systems. The first stage, broadly termed knowledge elicitation, produces a great deal of information from experts, generally in the form of typed, verbatim transcripts. Correlating this information according to common themes, and eventually organizing it into a hierarchical rule-base or decision tree is a mammoth task without the use of automated tools. A number of the larger AI toolkits now include hypertext-based tools for transcript analysis[34], and even induction mechanisms for finding patterns or rules in statistical data.

These patterns may be used in two ways: firstly to help authors structure their materials; secondly, to construct a dynamic user model rather than rely on the kind of limited stereotype or 'average' model implicit in most CBT applications. The need in particular for this second kind of model is discussed in depth by Berry and Broadbent[3], and also in Section 4.6.

The other side of the coin is structuring hypermedia materials so that even naive users can easily query the finished, self-contained system. This is desirable both to train new experts, and because it is highly dubious whether even the most subtle 'expert' system could ever be allowed to make unsupervized decisions. Thus users must be able to ask for justification; in many cases these requests are likely to be *ad hoc*, unforeseen by the system designers.

Again, hypermedia mechanisms have the power to provide a conceptually simple overview of the system's concepts and dialog interactions. This is a less hard-wired approach than that of conventional Help facilities, or of the Explain Decision option available in many expert system shells[31,35]. (Few expert systems allow users to browse through their databases or rule bases in an *ad hoc* fashion, distinct from their active decision-making modes.) The resulting dialog model offered by intelligent hypermedia is likely to resemble that of 'critiqing', where the system offers comments on a user's decisions but does not pre-empt or countermand them[32].

3.4   Hybrids and Connectionist Models

Consider once more the relative positions of hypermedia and semantic nets in Figure 3.3. Hypermedia tends to have a relatively sparse control structure, and less density of attributes than semantic nets. Of course, semantic nets are one of the main models for knowledge structures and control in expert systems. The provision of both facilities can be complementary, without becoming redundant. Expert systems approaches provide the means to proceduralize, to control. There are many domains where the necessary or available knowledge/data is so great in quantity, or complexity, that it is not feasible for humans to make effective decisions. Providing expert systems functionality can make these domains tractable[33]. Hypermedia, in turn, allows freedom to explore beyond the rather narrow channels of rule-based information. A number of successful hybrid systems are now commercially available — even for personal microcomputers. A good example is KnowledgePro[10]. This expert system shell not only supplies online context-sensitive help, but allows developers to combine AI and hypermedia techniques in their own applications, by means of its development language.

So far we have discussed only those approaches to artificial intelligence that incorporate explicit IF — THEN rules, in other words a top-down control architecture; but by no means all 'expert' systems, nor indeed all intelligent hypermedia rely on this approach. It is also possible to build a system that is initially 'unprogrammed', and acquires a structure of associative links according to the way that objects and their attributes are caused to interact over time. These bottom-up architectures are variously known as neural nets, parallel distributed processing or connectionist models. It seems increasingly likely that such mechanisms will be very significant in the hardware and software of the 1990s. For a comprehensive review of the field readers are referred to Rumelhart and Norman[41], which includes a full description of relevant algorithms.

Explicit references to the neural net/semantic net approach in relation to hypermedia development are made by Jonassen who states that: *"Hypertext browsing is the ultimate accretion medium."* In his model a semantic net structure learns from experience of users' browsing paths, gradually developing a richer, more elaborate knowledge base according to frequencies of association between nodes in the network. Eventually associations will form concept clusters, accretions, or aggregates[26]. Several other hypermedia models have employed semantic net-type implementations. These include NoteCards[17,18], and TOPIC[16]. TOPIC includes procedural weighting algorithms which cluster frames according to their content in relation to dominant concepts. However, we are yet to see a truly connectionist 'spreading association' hypermedia system.

SUMMARY

The representations used by AI and hypermedia systems are often similar — for instance hierarchical or network node-plus-link structures.

The fact that in both kinds of systems users' interactions cannot be fully predetermined requires that declarative or heuristic approaches to problem-solving are adopted.

What artificial intelligence has to offer hypermedia is automated reasoning strategies and heuristics — the means to make prohibitively large or complex knowledge domains more tractable. Automated reasoning may be deployed both in building hypermedia knowledge bases and in using them.

What hypermedia has to offer artificial intelligence is a different style of dialog and decision-making, centered on the user.

Hybrid, intelligent hypermedia systems offer the possibility of 'critiqing'. This may be a preferable approach to users who are themselves experts but work in domains where any mistakes must be minimized, and to those seeking computer-based tuition.

REFERENCES

1. Anderson, J. *Human Associative Memory*. Washington, DC: Winston, 1973.
2. Bartlett, F. *Remembering, a study in experimental and social psychology*, Cambridge University Press, 1932.
3. Berry, D. and Broadbent, D. Expert systems and the man-machine interface. Part Two: the user interface. *Expert Systems*, **4 (1)**, 1987, pp. 18-27.
4. Bertino, E., Gibbs, S. and Rabitti, F. document processing strategies: cost evaluation and heuristics. In: Allen, R. (Ed.) *Proceedings of the Conference on Office Information Systems*, March 23-25 1988, Palo Alto, California. *ACM SIGOIS* Bulletin, **9 (2-3)**, April and July 1988, pp. 169-181.
5. Carlson, P. Hypertext and intelligent interfaces for text retrieval. In: Barrett, E. (Ed.), *The Society of Text*. Cambridge, MA: MIT Press, 1989.
6. Chomsky, N. *Aspects of the Theory of Syntax*. Cambridge, MA: MIT Press, 1965.
7. Conklin, J. Hypertext: An introduction and survey. *Computer*, **20 (9)**, September 1987, pp. 17-41.
8. Eirund, H. and Kreplin, K. Knowledge based document classification

supporting integrated document handling. In: Allen, R. (Ed.) *Proceedings of the Conference on Office Information Systems*, March 23-25 1988, Palo Alto, California. *ACM SIGOIS Bulletin*, **9 (2-3)**, April and July 1988, pp. 189-196.

9.   Evans, R. Expert systems and HyperCard. *BYTE*, **15, (1)**, January, 1990 pp. 317-324.

10. Franklin, C. KnowledgePro: hypertext meets expert systems. *Database*, **12 (6)**, pp. 71-76.

11. Frisse, M. Searching for information in a hypertext medical handbook. *Communications of the ACM*, **31 (7)**, July 1988, pp. 880-886.

12. Frisse, M. From text to hypertext. *BYTE*, **13 (10)**, October 1988, pp. 247-253.

13. Gale, W. (Ed.) *AI and Statistics*. Addison-Wesley, 1986.

14. Gallant, S. Connectionist expert systems. *Communications of the ACM*, **31 (2)**, February, 1988 pp. 152-169.

15. Garg. P. Abstraction mechanisms in hypertext. *Communications of the ACM*, **31 (7)**, July 1988, pp. 862-70, 879.

16. Hahn, U. and Riemer, U. Automatic generation of hypertext knowledge bases. In: Allen, R. (Ed.) *Proceedings of the Conference on Office Information Systems*, March 23-25 1988, Palo Alto, California. *ACM SIGOIS Bulletin*, **9 (2-3)**, April and July 1988, pp. 182-188.

17. Halasz, F. Reflections on NoteCards: Seven issues for the next generation of hypermedia systems. *Communications of the ACM*, **31 (7)**, July 1988, pp. 836-852.

18. Halasz, F. Moran, T. and Trigg, NoteCards in a nutshell. *Proceedings of the ACM CHI+GI 1987 Conference*, Toronto, Canada, April 5-9, 1987.

19. Haselkorn, M. The future of ''writing'' for the computer industry. In: Barrett, E. (Ed.) *Text, ConText and HyperText*. Cambridge, MA: MIT Press, 1988.

20. Hawkins, D. Applications of artificial intelligence (AI) and expert systems for online searching. *Online*, **12 (1)**, January 1988, pp. 31-43.

21. Hawkins, D. Levy, L. and Montgomery, K. Knowledge Gateways: the building blocks. *Information Processing and Management*, **24 (4)**, 1988, pp. 458-468.

22. Hintzman, D. MINERVA 2: A simulation model of human memory. *Behaviour Research Methods, Instruments & Computers*, **16 (2)**, pp. 96-101.

23. Hintzman, D. 'Schema abstraction' in a multiple-trace memory model. *Psychological Review*, **93**, pp. 411-28.

24. James, G. Artificial intelligence and automated publishing systems. In: Barrett, E. (Ed.) *Text, ConText and HyperText*. Cambridge, MA: MIT Press, 1988.

25. Johnson-Laird, P. In: Johnson-Laird, P. and Wason, P. (Eds.) *Thinking: readings in cognitive science*, Cambridge University Press, 1977.

26. Jonassen, D. Semantic networking approaches to structuring hypertext. *Proceedings of Hypertext II*, University of York, June 29-30 1989.

27. Katz, B. Text processing with the START natural language system. In: Barrett, E. (Ed.) *Text, ConText and HyperText*. Cambridge, MA: MIT Press, 1988.

28. Kibby, M. and Mayes, J. Towards intelligent hypertext. In: McAleese, R. (Ed.) *Hypertext theory into practice*, pp. 164-172. Oxford: Intellect Books, 1989.

29. Knopik, T. and Ryser, S. AI-methods for structuring hypertext-information. *Proceedings of Hypertext II*, University of York, June 29-30 1989.

30. Koh, T. and Chua, T. On the design of a frame-based hypermedia system. *Proceedings of Hypertext II*, University of York, June 29-30 1989.

31. McAleese, R. The graphical representation of knowledge as an interface to knowledge based systems. In: Bullinger, H. and Shackel, B. (Eds.) *Human-Computer Interaction*, pp. 1089-1093, North-Holland, 1987.
32. Miller, P. *Expert Critiquing Systems: practice based medical consultation by computer*. Springer Verlag, 1987.
33. Minsky, M. A framework for representing knowledge. In: Winston, P. (Ed.), *The psychology of computer vision*. NY: McGraw-Hill, 1975.
34. Motta, E., Eisenstadt, M., Pitman, K., and West, M. Support for knowledge acquisition in the Knowledge Engineer's Assistant (KEATS). *Expert Systems*, **5 (1)**, February 1988, pp. 6-27.
35. Morrison, A. Hypertext and expert systems — experiences and prospects. *Proceedings of the Fifth International Expert Systems Conference*, 6 June 1989.
36. Niblett, T. and van Hoff, A. Structured hypertext documents via SGML. *Proceedings of Hypertext II*, University of York, 29-30 June 1989.
37. Nicolson, R. Towards the third generation: the case of IKBH (Intelligent Knowledge Based Hypermedia) environments. *Proceedings of Hypertext II*, University of York, June 29-30 1989.
38. Parsaye, K. *et al. Intelligent Databases — Object-oriented, deductive hypermedia technologies*. John Wiley and Sons, 1989.
39. Potter, N. and Trueblood, R. Traditional, semantic, and hyper-semantic approaches to data-modelling. *IEEE Computer*, **21 (6)**, June 1988, pp. 53-63.
40. Rich, E. *Artificial Intelligence*. NY: McGraw-Hill, 1983.
41. Rumelhart, D. and McClelland, J. (1986). *Brainy Minds: a critical review of Parallel Distributed Processing (Vols. 1 and 2)*, Cambridge, MA: MIT Press.
42. Salton, G. Another look at automatic text-retrieval systems. *Communications of the ACM*, **29 (7)**, July 1986, pp. 648-656.
43. Salton, G. *Automatic Text Processing*. Addison-Wesley, 1989.
44. Salton, G. and Buckley, C. Term-weighting approaches in automatic text retrieval. *Information Processing and Management*, **24 (5)**, 1988, pp. 513-523.
45. Schank, R. and Abelson, R. *Scripts, plans, goals and understanding*. Hillsdale, NJ: Erlbaum, 1977.
46. Sloman, A. Research and development in expert systems. In: Bramer, M. (Ed.) *Proceedings of the Fourth Technical Conference of the British Computer Society Specialist Group on Expert Systems*, University of Warwick, 18-20 December, 1984. Cambridge University Press.
47. Storrs, G. The Alvey DHSS Large Demonstrator Project Knowledge ANalysis Tool: KANT. In: McAleese, R. (Ed.), *Hypertext theory into practice*. Oxford: Intellect Books Limited, 1989.
48. Thompson, R. and Croft, W. Support for browsing in an intelligent text retrieval system. *International Journal of Man-Machine Studies*, **30 (6)**, June 1989. pp. 639-668.
49. Trigg, R., Suchman, L. and Halasz, F. Supporting collaboration in NoteCards. *Proceedings of the Conference on Computer Supported Cooperative Work*, Austin, TX, December 3-5 1986.
50. Walker. J. Supporting document development with Concordia. *IEEE Computer*, **21 (1)**, January 1988, pp. 48-59.
51. Walker, M. Framed documents. *Desktop Publishing Today*, **4 (5)**, May 1989. pp. 36-37.
52. Weyer, S. Questing for the "Dao": DowQuest and intelligent text retrieval. *Online*, **13 (5)**, September 1989, pp. 39-48.
53. Willett, P. Recent trends in hierarchic document clustering: a critical review. *Information Processing and Management*, **24 (5)**, 1988, pp. 577-597.

54. Winograd, T. *Understanding Natural Language*. NY: Academic Press, 1972.
55. Winograd, T. Frame representation and the declarative-procedural controversy. In: *Representation and Understanding*, Bobrow, D. and Collins, A. (Eds.). NY: Academic Press, 1975.
56. Woodhead, N. Master's Dissertation, Polytechnic of the South Bank, London, 1989 (unpublished).
57. Woods, W. 'What's in a link: foundations for semantic networks. In: Bobrow, D. and Collins, A. (Eds), *Representation and Understanding*. NY: Academic Press, 1975.
58. Younggren, G. Using an object-oriented programming language to create audience-driven hypermedia environments. In: Barrett, E. (Ed.) *Text, ConText and HyperText*. Cambridge, MA: MIT Press, 1988.

Electronic Publishing

"All I am proposing is to electronify literature".
Theodor Holm Nelson, 1989.

4.1   Introduction: Multimedia

There is nothing new about making references — either within a work to other parts of that work, or to external works. In academic literature there is a tradition thousands of years old of drawing on other documents for support, or contrast. In artistic media too, the use of allusions, of themes and 'borrowed' elements is almost universal. Neither is the idea of a non-linearly structured document strictly new; works such as dictionaries, anthologies, and reference manuals are rarely meant to be read from the first page to the last.

Taking a single written work as an example, for any one user there is likely to be considerable redundancy of information. The efficiency with which that user can extract the material sought depends largely on the facilities provided for categorizing, referencing or filtering information. In their most basic form, these facilities are conventions such as alphabetic indices, glossaries, tables of contents, bibliographies, chapter, section and sub-section headings; none of these is essential to the content of a work, but each enhances it in some way. However, the overall structure remains limited to a linear progression. In many works this linear path is the only feasible path for readers or viewers to take.

There is also a fundamental limit to the kind of material content that is supported for any one of our conventional media formats. For instance, the printed page is restricted to text, and to simple, static, two-dimensional graphics. Of course, it is possible to provide a video cassette, a computer or optical disk, or an audio cassette along with the book. Yet these in turn are organized in more or less linear fashions. There is no direct means of following a reference from one medium to the exact provenance in another. In other words, until very recently it has not been possible to browse between media using a single delivery device.

Furthermore, the actual corpus of available knowledge (as distinct from homogeneous data files) has already outstripped our capacity to manage and manipulate information. Despite having the basic physical means to access online information from remote locations, we do not yet have adequate means to sift out that which is relevant — with the exception of very specialized (and expensive) databases, most of which are manually cross-referenced or produced by processor-intensive brute force. Yet information is the currency of our culture, and those with better quality information have a considerable advantage over their competition. This quality depends on efficient processing of greater and greater quantities of low-grade or less relevant information.

Some publications, such as academic journals, do acknowledge the need of readers to access information at a variety of levels of detail, by providing additional, auxiliary features as abstracts, introductions, summaries, and conclusions. References to external works can be provided in the linear text, as footnotes, at the end of chapters, or as complete bibliographies at the end of a work. Furthermore, conventional references are often given at an unduly macroscopic level — to the title of a book or paper for instance, rather than to the page and paragraph number which is actually relevant.

Often there is considerable redundancy in providing such features — perhaps 10 or 20 per cent of most printed academic works consists of repeated bibliographical listings, overviews and summaries. Worse still, the entire publication may in some cases become redundant or obsolete because of the invalidation of a relatively small amount of information — changed prices or regulations, new addresses, better techniques. With static media it is often necessary to reproduce a whole volume or modular section when this occurs — an expensive and time consuming activity.

As well as the problems with repeated or obsolete information, there is considerable sacrificed space in a paper-based work; for instance, margins and section breaks. This is not strictly necessary, but is used to increase the work's aesthetic appeal or the ease with which a reader can identify breaks in the work's structure. And paper itself, apart from being an increasingly precious resource, is a bulky medium for storing large amounts of information. Hardcopy alternatives such as microfilm suffer from a lack of satisfactory delivery devices. A microfiche browser may be an acceptable way of checking library references, but few people given the choice would use one to read a periodical, let alone a text book.

By contrast, an average floppy disk can hold around half a million text characters (about as much as this book) in conventional format. CD-ROM disks can hold many times as much. Furthermore, both text and graphics can be compressed or archived by means of algorithms so that many more times as much information can be held on the same disk. Depending on the format and the access time criteria, compression ratios may be as much as two, three or even one hundred to one (e.g. IBM/Intel's DVI technology[34].). The appropriate algorithms can be built into software, or even ROM chips, so that decompression is performed dynamically, and transparently[38].

Thus, given a desktop computer and a hard disk or a small shelf, a researcher can have on hand a personal storage capacity equivalent to that of a reasonably sized library. Vannevar Bush's conjectures on this area have been borne out remarkably accurately (although he believed the medium would be microfilm): *"The Encyclopaedia Britannica could be reduced to the volume of a matchbox. The library of a million volumes could be compressed into one end of a desk.... Mere compression, of course, is not enough; one needs not only to make and store a record, but also be able to consult it..."*[8].

Printed media are limited and limiting then, in so far as they can be adapted to any given individual's requirements. If it is acknowledged that for many domains there are many possible, valid structures that can be overlaid upon that domain and between domains, and that ideas themselves are non-linear associations of concepts, there is no reason why a user's optimal structure should correspond to an author's. Yet printed materials do not support the same multiplicity of views — the extra navigational dimension — that is possible with hypermedia treatments.

The result is that authors are often forced to commit their works to an unduly narrow target audience. Arguably, this often means biasing a work to the lowest common denominator of users, because of commercial publishing pressures, or the need to achieve a minimum common educational standard. In contrast, many hypermedia systems support 'verbose' and 'fold-away' modes, in which annotations or auxiliary cue information is displayed to the full or repressed, respectively. Alternatively, it may be possible for the user to expand or suppress a specific class of attributes — such as graphical, technical or mathematical information. This can provide a novice with an initial overview presentation, or an expert with a specialist reading that is suited to a particular bias of interests, without presenting either with redundant material.

Another way in which the single, printed version is inferior to hypermedia is the ease with which the latter can achieve control over document distribution. Consider, for instance, the sensitive nature of many corporate and bureaucratic documents. To protect these at present, modular versions are produced. These are made available according to security access level or some analogous protocol. Providing physical security for them may entail considerable inconvenience. A preferable system would allow a range of users to view a single online document, or all corporate literature, with levels of detail (and transparency of detail) determined by their access level. The document is presented and protected seamlessly within the same delivery device.

Of course there are many areas in which a hypermedia approach is unsuitable — users do not have computers, cannot afford them, or need the portability of printed hardcopy. Some tasks make a visible and ordered edit/ version history desirable (especially where a number of developers are involved in one project) — and few hypermedia systems to date support this. Rather, edited materials tend to be stored online in the most recent version only. Furthermore, there are possible problems in converting hypermedia materials into flat file formats for tasks such as printing, which requires the imposition of just the sort of rigid form that hypermedia seeks to outmode. So it would be wrong to believe that hypermedia provides a publishing panacea. However, many observers are convinced that it will rapidly overtake, if not completely replace our present technologies in many contexts, and that these contexts will become more and more integrated.

The following recapitulates on the foremost reasons why a new approach is needed to integrate information and its sources:

- The amount of recorded information in the world doubles approximately every couple of years
- New media technologies continue to appear, each bringing new models and storage formats that are not directly compatible
- The physical locations of information continue to diversify
- More and better information is needed to advance and compete
- Better quality information need not cost more to produce.

Hypermedia offers a software approach to manage this information, and to integrate disparate software and media hardware resources, without necessarily demanding homogeneous protocols between all of these elements.

4.2 E-Books

Electronic literature exists already in a variety of forms, from scanned versions of 'literary' texts, online educational and reference manuals, to discussion forums and text-based databases or abstracts. However, although many of these services could easily be accessed or augmented with hypermedia functionality, few corporate producers or distributors to date have taken this next logical step. As with artificial intelligence, technology take-up has been only partial, both within the commercial and academic sectors. Even the now widespread use of 'desktop publishing' software has done little to change this attitude towards hypermedia; packages provide 'electronic paste-boards' — sets of tools based on those in use for centuries. The resulting products remain essentially two-dimensional, whether they are presented to readers on paper or on disk.

However, a number of ambitious projects are currently under way to realize the concept of a truly portable electronic book, or holistic personal information system[43]. These include Xerox PARC's Dynabook[21], the Australian Smart Book joint venture project, the Canadian Hi-lite optical Smart Card[38] and Apple's much heralded Knowledge Navigator. For instance, the Smart Book is a portable (225 x 155 x 30mm), rechargeable Reader system with an LCD screen and just six control buttons — of which four are dedicated to navigation. This will be used with ROM (Read Only Memory) texts packs ranging in (uncompressed) capacity from 1Mb to 8Mb — i.e. up to 45Mb compressed text.

Even when the above projects become robust enough for the mass market, they are likely to be less durable than the enduring book, and probably less portable; or if not less portable, then less easy to use with the human tools of hand and eye. This begs the question of why multi-billion dollar corporations develop such projects. The reason has already been hinted at; the 'Dynabook' or 'E-book' proper is more than a document wherein an electronic screen replaces the printed page. Electronic books potentially allow one host book format to contain a multiplicity of views. They encompass a variety of bespoke, virtual books which the user can tailor to his or her needs at any one usage, or across usages[36,46]. These views may be achieved via analogs of the sort of conventional access points mentioned above — indices, glossaries, etc. (see Figure 4.1). A major difference between these as found in print and in hypermedia is that in the latter they are actionable — selecting an embedded reference item results in direct access to its occurrence(s) (see Figure 4.2).

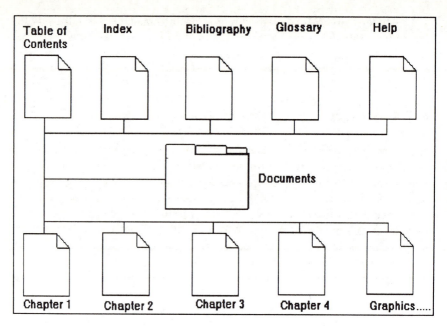

Figure 4.1 Many-to-many relationships of sections in an electronic book.

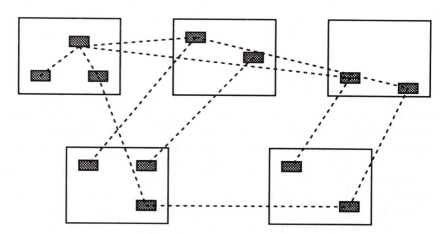

Figure 4.2 Embedded references from chunks to distant chunks.

It might be argued that this additional choice of structure entails additional complexity, and that this in turn would lead to a greater investment of time by users to accomplish their tasks. However, there is encouraging evidence to the contrary; Landauer, for instance, reports that experienced hypertext users (of the SuperBook browser) require only half as long in search tasks as do print readers[22]. A properly designed electronic book or interface to such works avoids this 'cognitive overhead' by providing support for direct access to items in the text at varying levels of granularity or abstraction. In addition, the active information processing tools provided by electronic books are far more powerful than the devices of conventional printed media — and might include text/pattern matchers, indexers, interactive maps and timelines (see sub-section 6.5).

In addition, there are a number of effects such as simulations and animations which simply cannot be achieved with conventional books[3,12]. Although electronic books require new skills, the learning curve for initial familiarization with hypermedia or electronic books appears to be relatively shallow. A study by Weyer demonstrates that college students can rapidly learn the basic features in such a system. Furthermore, Weyer's students and those in a study by Marchionini preferred the dynamic book to a simple online text or a paper text in question-answering tasks [28,46]. However, as a possible qualification to this enthusiasm, in a study of junior school pupils by Colbourn and Cockerton-Turner large individual differences were found in learning rates[10]. Then again, the potential benefit of the hypermedia approach is that materials can be provided for learners of all abilities and levels.

The book metaphor itself is in contrast to the pervasive software metaphor of the desktop — as supported by many hypermedia systems, such as Yankelovich et al.s' Intermedia[48,49]. Rahtz et al. suggest that its cues are likely to appeal to end users with minimal experience of computing[32]. But electronic books can come in as many formats as their paper forebears. In fact it is possible to distinguish several sorts of archetypal electronic book structures. For instance, the encyclopedia is relatively shallow, with many cross references within only a couple of levels of granularity[28,47]. The text book (or reference manual) has a narrower, deeper hierarchy, although with cross-references orthogonal to the main structure[25,29]. Interactive fiction can support a variety of paths based around themes and character 'views' as well as the more conventional, linear timelines[20]. Electronic journals and catalogs are also appealing possibilities, particularly in domains where samples or demonstrations from dynamic media are desirable. Electronic books are quite easy to develop from online text using standard off-the-shelf software. Figure 4.3, shows an interactive Table of Contents from this book, using OWL's Guide. Section 9.5 in the Contents is a Reference button that directly accesses its corresponding location in Chapter 9 (stored as a separate document file).

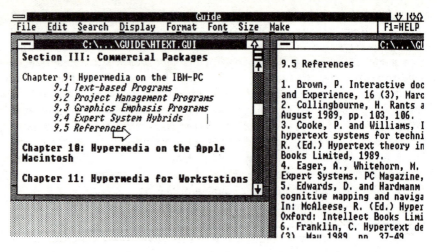

Figure 4.3 An E-book treatment of the present text.

Figure 4.4 presents a graphical Table of Contents or browser as supplied with HyperCard's online Help/Tutorial. Note that an Index is also available.

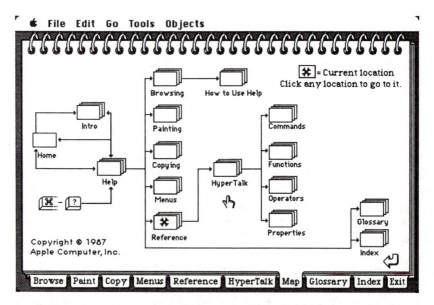

Figure 4.4 Help and Tutorial information from Apple's HyperCard.

Given so many apparently good reasons for electronic books, the reader may still be left asking why their take-up has been so inhibited. Among reasons that have been offered are a lack of consensus on the core features of hypermedia, and the perceived need to make links manually[24]. There are also issues of royalties, a lack of awareness, a lack of skilled staff, and ingrained prejudices developed from professional lives spent working with conventional, discrete media. However, as an incentive, and an indicator of the rapid advances new media can make in the marketplace once standards have been agreed, one only has to consider the compact disk; within five years this new medium has risen from obscurity and controversy to overtake the LP as the most popular format for recorded music. New possibilities of data compression make CD-ROM digitized video a likely extension of this industry[11,34].

4.3   B-Boards and E-Mail

Bulletin boards, online databases and electronic mail systems are also prime candidates to be enhanced with hypermedia. For instance, most E-mail systems are presently organized as hierarchical or ring networks. They do not have high-level graphical support, nor facilities for linking materials beyond the basic attributes of author, recipient, or subject heading. As Hawkins puts it, they are singularly lacking in those aspects of search which can be categorized as intellectual as opposed to mechanical[18]. Trigg's TEXTNET system implements networked hypertext as an object-oriented semantic net[42]. Categorization is by multiple features, which can include keywords as well as the standard attributes mentioned above. Eirund and Kreplin describe an experimental system, MULTOS, which goes a stage further toward intelligent hypermedia, by integrating content-analysis of documents with automatic mail distribution[13] (see also section 3.3).

4.4   E-Libraries

Creating one-off, electronic publications is only one half of the hypermedia ideal. The real challenge, as seen by pioneers such as Ted Nelson, is to create the 'docuverse' — an environment where it is possible for users to establish their own links among arbitrary materials, all made available in a virtual common format[30]. In Nelson's Xanadu system, users will access (and pay for) only those fragments of relevant knowledge which they require. This is a radical and controversial departure from the present world of discrete, 'private' documents, each with what amounts to an all-or-nothing royalty fee system. Furthermore, links in this system are not necessarily to documents or chunks. Although documents are seen as important anchorage points, new virtual documents may be created via 'transclusions' — a mechanism for overlaying layers of arbitrary-sized fragments or quotes. For an example of a hypermedia guided tour as applied to a library, readers are referred to Ertel[14]. The Apple Library Tour (a HyperCard stack) allows users to progress seamlessly via the computer from a topographical tour of the shelves, for instance, to lists of periodicals, to searching for keywords in articles.

4.5 Help Systems

Product reference materials have the following general characteristics: they are rigidly and uniformly organized into discrete sections, and contexts; they are organic in the sense that they expand gradually during their life cycles; they are not used in a linear fashion; as they grow they are difficult to manage, at any one time, and across historical versions. Consequently, they are also prime candidates for a hypermedia approach, both in relation to their production and maintenance, and in relation to their use.

Current online Help systems are certainly a great advantage over primitive error messages, and over systems that present no messages at all. However, the present generation of online Help is often little more than an electronic treatment of the user's Quick Reference Guide. Navigation strategies are limited, and there are few levels of abstraction in the degree of detail to which information is given. Perhaps most significantly, there are relatively few systems which give context-sensitive or 'intelligent' Help. In some systems the Help application is not even embedded within the main environment, but exists as an external reference work.

Context-sensitivity normally refers to the capacity of a system to locate relevant reference material automatically in response to a query relating to the user's cursor position. Help information is normally presented on the screen in a pop-up box or scrolling window which occupies a dedicated part of the screen (although the user may reconfigure this). Users are normally offered options to view related information topics, to move to an overview, to view other instances or contexts of the term/object in question, or to return to the main task domain.

A true hypermedia help system additionally provides multiple link structures and alternative levels of granularity. However, it is important to realize that a user in need of Help is not the same as a hypermedia user in need of a research tool; the former's immediate interests are local, and limited — the ability to browse through extended examples or material not directly related to the problem at hand is an unwanted distraction rather than a useful bonus. As Rubens points out, a good Help system should reduce the cognitive load of users, not add to it[35].

There is considerable cross-over between Help systems and more general educational aspects of hypermedia[10,17]. However, it is useful to distinguish where in the hierarchy of expertise users need what sort of learning facilities. For instance, Herrstrom and Massey[19] distinguish four developmental stages in users' familiarity with their systems, each of which requires Help information at the following levels:

1) overview;
2) tutorial;
3) procedural; and
4) reference.

Carroll and Aaronson contrast two different styles of 'intelligent' Help: How-to-do-it (step-by-step, procedural) and How-it-works (metaphoric, goal-based), concluding that the two have a complementary role — users can benefit from specific action-consequence instructions, and also from an overall rationale or conceptual model[9].

4.6 Education and Computer-based Training

Computer-based training (CBT) or computer-aided instruction (CAI) systems and their 'courseware' modules differ from online Help in that they are intended to be used as self-contained materials; they are not embedded in another application. Conventional CBT is characterized by the relatively inflexible structure of these materials — and by the fact that although the course is computer-based, it may also involve the use of supplements for other delivery devices, for instance audio or video. In the ideal hypermedia environment there would be no qualitative difference between embedded Help, CBT, and any other online materials; rather each is mutually accessible from any one context. Furthermore, the virtual structure of CBT materials would be determined dynamically by context, rather than precisely predetermined by its authors.

Several of the commercial hypermedia systems in Section III have been marketed with a primary emphasis on fulfilling the needs of the educational community, i.e. for microcomputer, for a finite library of materials, often for single user, with tools requiring no expert computer programming knowledge. These include Apple Computer's HyperCard and Office Workstations Limited's Guide for the Apple Macintosh (combinations of which are fast becoming standard equipment in US schools and colleges, where an increasing number of educators are designing their course materials as hypermedia). For the IBM PC and compatibles similar facilities are offered by Linkway, HyperPad and, again, Guide.

We are still some way from achieving the seamless information environment. However, there has been considerable speculation and a number of experimental studies to determine to what extent and how in particular this dynamic 'interactive' style of stand-alone CBT facilitates superior learning. In theory, not only does hypermedia encourage a 'hands-on' style of learning, but the structure of its materials is such that users can be guided into encountering central themes and crucial pivots many times as they interact with the system; material can be re-presented as browsing users backtrack to a 'home' or central crossroads location in order to explore another branch of the available information.

Learning can also be achieved by providing a series of modular, linked lessons, each of which is examined in relation to performance in a repeated or incremental task. Both the relatively passive and relatively active learning paradigms not only emphasize 'concept clusters' of information, but also support links to other clusters (perhaps emphasized by 'typed' links such as 'disagrees with' or 'alternative method'). In other words, although users have relative freedom to choose their own order of learning, some paths are 'easier' to follow than others — there are few long leaps forward into deeper material, and frequent or constant opportunities to return over material covered. The grouping of material into clusters allows easier abstraction (to navigation aids such as a graphical browser) and encourages users not to develop a completely 'deviant' conceptual model. However, the emphasis is on experimentation, discovery and synthesis, rather than on analysis and absorption of standard versions — only a small part of the material is actually repetitive in this idealized model.

From a psychological point of view, a number of findings support the superiority of active over passive learning paradigms. An empirical study by Stanton and Stammers confirms that providing a variety of possible learning styles (top-down, bottom-up and sequential) improves performance — it seems that more individual preferences are catered for[39]. By contrast, McKnight *et al.* report superior performance for linear styles, implying that caution and further research are called for in this area[25].

Guidelines for the design of educational materials, based on the analysis of objectives, are suggested by Franklin[15]. A similar emphasis on user analysis is recommended by Shneiderman[37]. Issues for authors are discussed in further detail in Chapter 6.

According to Franklin, in providing default paths or navigation strategies course designers should consider whether their aims are:

- To support the teaching of new skills
- To directly encourage the use of an existing skill
- To provide information to be used in conjunction with existing skills.

This may lead to the decision that one or more possible paths are essential, or redundant. Interestingly, most software support hypertext seems to fall into the third category — it is to augment existing basic skills, but only indirectly since the help system is a modular, separate entity to the main environment such as the editor or compiler.

Several recent projects have emphasized the need for a new model for the development of educational materials, as opposed to the traditional CBT production cycle[1]. An example of such a model is Intelligent Training Systems. The emphasis in ITS is in reducing the design, authoring and actual programming phases required, as well as validation and application maintenance, by providing high level toolkits (such as outliner, structurer for teaching strategies, user stereotyper). Course design and authoring are distinct phases; course material nodes are grouped into modular topics, which can be structured by the system to support a variety of teaching/ learning styles. A demonstrator application for this model, HITS, has been recently developed by Logica using HyperCard. As a coda to this it should be noted that Berry and Broadbent suggest that satisfactory educational systems will eventually need to have the capability of constructing individual, dynamic user models rather than stereotypes[4]. This is echoed by Colbourn and Cockerton-Turner's experimental findings of large individual differences in junior school pupils' understanding of the nature and use of help facilities[10].

4.7 Co-authoring and the Role of Writers

The information revolution is on the verge of converting even the most individualistic media forms from the unit production to the assembly line production paradigm. Even the literary work may be set to become less an isolated act by a single author, and more and more the product of a process in which the author is one of a group of several actors[2] — a group that eventually includes the 'reader'.

However, the most immediate implications of hypermedia and related technologies are for the users of large-scale technical documentation[44]. Several commentators expect the role of the technical writers and the numbers of their profession to be seriously undermined by the advances in software for electronic publishing tasks[5,6]. A more optimistic view is that there will certainly be erosion of the lines distinguishing the present roles of writers, editors and other publishing staff from their colleagues in other departments, but that the erosion is likely to be two-way; as technical writers become more generally 'computerate', they are as likely to assume some of the responsibilities of applications designers, systems analysts and database administrators, as such staff are likely to assume the role of writer[49,50]. The net amount of documentation in almost every field is growing — not least because the software has dramatically cut the cost of production. If anything, there is likely to be an increasing need for writing-related skills, no matter what the actual job title of the person possessing them.

The other side of the problem is the question of how to provide an adequate framework to support online documentation teams. Issues of collaboration — concurrent and/or editorial access to materials — are relevant both to authors and to end users. Production and research projects typically involve teams of co-operating specialists, each of whom is responsible for one aspect, but may have useful insights into a colleague's work. Many systems designers have taken the stance that users should normally be able to annotate existing materials created by others, but not allowed to permanently alter or delete the materials themselves. However, there are also questions of whether users should be allowed to create their own links, or to view all materials without restriction, and how to ensure consistent multiple updates to relevant versions of connected or derivative materials[24,40,41].

4.8 Reading and Writing Issues — an Introduction

Conventional media allow limited facilities for users to make customized, permanent versions of their own; beyond making marginal notes, or developing systems of notebooks, bookmarks and external file indexes, none of which is totally satisfactory. Ideally, in the opinion of the majority of commentators, hypermedia removes the author/user distinction[48], allowing the user to create new, actionable links, annotations, templates, and virtual documents which can be saved for later use.

Several far-sighted individuals have taken hypermedia to be the ultimate means of expressing freedom of speech[16,30]. However, readers should refer to Savoy for an exposition of why authors may prefer the canonical version of their materials to remain inviolate, and also McKnight *et al.*[26,27,36] for a further discussion. Most hypermedia systems make it a formality to create derivative documents which have a professional appearance indistinguishable from their source materials. (See also Section 7.3 for an elaboration of the template and style concepts).

However, this raises a number of practical considerations, particularly if originals are not protected from change (although an increasing number of systems allow edit protection). Then again, if a user can copy an original in a form that can then be cannibalized, and chooses to redistribute his own materials using 'borrowed' structures, issues of copyright are raised[41]. There is the fear that unprotected materials will be easily plagiarized and pirated. And, from the system designer's point of view, allowing collaborative, concurrent access at a writing/editing level to a multi-user network provides serious problems.

These problems can be broadly separated into the need to provide mutually coherent, consistent and intelligible structures to a corpus of users, and the problem of achieving a satisfactory compromise in the set of protocols adopted for permitting change[40,41]. Few commentators or developers have sought to tackle issues of versioning, royalties and intellectual property in a detailed or positive manner. Ted Nelson's Xanadu project, on the point of being launched as a complete commercial system, is a notable exception[30,31].

The problem of providing consistency to users, in terms of presentation and the density of references, depends to some extent on the form of material prior to the addition of hypermedia functionality. Works such as reference manuals often have a strong, intrinsically regular structure of sections and sub-sections. However, providing consistently sized 'chunks' of information, and consistent numbers of links may be problematic with materials such as dictionaries[32]; in the Oxford English Dictionary 5% of entries accounts for 48% of the bulk of text. Furthermore, this study points out that works which have developed chronologically may suffer from a bias towards retrospective references. In fact, with some hypermedia systems this can be easily remedied. For instance, InterLex, Houghton Mifflin's version of the American Heritage Dictionary (which can be used in conjunction with Intermedia 3.0) supports 'concept-oriented' searches, using sub-terms, wildcards and suffix-stripping[45]; in other words structure is implicit in the associations of content, rather than explicit in predetermined links.

By analogy, for systems in which virtual documents may be compiled on the fly, inference (e.g. of which cues are appropriate for presentation) may be the only tenable model. But will users be able to adapt to the extra level of decision-making required to initiate this dynamic association or presentation? The answer seems to be affirmative; Marchionini observes that encyclopedias are default knowledge sources for secondary/high school grade pupils, and confirms that electronic encyclopedia techniques can be easily accommodated by means of appropriate, simple mental models[28].

Further practical authoring issues are examined in the Chapters 6 and 7.

SUMMARY

The literary act of referencing materials is not new, but hypermedia offers the novel possibility of interactive, immediate access to referenced materials.

A new information paradigm is needed to manage the growth of information in general. Hypermedia can provide both the framework for production and the (online) means of distributing the finished products. This chapter has sought to demonstrate that hypermedia can and should be adopted as a methodology that augments our present print-based and electronic publishing industries, and integrates them with the other media; the divisive text or graphics-based approaches of other software can be fruitfully combined.

This is not to say that hypermedia software is synonymous with desktop publishing systems. The emphasis is quite different — hypermedia being more suited to the demands of long life-cycle, referential materials rather than to the shorter, typically simpler, one-off (printed) documents that are the domain of DTP.

Not only is it conceptually possible for medium-scale (local networks) and even large-scale (wide-area, heterogeneous networks) hypermedia systems to be implemented, it is also seemingly imminent. However, there are still major problems to be overcome in establishing the necessary co-operative infrastructure and for the envisaged large-scale electronic library. At the other end of the spectrum hypermedia also offers the possibility of portable, dynamic electronic books.

Even where basic electronic media have already been adopted for distribution (for instance for bulletin boards and electronic mailing systems) hypermedia can improve the presentation quality and utility of information.

Hypermedia's suitability for developing context-sensitive applications, and for seamlessly integrating them makes it an ideal paradigm for online Help and CBT. The main rule for hypermedia educational materials is that a good structure should encourage synergy rather than narrow determinism. The emphasis on explicit structure is likely to encourage an understanding of relationships between concepts. It will also permit the construction and integration of dynamic materials such as animated models, in addition to the traditional communication of linear, factual knowledge. Most importantly, hypermedia offers the freedom to interpret structure and to display information in many alternative ways.

However, freedom to alter the structure of materials during a user's session may lead to permanent corruption of the originals, which is likely to be contrary to authors' interests.

Hypermedia systems are also available that support collaborative authorship. However, some change in the role and status of authors may be entailed.

At least for the foreseeable future, there will continue to be a complementary role for hardcopy versions.

REFERENCES

1. Barden, R. Using hypertext in building intelligent training systems. *Interactive Learning International*, **5**, 1989, pp. 109-115.
2. Barrett, E. Textual intervention, collaboration, and the online environment. In: Barrett, E. (Ed.), *The Society of Text*. Cambridge, MA: MIT Press, 1989.
3. Benest, I., Morgan, G. and Smithurst, M. A humanized interface to an electronic library. In: Bullinger, H. and Shackel, B. (Eds.) *Human-Computer Interaction — INTERACT'87*, pp. 1089-1093, North-Holland, (1987).
4. Berry, D. and Broadbent, D. Expert systems and the man-machine interface. Part Two: the user interface. *Expert Systems*, **4 (1)**, 1987, pp. 18-27.
5. Brockman, R. Exploring the connections between improved technology — workstation and desktop publishing and improved methodology — document

databases. In: Barrett, E. (Ed.) *Text, ConText and HyperText*. Cambridge, MA: MIT Press, 1988.

6. Brockman, R., Horton, W. and Brook, K. From database to hypertext via electronic publishing: an information odyssey. In: Barrett, E. (Ed.), *The Society of Text*. Cambridge, MA: MIT Press, 1989.

7. Brown, P. Interactive Documentation. *Software — Practice and Experience*, **16 (3)**, March 1989, pp. 291-299.

8. Bush, V. As we may think. *Atlantic Monthly* **176 (1)**, July 1945, pp. 101-108.

9. Carroll, J. and Aaronson, A. Learning by doing with simulated intelligent Help. In: Barrett, E. (Ed.), *The Society of Text*. Cambridge, MA: MIT Press, 1989.

10. Colbourn, C. and Cockerton-Turner. Using hypertext for educational 'Help' facilities. *Proceedings of Hypertext II*, University of York, June 29-30 1989.

11. Cook, R. Desktop video studio. *BYTE*, **15 (2)**, February 1990, pp. 229-234.

12. Dufresne, A., Jolin, N. and Sentini. Hypertext documentation for the learning of procedures. *Proceedings of Hypertext II*, University of York, June 29-30 1989.

13. Eirund, H. and Kreplin, K. Knowledge based document classification supporting integrated document handling. In: Allen, R. (Ed.) *Proceedings of the Conference on Office Information Systems*, March 23-25 1988, Palo Alto, California. *ACM SIGOIS Bulletin*, **9 (2-3)**, April and July 1988, pp. 189-196.

14. Ertel, M. A tour of the stacks. HyperCard for libraries. *Online*, **13 (1)**, January 1989, pp. 45-53.

15. Franklin, C. The hypermedia library. *Database 11* **(3)**, June 1988, pp. 43-48.

16. Hanson, R. Toward hypertext publishing. *Sigir Forum*, **22 (1-2)**, Fall/Winter 1987-88, pp. 9-27.

17. Hardman, L. Evaluating the usability of the Glasgow Online hypertext. *Hypermedia 1* **(1)**, Spring 1989, pp. 34-63.

18. Hawkins, D. Applications of artificial intelligence (AI) and expert systems for online searching. *Online*, **12 (1)**, January 1988, pp. 31-43.

19. Herrstrom, D. and Massey, D. Hypertext in context. In: Barrett, E. (Ed.), *The Society of Text*. Cambridge, MA: MIT Press, 1989.

20. Howell. G. Hypertext meets interactive fiction. *Proceedings of Hypertext II*, University of York, June 29-30 1989.

21. Kay, A. and Goldberg, A. Personal dynamic media. *IEEE Computer*, **10 (3)**, March 1977, pp. 31-41.

22. Landauer, T. Tasks, text and functionality (symposium remarks). *Proceedings of Hypertext II*, University of York, June 29-30 1989.

23. Lewis, B. and Hodges, J. Shared books: collaborative publication management for an office information system. In: Allen, R. (Ed.) *Proceedings of the Conference on Office Information Systems*, March 23-25 1988, Palo Alto, California. *ACM SIGOIS Bulletin*, **9 (2-3)**, April and July 1988, pp. 197-204.

24. McClelland, B. Hypertext and online... a lot that's familiar. *Online*, **13 (1)**, January 1989, pp. 20-25.

25. McKnight, C., Dillon, A., and Richardson, J. A comparison of linear and hypertext formats in information retrieval. *Proceedings of Hypertext II*, University of York, 29-30 June 1989.

26. McKnight, C., Richardson, J. and Dillon, A. The construction of hypertext documents and databases. *The Electronic Library*, **6 (5)**, October 1988, pp. 338-342.

27. McKnight, C., Richardson, J. and Dillon, A. The authoring of hypertext documents. In: McAleese, R. (Ed.) *Hypertext theory into practice*. Oxford: Intellect Books (1989).

28. Marchionini, G. Making the transition from print to electronic encyclopedias: adaptation of mental models. *International Journal of Man-Machine Studies*, **30 (6)**, June 1989, pp. 591-618.

29. Monk, A. The Personal Browser: a tool for directed navigation in hypertext systems. Interacting with Computers, *The Interdisciplinary Journal of Human-Computer Interaction*, **1 (2)**, August 1989, pp. 191-196.

30. Nelson, Literary Machines. Swathmore, PA: Nelson, 1981.

31. Nelson, T. Managing immense storage. *Byte*, **13 (1)** January 1988, pp. 225-238.

32. Rahtz, S., Carr, L. and Hall, W. Creating multimedia documents: hypertext-processing. *Proceedings of Hypertext II*, University of York, 29-30 June 1989.

33. Raymond, D. and Tompa, F. Hypertext and the Oxford English Dictionary. *Communications of the ACM*, **31 (7)**, July 1988, pp. 871-879.

34. Robinson, P. The four multimedia gospels. *BYTE*, **15 (2)**, February 1990, pp. 203-212.

35. Rubens, P. Online information, hypermedia, and the idea of literacy. In: Barrett, E. (Ed.), *The Society of Text*. Cambridge, MA: MIT Press, 1989.

36. Savoy, J. The electronic book Ebook3. *International Journal of Man-Machine Studies*, **30 (5)**, May 1989, pp. 505-523.

37. Shneiderman, B. Reflections on authoring, editing and managing hypertext. In: Barrett, E. (Ed.), *The Society of text*, MIT Press, Cambridge MA, 1989.

38. Smart Card storage technologies — Technical Notes (unattributed). *The Electronic Library*, **6 (6)**, December 1988, pp. 432-438.

39. Stanton, N. and Stammers, R. Learning styles in a non-linear training environment. *Proceedings of Hypertext II*, University of York, June 29-30 1989.

40. Trigg, R. and Suchman, L. Collaborative writing in NoteCards. In: McAleese, R. (Ed.) *Hypertext theory into practice*. Oxford: Intellect Books Limited, 1989.

41. Trigg, R., Suchman, L. and Halasz, F. Supporting collaboration in NoteCards. *Proceedings of the Conference on Computer Supported Cooperative Work*, Austin, TX, December 3-5 1986.

42. Trigg, R. and Weiser, M. TEXTNET: a network-based approach to text handling. ACM Transactions on Office Information Systems, 4 (1), January 1986. pp. 1-23.

43. Van Dam, A. Hypertext '87 keynote address. *Communications of the ACM*, **31 (7)**, July 1988, pp. 887-895.

44. Walker. J. Supporting document development with Concordia. *IEEE Computer*, **21 (1)**, January 1988, pp. 48-59.

45. Walter, M. IRIS Intermedia: pushing the boundaries of hypertext. *The Seybold Report on Publishing Systems*, **18 (21)**, August 1989, pp. 21-32.

46. Weyer, S. The design of a dynamic book for information search. *International Journal of Man-Machine Studies*, **17 (10)**, July 1982, pp. 87-107.

47. Weyer, S. and Borning, A. A prototype electronic encyclopaedia. *ACM Transactions on Office Information Systems*, **3 (1)**, January 1985, pp. 63-88.

48. Yankelovich, N., Meyrowitz, N., and Van Dam, A. Reading and writing the electronic book. *IEEE Computer*, **18 (10)**, October, 1985, pp. 15-30.

49. Yankelovich, N., Haan, B., Meyrovitz, N. and Drucker, S. Intermedia: The concept and the construction of a seamless information environment. *IEEE Computer*, **21 (1)**, January 1988, pp. 81-96.

50. Zimmerman, M. Reconstruction of a profession: new roles for technical writers in the computer industry. In: Barrett, E. (Ed.), *The Society of Text*. Cambridge, MA: MIT Press, 1989.

Section II

Owners, Authors and Users

Introduction

This section examines hypermedia from three broadly different perspectives: those considering buying or commissioning hypermedia; those producing hypermedia materials; those using such materials. Particular emphasis is given to needs of the second group — hypermedia authors. Separate chapters describe the basic tools that can be used to build hypermedia applications, and how these benefit from a structured overall style or model. Experimental findings are examined in relation to both human and computer-based model building.

Readers in need of in-depth guidance should use this section as a menu or shopping-list. Bibliographical references draw together some of the latest material from a wide range of disciplines, and point to the directions in which hypermedia research is headed.

5 Owner Issues — Hypermedia and Management

5.1   Introduction: Strategic Software Resources

This chapter examines hypermedia systems from the point of view of systems owners and potential owners, and of systems department managers; the emphasis is on the commercial possibilities of the technology, and of general criteria for evaluating hypermedia systems. More specific considerations, including the kinds of functionality which authors/designers and users may require are examined in turn in the next three chapters.

The potential for applying hypermedia to commercial domains is vast. In the short-term, most of these solutions are likely to be biased towards text organization and management; hypermedia can provide a link from the operational to the strategic levels of information. However, there are already a number of software companies marketing products which can integrate the media of the printed page with forms such as interactive video and even digitized sound. Commercial applications of hypermedia can be categorized according to size (whether systems are developed by individuals or companies), by target user (personal, in-house or open software market), and by tool function (add-on feature, shell, bespoke solution, or third-party shellware).

5.2   Commercial Potential

5.2.1   Corporate Markets

In addition to low-level data, most organizations generate increasingly large quantities of information which is not amenable to storage in a conventional database. The contrast is qualitative — information is needed to support, interpret and apply data. This information may be directly related to the production of the primary service (increasingly information is the product or service), or it may be a by-product of more general administration[20,31]. Information systems have become so much a part of our corporate culture that they frequently mirror the actual structure of the corporation itself[13]. However, these 'systems' are often hybrids with computerized and manual components; and as one progresses from the lowest levels of day-to-day data processing and operational control through tactical and strategic management information levels, the role of computers, perceived or implemented, typically diminishes. Computerization, although it has been effective in harnessing and processing data, has failed to make the same impact on information[7,25].

The predominant format in which information is stored and distributed remains the paper-based or electronic filing system, augmented by manuals, messages, minutes, reports and catalogs. Neither format is optimal in terms of physical or functional efficiency. Paper is bulky, requires many copies to be produced and distributed and the traditional, multi-stage print production cycle is both laborious and costly. In the case of professionally printed material, revisions and updates can be extremely expensive, although both the proportion of material altered, and number of copies needed tend to be relatively small. Conventional solutions generally involve the production of modular reference manuals — errata are compiled until they warrant the revision of a particular module, which is then reprinted, and replaced in each manual.

With the online manual solution, a single 'canonical' version is available to all users. Each error can be corrected directly as it is identified. Moreover, if an error occurs in more than one section, it is far easier to trace and replace automatically with online systems. Equally, if a new section is inserted or the structure needs to be altered in some other way, it is normally possible to automatically relate the entire contents to the new structure. However, electronic solutions for office automation and 'Management Information Systems' are often modeled on their physical, hard copy predecessors — employing the lowest common denominator of structure because of the heterogeneity of materials they must encompass. As discussed in Chapter 2, file-based, hierarchical or flat text databases employ the most basic facilities of conventional data processing software, and fail to realize the most useful relationships, the potential point-to-point connectivity, between their content objects. The lack of structure, weighted term lists or coded attributes also means that the investment necessary to develop an exclusively AI-oriented solution may not be worthwhile. However, the new multimedia technologies make possible the development of enormous databases, including very diverse storage and delivery devices[27]. Hypermedia structure is seen as the necessary and sufficient paradigm for managing these databases.

The hypermedia/multimedia model can integrate arbitrary functional levels or sources of information; applications for electronic publishing, office automation and MIS, for instance, can be accommodated in a single, seamless conceptual framework, regardless of whether the corporate structure is hierarchical, network, web-like or hybrid. Different departments may identify quite different domains in which a hypermedia system would increase the utility of existing information. For instance, the production department might use a commercial package as a means to distribute and maintain technical documentation, while the marketing and research departments use the same package as an electronic mail system and as a platform for collaborative development of ideas and management of their provenance sources. This may call for joint discussions by systems evaluators from all departments, or for far-sighted decisions if corporate purchasing is made centrally.

The model is also adaptable over time — it can adapt and grow organically along with the organisation. Just as importantly, users of a specific application are not bound by the default structures provided in local information, but can instigate their own forms of reference and cross-reference on the fly. For instance, a user needing to trace all occurrences of a term or part can locate them and save the references under a new section heading dealing specifically with the term. This is very similar to constructing and saving a view in a relational database, except that no homogeneous, tabular organisation of the base materials is required. Indeed, within such a flexible framework there may well also be tools that employ AI techniques, but these will only be used for very specific purposes; they are secondary features of the environment, rather than its core.

The kinds of organization likely to provide an immediate market for off-the-shelf multimedia shells and shellware are manufacturing and hi-tech industries; in particular those with large, rapidly moving stock and evolving products. Professionals needing to extract very high quality information that cannot be easily predicted, from a large corpus of irrelevant material, will also benefit.

5.2.2 Private Users

Many of the available hypermedia packages for microcomputers employ menu-driven interfaces and have the facilities of simple CASE tools; i.e. they require little more than basic keyboard or mouse skills to be able to begin using them, and relatively limited general computer knowledge to implement personalized applications. The main obstacles are likely to be methodological then — the ease with which a user can begin to author his or her own materials can belie more subtle difficulties, such as the spaghetti hypertext syndrome, that may arise in using the finished product. Like databases, hypertext applications benefit from forethought, and preferably an explicit, albeit very general, structured plan.

5.2.3 In-house Users

Organizations large enough to support their own computer and publishing departments in house are likely to have most of the necessary skills to develop sophisticated, bespoke hypermedia systems for themselves; they will almost certain to be able to deploy a shell without resorting to external advice beyond supplier support. However, even more so than for individuals coming to the area, specific experience of hypertext methodological issues is desirable. The alternatives for smaller, or non-computerate companies who have identified a need for hypermedia are to hire specialist consultants, or possibly to buy both shells and third-party software off the shelf, and invest in staff training courses.

5.2.4 Tools, Shells and Bespoke Systems

These come in several degrees of development investment. At the simplest extreme, an increasing number of software products (such as some expert systems) include facilities for providing hypertext-style links between sections of documentation, and even for making these sensitive to context.

Organizations that require a greater range of supplied hypermedia features will need to examine the specific facilities provided by hypermedia shells, such as the examples mentioned in Section III. There are two basic problems with buying a commercial shell product: too much functionality, or too little functionality — in other words a trade-off between flexibility and complexity[22,33]. In the former case it may be initially tempting to buy a product with sophisticated graphics facilities, only to find that these are never used, but cannot be stripped down from the run-time application — thus taking up valuable memory and detracting from the performance that might have been achieved with a slimmer product. In the latter case, a program may lack much needed development support features, or the range of link types that would have provided users with a richer choice of access strategies. Worse still, a program whose architecture is not sufficiently open may prevent systems developers from adding adequate auxiliary tools.

In many cases where auxiliary features are required, it will be possible to develop them using the system's own application language — although some are very limited in scope. The more powerful shells are particularly useful for rapid prototyping of applications which may eventually be implemented from scratch using a conventional programming language. Alternatively, some hypermedia systems' protocols have been left sufficiently open to allow external development of tools.

Caution is also needed in relying on the macro or structured application development languages provided with many packages: Is it compiled or interpreted? Will it actually be easy to learn, or merely encourage 'bad' programming style? Can applications be run without the main development environment — either with a run-time system, or as a compiled self-entity? In fact, the good news is that many packages are supplied with relatively open interfaces to the outside world, and that facilities can be tacked on, or stripped down with very little effort. This is a task that can either be delegated to in-house programmers, or possibly negotiated with the shell developers, who may support bespoke (or 'modular' bespoke) solutions.

The most ambitious option is to build a hypermedia system itself from scratch. This will be necessary where users' requirements include a very specific constraint, such as a run-time access speed that a shell's range of features may preclude, or real-time monitoring capabilities.

5.2.5 Shellware

Copyright material issued on electronic media now includes market reports and professional updates. As with in-house materials, the advantage of using this medium is that large publications containing quickly outdated information can be revised regularly, and existing users supplied with an update at relatively low cost. A further possible consideration is that the added utility of a hypermedia structure, and the ease with which a subject may be penetrated, will increase the marketability of the information itself.

The hypermedia market for third-party authors and publishers can be divided into two broad categories: providing packaged information releases; providing utility programs. These are used in conjunction with off-the-shelf hypermedia shells; in some cases they are stand-alone applications using a shell's run-time library, which generally gives the user a stripped-down, read-only version of the shell. (It should be noted that not all shell developers allow royalty free distribution of the run-time or read-only packages).

To date only HyperCard — the first shell to achieve large-scale success

— has spawned a large number of third-party programs (known as StackWare, after HyperCard's stack-based files). However, already there are third party applications beginning to appear for some of the PC packages, such as KnowledgePro and Hyperdoc. The publishing house Longman plans to produce a series of regular business communications to be read with the HyperBook system. However, there are still vast untapped resources of information in the public domain for enterprizing 'knowledge authors' to enhance with the added value of a hypermedia structure. In many cases there is relatively little need for creativity in terms of authoring original content materials — merely identifying key terms and relating their occurrences will provide considerable added value. However, for those wishing to plan, develop, and refine materials in a single environment, hypermedia tools can provide support at all stages from brainstorming to publication[9].

Shellware may be a better generic term for applications developed for use with the broad range of shell products, not all of which employ a stack metaphor. Shellware has two advantages over conventional publishing for start-up companies or part-time, individual authors: it is cheap to produce, and cheap to distribute. Because the market for many of these products is of specialist interest, or due to the authors' limited resources, a common means of distribution is via the shareware networks. Listings of some notable shareware and stackware products are to be found in the Appendices.

5.3   Who Should Consider Hypermedia Systems?

5.3.1   Purchasing and Stock Control

A number of large-scale hypertext systems already in use by corporations in Europe and the US have been designed to deal with stock control databases. A major advantage of hypermedia stock control is that it is easy to include graphical information along with descriptions, figures. Thus workers on the assembly line can select items they use by point-and-click mouse commands, without having to fill out order forms or work from obscure catalogue numbers. Once built, the same graphical database of products has the potential to be used for diagnostic or training purposes. Good examples of systems suitable for this purpose include HyperCard, Guide/Idex and Hyperdoc.

5.3.2   Project and Application Management

The traditional production cycle model, still very common even in hi-tech industries, begins with research and development, and ends with marketing. More recently, management science has shifted towards an emphasis of user requirements as the starting point in product development, and as source of feedback in an iterative cycle[15]. Structured methodologies for the design of software systems also begin with an analysis of the expert's subject knowledge and/or the user's requirements. However, these are primarily designed for the integration of paper-based processes in a computer-based environment. There is still a need for formal methodologies to evaluate human-computer interaction. Hypermedia tools may prove to be an invaluable experimental paradigm for this evaluation, because of the ease with which applications may be prototyped, and due to the freedom they give in possible strategies for application use.

Software tools for the management of projects have become major products in their own right. The term project management tool is often understood to be exclusive to IPSEs (Integrated Project Support Environments, or software which is an implementation of one of the paper-based formal methodologies or techniques, such as SSADM, CPM/CPA or PERT). However, it can also be applied to tools which support the textual documentation of projects, including software development projects[30].

There is an increasing realisation that this documentation should begin at an early stage in the development cycle, and that due to the growing complexity of projects (particularly software development) this documentation needs to be collaborative. It is not sufficient to complete a product and then hand it over for technical user documentation. As Haselkorn points out[16], the technical writer's role can be expanded to include specification of the user requirement, in-house annotation of the product components and online 'Help' documentation as well as the accompanying, printed user manual.

Hypermedia systems are available with facilities both for concurrent, multi-user collaboration, and for controlling the evolving end-product materials. Some hypermedia systems such as KMS and NoteCards also support versioning management; as items are changed, historical copies are stored in such a way that a user can backtrack through previous versions for that item, as well as between separate items[1,32]. This can be particularly useful in collaborative developments, for instance to be able to see a 'clean' copy of a document without annotations. It is also an additional means of insuring against data loss.

Hypermedia functionality is also beginning to be incorporated in software packages explicitly marketed for project planning, management and systems analysis. An example of a hypermedia approach to Petri Nets is provided by Furuta and Stotts; in their prototype an explicit separation is made between a model's structure, content, and context[12,29]. Similarly, the hypermedia paradigm's capacity for levels of abstraction and multiple views could be easily applied to methodologies needing to separate logical from physical models (see sub-section 5.3.4). Good examples of project management tools featuring hypertext are Lotus Agenda and Web Information Assistant.

5.3.3   Software Projects

"I believe the time is right for significantly better documentation of programs, and that we can best achieve this by considering programs to be works of literature."   Donald Knuth, 1984[19].

Software development itself provides an example of project management where comments and organized development versions may be invaluable; storing comments as linear parts of the code leads to monolithic documents; alternatively, 'nested' hypertext annotations can either be folded away to reveal more of the code itself, without the need to scroll away from the main point of interest, or they can be expanded and used to follow up cross-references. Hypermedia links can also be used as sophisticated search mechanisms — to locate all occurences of a procedure, and to manage them in what is effectively a data dictionary. A facility that allows links to be updated to all occurrences of a given term (as provided by Web Information Assistant) can be invaluable.

Examples of prototype tools developed specifically for software code documentation include Knuth's Web[19]; different from Web Information Assistant above), the derivative CWeb[30], and DOCMAN[11]. Using such tools, programming teams can effectively cross-reference procedures and objects by means of annotations, which are organized into an encyclopedic structure. The approach also allows for integrated top-down and bottom-up development; as Knuth points out, a program's real structure resembles not so much a tree as a web, i.e. with many vertices of communication and control. Furthermore, documentation or program levels can be folded away or expanded to reveal an appropriate level of granularity. Alternatively they can be extracted to provide a summary of code modules. This form of commentary can help to reduce the time spent after development in product maintenance — even if team members change. Knuth's Web system, based on the TeX document formatting language, goes a stage further than annotation by providing the means for typesetting code and related documentation, so that printed or WYSIWYG reference works can be easily produced[19].

5.3.4   Modeling

Hypermedia offers a means of providing users with possible parallel structures in materials, each of which may suit different users at different times. These structures fall into the following categories:

(1)   Logical Structure — a canonical interpretation of the semantic relationship between items;

(2)   Pragmatic Structure — ad hoc 'views' of relationships which may emphasise or minimize aspects of (1);

(3) Dynamic Structure — how relationships and values interact over time; systems such as HyperCard and SuperCard allow variables to be manipulated by users to affect outcomes representing particular contexts such as weather conditions; true hypermedia programs allow the incorporation of animations and dynamic video or sound.

5.3.5 Legal and Medical

Lawyers and doctors have been among the first professionals to embrace advanced computer developments such as expert systems. One of the main difficulties in building a reliable expert system in these areas is that the subject domain is both vast, and partially 'soft' (areas are either unknown, uncertain, or unpredictable). A purely rule-based system needs to manage uncertainty, often by pruning or truncating the possible decision tree. In doing so it is in danger of rejecting alternative material which may have been of interest to the user, although in conflict with or irrelevant to the 'best' solution. Thus the lengths that developers go to in real life to disclaim liability for their expert systems shells and third-party applications, as being designed purely for tutorial use.

A hypermedia approach, as applied to legal case history, or perhaps to medical symptomatology, leaves more of the actual decision making in the hands of the expert (or student). The user is provided with information and choices concerning further information; default paths may indicate precedented or likely decisions. This is similar to the AI 'critiqing' approach, and can considerably enhance the speed and efficiency with which the user interacts with the available information. Machine and human can each be given priority in the tasks at which each is best. Deciding the level of granularity to favor at any one point can be left to the user — a notoriously difficult aspect for blackboard architecture expert systems. Deciding probabilities on the basis of a human decision, and collating all the possibly relevant material, or the user's selected material, can be left to the expert system.

Furthermore, hypermedia offers the hitherto impracticable possibility of integrating textual records or numerical data with media such as video or animated graphics: legal applications might include videoed witnesses' depositions; medical applications might include selective animations of individual organs or physiological systems. A choice of powerful hybrid AI/hypermedia shells is now available to developers; these are likely to be quite adequate for the development of all but the largest of such systems.

5.3.6 News and Financial

Hypermedia is set to revolutionize the way we receive news, and in particular the way financial institutions use it. At present most electronic news wire services are organized by alphabetic and/or subject categories. However, the categories are very general and there is no way of accessing material which is synonymous with, similar or closely related to any given topic. Furthermore, in most systems a story is categorized only by its most salient feature. Hypermedia solutions allow for the provision of (possibly) auxiliary strategies: hierarchical and attribute-based linking of categories, graphical browsing, and non-linear default paths. Hypermedia can also be combined with automatic text indexing tools to generate expanded category indices in real time, and to reduce the need for human monitoring of incoming material.

In volatile situations, such as financial trading, any small advantage in the quality of information provided can lead to considerable gains (see Figures 5.1 and 5.2). Real-time monitoring in hypermedia is thus an area of research which is attracting great interest. It should be noted that at present few of the shells considered in Section III have the facilities or speed required for complex, large-scale tasks of this kind. These issues are further discussed below and in sub-section 6.5.8.

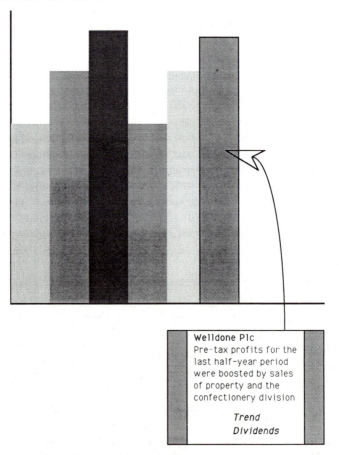

Welldone Plc
Pre-tax profits for the
last half-year period
were boosted by sales
of property and the
confectionery division

Trend

Dividends

Figure 5.1 Hypothetical hypermedia news system accessed from graphical hot-spot.

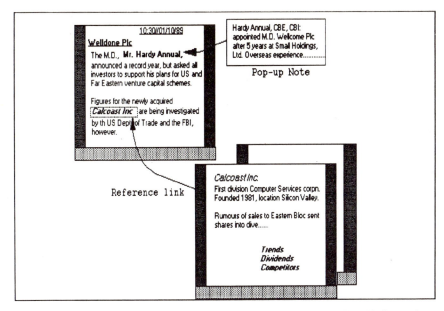

Figure 5.2   News system story shows means of direct access to related information.

5.3.7   Interactive Video

Readers of Section I will recall that hypermedia is taken to be a subset of the larger multimedia industry — not all of which supports hypermedia's emphasis on structural organization. Hypermedia shells provide an ideal front end with which to manage digitized video and audio information. In fact, the facilities provided can approach those of a basic video editing suite, and at a fraction of the cost (Cook). Several film schools in the UK and USA, as well as the BBC's Interactive Television Unit, are now using programs such as HyperCard, SuperCard and LinkWay as front ends to assignments, class materials and presentations. The Elastic Charles is an example of a hypermedia journal which uses HyperCard as a base; it also features advanced tools for segmentation and management of dynamic frame sequences via 'micons'[5].

More ambitious environments are also under development with support for the dynamic requirements of video-disk management[14,24]. An available off-the-shelf program with particular emphasis on video-disk technology is Hyperdoc; in addition to its control features, its storage algorithms are noteworthy for their fast, efficient data compression ratios. Intel's recent DVI real-time (de-)compression products for the IBM PC appear to be a watershed in technology take-up for computer-based multimedia — and particularly video[26]. Again readers of Section I will recall that hypermedia is taken to be a subset of the larger multimedia industry — not all of which supports hypermedia's emphasis on structural organization.

The BBC ITU is also developing a multimedia system — MediaMaker — which runs on the Apple Macintosh II computer, and is due to be marketed in 1990 [6]. MediaMaker is partially implemented in SuperCard, and allows 10-minute presentations to integrate material from many sources with a central, fast-access videotape. File items are represented by 'picons'. These can be calibrated by time, condensed or expanded, and internally 'chunked' into content picons. One of the problems to be tackled in developing sophisticated graphical hypermedia is some means (preferably consistent, if not automated) of indexing images; and for managing the time dimension of materials. A prototype model for indexing and browsing time-driven materials is presented by Christodoulakis and Graham[8]. Running on a Sun workstation, this uses a calibration system similar to that employed in MediaMaker to create icon hierarchies, which are linked together into an acyclic directed graph. Materials may then be browsed sequentially or at random. The authors suggest that icons for video or animation sequences should be key frames, and a form of automated generation is available; however, for audio sequences this issue is less clear.

5.3.8 Hypermedia Entertainment

The success of interactive, text-based adventure software points towards a vast potential market for hypermedia/multimedia entertainment applications. The first of the true 'hyperware' generation of games software are already rumored to be in production. Participants and story-lines in these scenarios correspond roughly to 'views', and the approach has much in common with object-oriented programming; increasingly there is a move away from deterministic outcomes towards more subtle possibilities achieved with AI techniques. The medium-term future holds out the promise of sophisticated video and animation backgrounds, together with virtual environment interfaces — a new generation of peripherals such as data gloves and helmets allowing realistic 3-D interaction with multi-sensory feedback. Taking all this into account, some analysts predict that the entire multimedia industry could be turning over as much as $17 billion by 1994[21].

5.3.9 Public Services Hypermedia

One of the problems with providing the general public with access to databases of public services is the level of skills needed to interact successfully with the software. In contrast, hypermedia requires only the most simple of keyboard commands or pointer skills, and uses familiar, everyday organizational metaphors. This permits complex information to be made available in a structure which each user can tailor to his or her own needs. One example of this approach as designed for tourists is Glasgow Online, a HyperCard-based system that allows visitors to navigate through the city graphically, or by use of special interest categories[2]. A similar town prospectus is now under development for Preston using Hyperdoc.

Teletext or television information services are also likely to move toward hypermedia indexing — the present hand-held, number-based control units require an unduly laborious number of commands to access a given screen. A lesser number of buttons, providing a means of jumping from one embedded key term to the next would seem to be highly desirable, as would a more sophisticated graphical overview of available information. Telephone shopping by item lists has so far proved to be unpopular, but might be encouraged by use of familiar graphical maps, aisles and shelves, particularly with the eventual arrival of larger, higher definition television screens.

5.3.10   Social and Government Hypermedia

Local and central government are among the largest producers of textual information. It has been estimated that the amount of information produced in the United States by public bureaucratic organisations alone is such that computerization would provide permanent employment for up to two million people. In fact, by 1970 nearly half of the US population were classified as 'information workers'[25], and this trend seems set to continue [15]. Hypermedia is likely to provide an ideal paradigm for areas such as departmental procedures and regulations, in that the quality of information would be substantially improved without requiring a large number of specialist, expert computer staff. There is a consensus that we are seeing the beginning of a significant 'information revolution'. However, unlike the earlier agrarian and industrial revolutions the present revolution has yet to result in any generalized increase in productivity. Hypermedia may become a crucial technology in achieving this increase, in that it can provide a consistent interface across applications, and integration between the current diversity of software.

5.3.11   Military Hypermedia

Military applications are also likely to provide systems designers with a major market. One much publicized example is the ZOG system installed on the US Navy's nuclear-powered aircraft carrier, Carl Vinson; this integrates information from a weapons planning system with more general sources throughout the ship.

The cost of field manoeuvres means that modern officer training includes an increasing emphasis on logistics and computer-based simulations. An interesting study of officers' cognitive mapping skills is provided by Klein and Cooper[18], who demonstrate that performance and confidence are related to the richness of cognitive maps, which can itself be improved by training. Furthermore, in crises officers were found to be likely to move in for a 'fine-grain' strategy, often losing sight of the general 'big picture'. A hypermedia solution could provide a maintained view of several levels of granularity, thus reducing the cognitive overhead of decision makers in complex or stressful conditions.

Section 8.2.1 describes the particular relevance of hypermedia to cognitive mapping and to hypergames, another 'soft' Operations Research technique that has been applied in military settings. Hypergames attempt to represent multiple alternative models or perceptual games. Bennett and Dando claim that the use of a more sophisticated hypergame strategy by the German High Command than by the French in the Ardennes Campaign of 1940 was a significant contributor to the Fall of France[3]. (Computer historians may be interested to know that German hypergame superiority owes much to a certain Von Neumann...) The capacity of a hypermedia framework to implement such an approach, representing multiple views and strategies, should be obvious. Applications of hypermedia to sensitive data and to battlefield scenarios will obviously require the same kind of advanced security administration features as other military software — such as encryption, password access and real-time data validation, as well as positive vetting of contractors.

5.3.12   Educational

The application of hypermedia in educational organizations and contexts, and by third-party CBT developers, has already been extensively discussed in section 4.6, and is mentioned here for the sake of completeness.

5.4   Cost Benefits of Hypermedia

Hypermedia has complementary aims to those of expert systems technology — 'automation' or computer support for areas of high-quality information (knowledge). A sufficiently good application can to some extent substitute for the scarcity or expense of experts themselves. Furthermore, the emphasis in hypermedia is on assisting the naive user — thus knowledge is being transformed from a specialist commodity into something with a far greater potential audience. And once it has been computerized it can be mass produced and updated with minimal effort.

But even for the most mundane of electronically produced materials there is likely to be an immediate and substantial reduction in the time needed relative to the conventional production cycle. Brockman[4] cites 3 days in contrast to 18 for a document produced with the Xyvision Integrated Publishing System as opposed to a traditional cycle. This saving can be reinvested in raising the quality of documents (adding alternative hyperme-dia paths, extra views) or in producing a larger number of documents for the same staff costs[17]. These possibilities are discussed in turn below.

For most organisations the primary benefits of producing high quality documentation relate to product and corporate reputation. In some in-house contexts such as financial trading systems, high quality may also be useful in that it allows users to make more rapid decisions. There may also be secondary benefits in terms of reduced telephone hotline costs or in-house training[28].

The issue of staff costs is rather more controversial. Just as with the new expert systems professions such as knowledge engineers, there is the potential for a skills shortage to drive up the market price of technical writers and systems designers with hypermedia experience; at least in the short to medium term. Hypermedia authors are likely to be knowledgeable generalists. This is discussed further in the next chapter. As Shirk[28] puts it, *"the technical writer who creates online documentation must become a special kind of computer scientist, with skills drawn from many fields."*

However, there is also the potential for the 'de-skilling' of the writing process. In environments where stereotyped document database structures are imposed over relatively factual (as opposed to relatively interpretive) material, the task of creative writing is transformed to one of repetitive clerical work[4]. It is equally possible that many of the tasks grouped together presently under the technical writer's job description will be assimilated by other professionals as part of their own workloads[34,35,36]. In such cases it becomes more difficult to assess the proportion of time spent purely on writing-related activities, and what these ultimately cost.

5.5 Corporate Deployment Planning

A number of useful assessment criteria tables exists in the hypermedia literature[7]. Even where the specific data has been outdated, the criteria themselves can be used as the basis of an evaluation study. Excellent criteria for the evaluation of general text storage and retrieval software are given by Nieuwenhuysen,[23]. Generally speaking, it is not necessary to perform the same kind of rigorous data analysis prior to implementing a hypermedia system that would be desirable prior to implementing a conventional database. Indeed, it should be clear that the heterogeneous nature of materials that may be combined using a hypermedia system may preclude more than the most general of qualitative or quantitative analyses. Some fundamental guideline questions with more specific relevance to deciding on a hypermedia solution are offered below. Questions dealing with data/user issues in the first section are complemented by software-specific questions in the second section.

Data/User Issues:

- Does a corpus of textual/multimedia information exist?
- Do users require non-linear access to parts of this information?
- Does the information benefit from versioning or regular updating?
- Is the information of specialist interest or sensitive in nature?
- Is the present size of the information presently unmanageable?
- Is or can the information be computerized?
- Will computerizing or accessing the information infringe copyright?
- Do a number of users require concurrent access to the information?
- Will a hypermedia system save time and/or money?
- Do users have sufficient skills/aptitude for a hypermedia system?

System Issues:

- Does the system support the data types and storage devices required (e.g. compressed graphics, video-disk drives)?
- Does the system support the desired kinds of linking structure (e.g. embedded item-to-item links, multiple hierarchies, multiple open documents)?
- Does the system support versioning and/or online updating?
- Does the system provide administrative control facilities or read-only access?
- Does the system support applications of the envisaged size, and with acceptable run-time performance?
- Can the system import/export dynamic data, compatible with formats used by other software?
- Does distribution of applications require a special license or is a free reader-only provided for multiple copying?
- Does the system support networking?
- Is the system compatible with existing hardware configurations (especially color graphics mode and RAM requirements)?
- Does the system provide context-sensitive help and/or graded user levels?

Figure 5.3 gives a summary of the broad areas to which hypermedia can be applied in organizations, and the relative time scale each implementation is likely to require.

Details	Timescale	Application

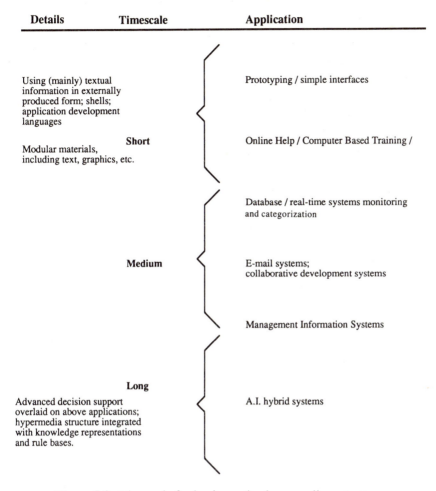

Using (mainly) textual information in externally produced form; shells; application development languages

Modular materials, including text, graphics, etc.

Short

Prototyping / simple interfaces

Online Help / Computer Based Training /

Database / real-time systems monitoring and categorization

Medium

E-mail systems; collaborative development systems

Management Information Systems

Advanced decision support overlaid on above applications; hypermedia structure integrated with knowledge representations and rule bases.

Long

A.I. hybrid systems

Figure 5.3 Timescale for implementing hypermedia systems.

SUMMARY

Hypermedia has the potential to become the dominant software paradigm for the 1990s; there is an urgent need to integrate heterogeneous information and improve its quality of in ways that are not feasible with present procedural data manipulation, nor with current AI techniques. Hypermedia as it is now marketed can bridge the development gap. Ultimately it is quite possible that hypermedia systems *per se* will be integrated into operating systems and generalized interfaces that integrate techniques from many different areas of computer science.

Just as a consensus of the full role of hypermedia is yet to emerge, so too there is disagreement about how the basic tasks that constitute the role of hypermedia should be achieved themselves. These issues are primarily the concern of systems developers and hypermedia authors, and are discussed in depth in the following two chapters.

REFERENCES

1.   Akscyn, R., McCracken, D. and Yoder, E. KMS: A distributed hypermedia system for managing knowledge in organizations. *Communications of the ACM,* **31 (7),** July 1988, pp. 820-835.
2.   Baird, P. and Percival M. Glasgow Online: Database development using Apple's HyperCard. In: McAleese, R. (Ed.), *Hypertext, theory into practice.* Oxford: Intellect Books, 1989.
3.   Bennett, P. and Dando, M. Complex strategic analysis: a hypergame study of the Fall of France. *Journal of the Operational Research Society,* **30 (1),** January 1979, pp. 23-32.
4.   Brockman, R. Exploring the connections between improved technology — workstation and desktop publishing and improved methodology — document databases. In: Barrett, E. (Ed.) *Text, ConText and HyperText.* Cambridge, MA: MIT Press, 1988.
5.   Brondmo, H. and Davenport, D. Creating and viewing the Elastic Charles — a hypermedia journal. *Proceedings of Hypertext II,* University of York, June 29-30 1989.
6.   Cawkell, T. From Memex to MediaMaker. *The Electronic Library,* **7 (5),** October 1989, pp. 278-286.
7.   Checkland, M. *Systems Thinking, Systems Practice.* John Wiley, 1981.
8.   Christodoulakis, S. and Graham, S. Browsing within time-driven multimedia documents. In: Allen, R. (Ed.) *Proceedings of the Conference on Office Information Systems,* March 23-25 1988, Palo Alto, California. *ACM SIGOIS Bulletin,* **9 (2-3),** April and July 1988, pp. 219-227.
9.   Conklin, J. Hypertext: An introduction and survey. *Computer,* **20 (9),** September 1987, pp. 17-41.
10.   Cook, R. Desktop video studio. *BYTE,* **15 (2),** February 1990, pp. 229-234.
11.   Fletton, N. A hypertext approach to browsing and documenting software. *Proceedings of Hypertext II,* University of York, June 29-30 1989.
12.   Furuta, R. and Stotts, P. Separating hypertext content from structure in Trellis. *Proceedings of Hypertext II,* University of York, June 29-30 1989.
13.   Handy, C. *Understanding Organisations.* Penguin, 1976.
14.   Gartshore, P. Hypertext as a programming environment for the authoring and production of interactive videodisk training packages. *Proceedings of Hypertext II,* University of York, June 29-30 1989.
15.   Grice, R. Information development is a part of product development — not an afterthought. In: Barrett, E. (Ed.) *Text, ConText and HyperText.* Cambridge, MA: MIT Press, 1988.
16.   Haselkorn, M. The future of ''writing'' for the computer industry. In: Barrett, E. (Ed.) *Text, ConText and HyperText.* Cambridge, MA: MIT Press, 1988.
17.   James, G. Artificial intelligence and automated publishing systems. In: Barrett, E. (Ed.) *Text, ConText and HyperText.* Cambridge, MA: MIT Press, 1988.
18.   Klein, J. and Cooper, D. Cognitive maps of decision-makers in a complex game. *Journal of the Operational Research Society,* **33 (1),** January 1982 pp. 63-72.
19.   Knuth, D. Literate programming. *The Computer Journal,* **27 (2),** 1984, pp. 97-111.

20. Levine, L. Corporate culture, technical documentation, and organization diagnosis. In: Barrett, E. (Ed.) *Text, ConText and HyperText*. Cambridge, MA: MIT Press, 1988.
21. Lippincott, R. Beyond Hype. *BYTE,* **15** (2), February 1990, pp. 215-218.
22. Marchionini, G. and Shneiderman, B. Finding facts *vs.* browsing knowledge in hypertext systems. *IEEE Computer,* **21 (1)**, January 1988, pp. 70-80.
23. Nieuwenhuysen, P. Criteria for the evaluation of text storage and text retrieval software. *The Electronic Library,* **6 (3),** June 1988, pp. 160-166.
24. O'Connor, B. Access to moving image documents: background concepts and proposals for surrogates for film and video works. *Journal of Documentation,* **41 (4)**, 1985, pp. 209-220.
25. Porat, M. Global implications of the information society. *Journal of Communication (University of Pennsylvania Press)*, Winter 1978, pp. 70-80.
26. Robinson, P. The four multimedia gospels. *BYTE,* **15 (2)**, February 1990, pp. 203-212.
27. Shetler, T. Birth of the BLOB. *BYTE,* **15 (2),** February 1990, pp. 221-226.
28. Shirk, H. Technical writers as computer scientists: the challenges of online documentation. In: Barrett, E. (Ed.) *Text, ConText and HyperText*. Cambridge, MA: MIT Press, 1988.
29. Stotts, P. and Furuta, R. Petri-Net-based hypertext: document structure with browsing semantics. *ACM Transactions on Information Systems,* **7 (1),** January 1989, pp. 3-29.
30. Thimbleby, H. Experiences of 'literate programming' using CWEB (a variant of Knuth's WEB). *The Computer Journal,* **29 (3)**, pp. 201-211.
31. Toffler, A. *The Third Wave*. NY: William Morrow, 1980.
32. Trigg, R. and Suchman, L. Collaborative writing in NoteCards. In: McAleese, R. (Ed.), *Hypertext theory into practice*. Oxford: Intellect Books Limited, 1989.
33. Trigg, R. Guided tours and tabletops: tools for communicating in a hypertext environment. *ACM Transactions on Office Systems,* **6 (4)**, October 1988, pp. 398-414.
34. Weiss, E. Usability: stereotypes and traps. In: Barrett, E. (Ed.) *Text, ConText and HyperText*. Cambridge, MA: MIT Press, 1988.
35. Zimmerman, M. Are writers obsolete in the computer industry? In: Barrett, E. (Ed.) *Text, ConText and HyperText*. Cambridge, MA: MIT Press, 1988.
36. Zimmerman, M. Reconstruction of a profession: new roles for technical writers in the computer industry. In: Barrett, E. (Ed.), *The Society of Text*. Cambridge, MA: MIT Press, 1989.

6 Authoring Issues I — Tools

6.1   Introduction: General and Task-specific Functionality

Section I of this book emphasizes the ways in which the role of a hypermedia package in an organisation is potentially more eclectic than that of more traditional software such as databases and spreadsheets. This chapter is for

97

the benefit of potential authors or designers. It aims to highlight the possible kinds of functionality of hypermedia systems, in terms of a palette of tools. This palette should be interpreted as a superset of the specific sorts of functionality which empirical studies have indicated is actually desirable in certain contexts — an area which is discussed in the next chapter. There will obviously be some overlap, and some of the sections below have been allocated according to an apparent aggregate emphasis rather than any definitive and exclusive relevance. In terms of target readership, it is probably the case that authors will want to read the next chapter; it is not necessarily true that those with a mainly psychological interest in the area of HCI will want to read this chapter.

6.2   From Paper to Disk

In many cases, hypermedia applications are implemented with existing bodies of information, in printed or electronic form. The most cost-effective way of translating the former into the latter is by means of OCR (optical character recognition) scanners. These devices can scan text into machine-readable form and now have high degrees of reliability (95-99 + %) over a wide range of typeset, laser-printed and even hand-written styles. The resulting data files can then be cosmetically treated with software such as spell checkers, style formatting or automated mark-up software, and file format converters to produce information in a form e.g. ASCII that can be directly imported by hypermedia applications[17,30].

One problem with such an approach is that a hypermedia application is not just a book delivered on a screen rather than on a printed page. Over the last 600 years the Western printing and publishing industries have developed an elaborate set of protocols and cues that guide readers as to a book's internal structure and contents, as well as its external references. Readers absorb these from childhood, often in informal settings. Electronic publishing has a good deal of catching up to do, and it may be that some of the conventions we accept at present will give way to better methods of communicating information over the next several decades.

To give an analogy, let us examine conventions from the early days of printing. The first type styles were designed to imitate the style of contemporary quill pen and ink. Eventually it was realized that styles could be more economic visually, and they began to reflect other media, including carved lettering. Techniques such as kerning or proportional spacing between letters, the addition of italic and bold styles, and the use of extra leading and hyphenation to justify line endings are relatively late developments.

The advent of electronic publishing has led to an apparent increase in the speed with which the technology and its conventions are changing. It is interesting to place this in historical perspective. Font design over the centuries has often drawn on other media for inspiration. For instance, in the Renaissance serif fonts looked to calligraphy, and in the 19th Century, styles influenced by engraving became fashionable. But fonts are no longer restricted to paper. Already there have been attempts to design display fonts for easier screen reading or machine scanning, and fonts that are equally easy to read on screen and on paper. With hypermedia, there is also the potential to use typographic cues to indicate that text objects are actionable. This is a preliminary step that is likely to be augmented by more radical revisions of established formats — of document structure itself.

The problem is that at the moment there are only local (inter-organizational) guidelines to style and structure for the electronic media; there is much more scope than ever before for individual authors to impose ad hoc structures of their own choosing. Although heralded by some as a great force for personal and information freedom[25], this trend also has the potential to lead to anarchy, lowered standards of aesthetics, and above all confusion for the user.

A major problem to overcome is that few literary or technical authors have even an informal training in graphic design, let alone and awareness of HCI design issues[26,34]. The implication is that professional applications will need co-operation by teams of specialists; there may be less scope for the maverick author than has been suggested in Chapter 5. One possible, partial solution to this problem in the short term is the provision of declarative formatting and task-oriented templates[4]. However, developing a new rhetoric for hypermedia remains a controversial issue; it is explored further in Section 7.3 on Style and House Styles.

6.3 Necessary Knowledge

There are two possible answers to the question of what specialist knowledge is needed by hypermedia authors and developers:

- **A great deal:** as in knowledge engineering, a multi-disciplinary awareness is probably desirable.
- **Very little:** packages are relatively easy to learn with a small kernel of commands and strategies; there is no need to be completely right first time — incremental prototyping is feasible, and probably even desirable.

In other words, good hypermedia systems developers, authors and interface designers are likely to be generalists. Wherever possible, it is desirable to work from elicited user requirements, using an iterative, incremental process of validation and modification. This requires good interpersonal communications skills. In addition, although hypermedia implementation does not require the same monolithically logical structuring as conventional database design, authors require good analytic and linguistic skills to:

● Interpret materials and/or experts' interview transcripts
● Overlay the functionality that their reders will require.

In cases where original content materials are to be produced, authors will also require:

● Creativity
● In-depth domain knowledge

(Note that there will be many cases where information exists on paper, or even online, and a hypermedia system is proposed to increase its utility — i.e. the author's task is mainly to interpret relationships between objects, and to use these relationships in overlaying a suitable hypermedia structure.)

However, in other cases it is inevitable that authors will have to acquire new and unfamiliar production techniques. Developers of multimedia applications will need to co-ordinate with and understand, for example, video/CD-ROM specialists and sound engineers.

Even where material is purely textual, graphic design skills (choice of page layout and typography) can considerably enhance readability. However, formal graphic design training takes no account as yet of hypermedia; it is important to realize that hypertext has an important secondary graphic function that is only hinted at in print precedents — i.e. some words are actionable links, some conceal a secondary level of expansion, others are keyword synonyms or exist in a context elsewhere.

Many graphic design professionals have been relatively slow to take up the computer as a new tool of their profession. There is no longer any good reason for this. Most hardware configurations now permit **WYSIWYG** screen displays; fonts can be combined experimentally, redesigned, or scaled to arbitrary point sizes without compromising resolution. Artists and draftspersons can select specialist graphics software packages that will allow them to create materials for a range of purposes across the whole spectrum: from simple line art to full-color, 3-D animations. However, there is a clear 'skills dichotomy' — between individuals with professional graphics training and skills, and those with computer skills. To some extent this is reflected in the compromises made by multi-purpose software suites trying to cater to as wide a market as possible. In turn, the fact that integrated packages are available has encouraged the beliefs that each task is easy, and that all tasks can be accomplished by the same person. Cross-training from one discipline to the skills of the other tends to be on the job.

As noted above, this means that authors have several tasks to bear in mind simultaneously[35]; in addition to their traditional concerns of content and structure they are responsible in many cases for the 'desktop publishing' aspects of the application — its final appearance (although use of templates/ style sheets may expiate this). Furthermore, the previously more informal aspects of document management, 'meta-information' such as version editing history, now need to be incorporated — particularly in collaborative projects[20]. And finally, but not least, authors should be aware of the models users bring to the system[16,24]. This last issue is examined in greater depth in the next chapter.

For those using proprietary hypermedia shells, actual computer-related skills centre around human-computer interface design, and overlap with skills mentioned above. Large applications may also require specialists in such fields as networking, tool building and hardware configuration (perhaps non-standard input devices such as touch-sensitive screens will be desirable). Similarly, Barden[2] makes the useful distinction between subject expert authors and course design experts, who determine the format and packaging of applications.

In summary, a large hypermedia development team should have a core team consisting of the professionals in the table below:

Primary Developers:
- Technical author(s)
- Hypermedia specialist programmer(s)

Auxiliary Specialists:
- Computer graphics designer
- Cognitive psychologist
- Systems analyst
- Networking specialist
- Systems programmer
- Knowledge engineer
- Video technician
- Sound engineer.

If this roll call sounds daunting, bear in mind that it is quite feasible for a single person with limited micro-computing knowledge (and no actual programming language skills) to construct educational applications with hundreds of links in a matter of a few weeks, working part-time. For evidence of this, consult the ShellWare appendix. Another interesting possibility is collaborative development by remote authors (journal-style hypermedia applications such as the Elastic Charles). These provide a common forum for topic-related discussion, but allowing a greater degree of inter-document annotation and cross-referencing than printed journals.

6.4   Route Planning

6.4.1   Default Paths

Default paths can follow a variety of models such as hierarchy or 'guided tour', and relate to the canonical skeleton chosen for the application (see Sections 7.1 and 7.2 in the next chapter); i.e. they will be constrained by the form and possible relationships of the node objects, and the available range of link types. Providing default paths is an important consideration in large applications — where it is easy to become disoriented — if users are likely to be less than experts in the subject domain, for instance with CBT materials. However, this is not to say that users should be unable to veer from the default or guided tour path, at any time they wish.

6.4.2   Navigating or Browsing?

Studies suggest that the naive user of a hypermedia system employs quite different search and exploration strategies to those of the expert user. The former seems less willing to explore deeply nested or distant information for fear of getting lost. To some extent this reluctance can be countered by providing backtrack or audit trail facilities. Experts make use of more sophisticated control strategies, and of navigation aids.

It is also useful to distinguish the two different styles with which it is possible to traverse the information space. The names generally given to these main categories are navigating and browsing, the two ends of a spectrum measured by the degree to which a user is concentrating on the macro (structural) features of the information, or its microfeatures (actual information nodes), respectively.

Perhaps an analogy will be useful in visualizing this difference. Consider a seafaring explorer of the last century, who relied on certain tools and methods to navigate between islands and to examine the flora and fauna living there. Navigation tools are the compass, map and sextant. Browsing tools are the magnifying glass, notebook and butterfly net. Sometimes a tool can be used for both tasks — such as the telescope. The analogy with the sorts of tool metaphor adopted by many software packages should be becoming obvious. Several commentators have taken pains to distinguish these two modes, yet have then confused the issue by using the terminology of one to describe the other. For instance, McAleese [21] comments that *"navigation involves the use of a graphic aid such as a browser...''* This is easily done, and in practice there is a grey distinction.

In fact each of these categories can be further broken down according to whether and to what degree they are constrained; whether they are inquiries of a specific or general nature; whether search patterns are systematic, or casual. Navigation can be towards a specific or general location at which to browse, and browsing can be directed towards locating a single, known fact, something that fulfills a certain criterion, or just in the hope of discovering something interesting. Conceptually, navigation falls closer to the strategic end of the spectrum and browsing closer to the tactical. In fact, even strategies are generally expedient — Wright and Lickorish[38] observe that a system's provided functionality heavily influences users' strategies. Users can make use of complementary support facilities local to the software (with the important proviso that it should be obvious the facility exists and how it should be used).

As was observed in Section 4.6, it is incumbent on systems/materials designers to provide adequate support for their users' anticipated strategies, or their lack of them. In particular designers need to support those users without an expert knowledge of a domain, for instance by differential node clustering and/or link typing. Note that it is not fully appropriate to equate hypermedia users' search strategies with those of conventional algorithmic approaches to databases, such as depth-first and breadth-first search. Canter *et al.* observe five identifiable strategies by which users manually peruse a (conventional) database[5]:

- Scanning — closest to breadth first search, though less systematic
- Browsing — serendipitous path experiments
- Searching — for a specific goal; little deviation from route on backtracking
- Exploring — extremes of information sought rather than neighbourhoods
- Wandering — unmotivated, unsystematic.

Note that systematic browsing may itself be further broken down into strategies which are:

- Spatial — the one-off search through all relevant materials
- Temporal — regular browsing of certain periodicals, for instance.

Several other studies have sought to evaluate users' preferences when offered alternative hypermedia navigation modes[5,9,28,38]. The results are by no means consistent, and no consensus is available — perhaps somewhat due to the kind of non-standard terminology described above. For instance, Cove and Walsh comment that: *"Browsing is essentially visual... associated with 'shapes' and patterns both in terms of pictures and the distribution of text on the page or on the VDU screen"*[9]. On the other hand, McAleese[21] concludes that: *"There is a tendency for the graphical interface (Type 2) to encourage users to seek the extent of the knowledge/information and produce unstructured journeys, whereas, Type 1 (textual) interfaces are more likely to produce browsing and scanning..."* A further aspect of this confusion is due to the fact that both browsing and (possibly) navigation can be concerned with the semantic aspects of information.

Simpson and McKnight observe that users perform better with a hierarchical table of contents than with an alphabetic index[30]. This may need to be qualified with the proviso that both were non-interactive, and by the finding of Monk *et al.* that non-interactive navigational aids are in themselves of significant use[24]. Wright and Lickorish offer a useful alternative contrast between browsing and navigation; the former deals predominately with internal links in a document, the latter mainly with external links. They conclude that there is probably no universally best navigational mode — deciding which to support should depend on an analysis of the users' tasks, the nature of the media, and the secondary functionality required[38].

6.5 Tools for Trails

6.5.1 Access Points

Access points in a knowledge source such as a book, or a database, are the locations from which users can retrieve actual occurrences of information. The tools described below are typically in addition to the sorts of conventional document/database access points described in Chapters 2 and 4. Deciding which tools will be most useful in general-purpose systems, and how to facilitate their use for any given domain are important considerations for designers and authors [23].

The simplest tools to be used in conjunction with access points is a range of button types, each accessing information in a different way. Figure 6.1 shows the graphical appearance of the cursor over button types in OWL Guide. For instance, an important link to an extended piece of text may merit a reference button, but a glossary style explanation of a word probably only requires the use of a Note (pop-up) or Expansion (Fold-out/Fold-away) button.

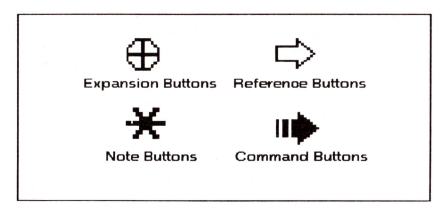

Figure 6.1 Guide's button types are indicated by distinctive
graphical cursors.

6.5.2 Browsers

As noted above, the term browser has variously been applied to navigation or
orientation aids which operate at a level abstracted from actual node
information, and to devices which search for information at the nodes
themselves. Examples of the former include fish- or bird's-eye graphical
browsers. These present an abstract view of the information available —
'terrain knowledge' rather than 'street knowledge'[20]. Fish-eye browsers are
so called because they give disproportionate emphasis to the most central
information displayed. Trigg points out that the kind of overview offered by a
browser can be an invaluable brainstorming tool for authors[33]. Visual
browsers have a relatively low cognitive overhead, but provide the most
basic, and often inflexible forms of support for users' strategies[22].

A major problem with graphical browsers is that often the author's
preconfigured view is the only one possible — selection is by a single
criterion such as node name, category, or creation date. Furthermore,
graphical browsers are limited to an essentially two-dimensional view of
information. Cooke and Williams[7] and Monk[23] observe that these problems
become more serious with large hypermedia databases than with small — as
screens have limited resolutions, and can only display a fraction of relevant
materials.

More sophisticated browsers can filter information according to the
user's query specification. Again, in a complex system it is difficult to know
which attributes can be retained and which to filter out. Possible solutions to
these problems include browsers such as gIBIS which can display information at several layers of granularity[8]. Other proposals include devising a
browser that is updated dynamically during a user's session[28], is reconfigured before a session[3], or employs analytic techniques such as those of
Petri Nets[31].

The term browser has also been used (more rarely but perhaps more appropriately) to describe tools or techniques for examining a large number of nodes according to a given strategy. An example of the latter might be HyperCard's Address stack Browse button for automatic presentation and HyperTalk's Sort command for reordering of cards in a stack. In addition, HyperCard's Find option can be used for single text strings or field items — and the underlying script easily modified to allow multiple searches[16]. Other browsing tools/methods offered in commercial packages and experimental systems include:

6.5.3 Backtracking/Audit Trails

Again, HyperCard's Recent option/card provides a convenient example, allowing the user to return to one of up to 42 most recently accessed cards, grouped together as miniatures on the Recent card (see Figure 6.2). Hyperdoc also maintains a dynamic audit trail, representing each accessed object by its type — e.g. document or graphic.

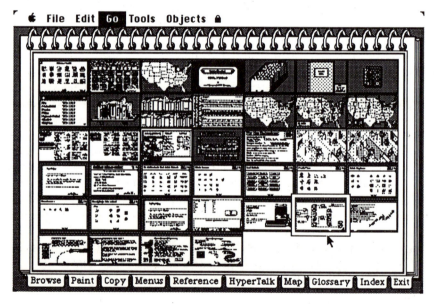

Figure 6.2   Use of the Recent option in HyperCard allows direct access to one of up to 42 recently visited cards.

Alternatively, many systems offer users backtrack buttons or icons on each card. Guide allows users to set personal preferences as to whether backtracking should include notes and replacements, or just references (see Figure 6.3).

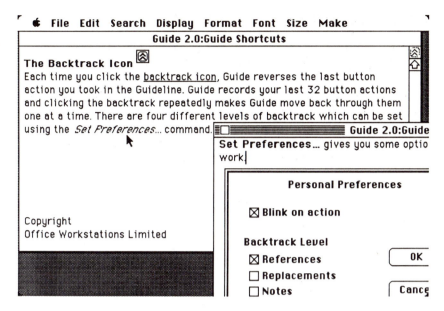

Figure 6.3 Guide supports graded levels of backtracking via an icon.

6.5.4 Clipboards/Notebooks

At their most simple, clipboards are provided by Microsoft Windows (as required to run Guide), and as a desk accessory on most Macintosh system disks. These can be called up to allow the user to cut and paste references or other relevant material found during a browsing session, or to transfer information within the host environment from one application to another. More complex, dynamic or 'intelligent' tools are able to build up a picture of the user's session, or a desired session. These are described below, as well in Section 3.2, on intelligent information retrieval.

6.5.5 Declarative Querying

As was discussed in section 3.2.5 on heuristics, it is sometimes not possible to describe exactly the information that is required, in terms that a conventional procedural search algorithm can employ. Sometimes it is necessary or preferable to use instead a more general 'declarative' description. An example of this approach is utilized by Chen *et al.*'s object-oriented hypermedia system, Panorama, being developed by Texas Instruments Inc. In this system, a user's query includes both a retrieval specification (Boolean criteria) and a non-procedural display specification[6].

6.5.6 Filters/Dynamic Attribute Selection

Here the distinction between navigation and browsing is particularly blurred; the aim is to reduce the complexity or quantity of information satisfying a search criterion, resulting in presentation at a suitably abstract level. This kind of facility can be used for authors structuring information[11], and for users' tasks such as ripple searching. The latter consists os starting with a rigorous set of criteria such as definite location or time-stamp, and gradually relaxing the criteria so that the search proceeds outwards like a ripple, until satisfactory information is found (see Figure 6.4.).

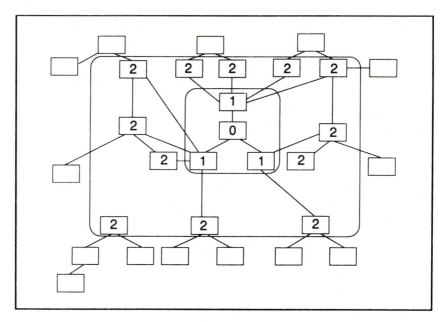

Figure 6.4   Ripple searches spread out from a central point as criteria
are relaxed.

6.5.7 Fold-away/Verbose Display Options

These options may operate for information displayed about node icons in a general graphical browser, or for the way information at a specific expanded node is displayed; for instance, documents may be folded down to a list of headings, or fully expanded to reveal nested sub-headings. It may be possible to set an overall preference from a menu, or to expand each heading individually. Examples of systems which provide this type of facility include Guide (Expansion buttons) and Hyperdoc.

6.5.8 Keyword Comparison/Inverted Indexing

In a sense a list of keywords is itself a kind of filter. It can be particularly useful in indexing dynamic databases; as new information arrives it is compared with terms in the keyword list, and for each positive match a pointer is added to the new information; the keyword list can then be used as an actionable index — allowing access to all occurrences of a given term. Alternatively, a user can have his or her own personalized keyword list which is used to search materials as required[9]; Figure 6.5 describes the use of a string search and timeline browser in a hypothetical news system.

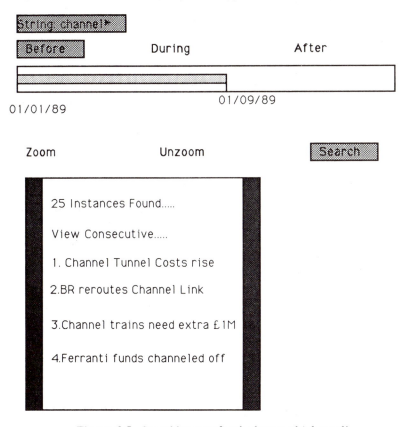

Figure 6.5 Searching text for the keyword 'channel'.

In inverted indexing, all semantic terms in a new document are immediately compiled into an index; i.e. there is no vetting against keywords. Resulting indices may be alphabetic, or in terms of linear or hierarchical category listings. Edwards and Hardman provide some evidence that (personalized) hierarchical indices — a form of cognitive map — may be more efficiently adopted by users than alphabetical indices[12].

6.5.9 Local Maps

Local neighbourhood and context maps are similar to bird's-eye browsers, except that their emphasis is typically at a more microscopic informational level[33]. They are thus relevant to both browsing and navigation. Their selection is in terms of proximity — which may be physical, chronological, or according to some other clustering attribute(s).

6.5.10 Multi-windows/Multi-tasking

Systems such as Guide and NoteCards allow an arbitrary number of distinct items to be displayed on the screen together. This is in contrast to HyperCard, for instance, which currently (version 1.2.1) only supports one card per screen. OS/2 software and some Unix workstation packages not only allow multiple display, but also actual multi-tasking, i.e. more than one item can be 'live' concurrently. This is particularly valuable with real-time databases and multimedia. In the latter case, for instance, a user might wish to browse through separate sound, video and text sources together.

6.5.11 Natural Language Parsers

Natural language algorithms can be used to scan text for keywords that are *a priori* unspecified[19,26,27]. Discounting common connectives, participles and other non-distinguishing words, they may select words according to one or more of the following criteria: word association (near or common neighbors); word frequency (implying thematic importance); first or last sentence of paragraph (used to give a summary of the text); random (to give a flavour of the text); synonyms (generated by a thesaurus, e.g. InterLex[36]). The theoretical problems with natural language processing are discussed in section 3.3.2.

6.5.12 Scrollers

Scroll bars are provided by many software packages, allowing users to move the virtual page or desktop up, down or across in relation to the screen by means of clicking or dragging with the mouse. Scrolling is necessary in applications that do not present information in screen-sized cards or chunks. This is one of the simplest forms of browsing, requiring little cognitive overhead or specific knowledge of the software. Indeed, Monk *et al.*[24] demonstrate that for small text documents, scrolling users performed tasks significantly faster than users with other forms of browser.

6.5.13 Summary/History Trees

These are similar to the backtracking facility provided by HyperCard's Recent card and are designed to be used in conjunction with the more common 'global overview' browser. However, they are more flexible in that attention is given to the degree of granularity provided in the browser[38]; for instance, whether they specify the exact information nodes visited, or merely the file/folder/stacks which are accessed. Examples of Summary and History Trees have been implemented in NoteCards, and support notetaking by users[14].

6.6 Storage and Dissemination

An increasingly common means of distributing large amounts of pre-structured information is on CD-ROM disks. These have relatively large storage capacities (up to around 600 megabytes), and are cheap to duplicate commercially. The main advantage of CD-ROM technologies would seem to be for pictorial information, which requires large amounts of storage space. At present, however, CD-ROM amounts to read-only publication, or what Nelson terms 'closed hypermedia'[25]; although erasable CD-ROM technology is available publishers have chosen to avoid it. Not only are the drives and disks more expensive, but the controversial question of creative integrity is brought up.

Commentators are divided as to the overall advantages of read-only distribution. James, for instance, believes it is crucial to protect originals from tampering[17]. However, users of read-only material are almost entirely at the mercy of the authors. Even if their hypermedia system allows new structures to be created during a session there will be no way of permanently saving these structures together with the originals of their corresponding contents; saving them externally is likely to require duplication of original contents, which is both storage intensive, and probably in breach of copyright. Furthermore, the new structural possibilities of hypermedia have hardly begun to be incorporated in CD-ROM publications; early examples of 'electronic encyclopedias' are remarkably unambitious, offering little more than a novel presentation medium and a possible marginal advantage in locating individual items.

6.7 Modification and Integrity

To date, issues of modifying online materials have been addressed in greatest depth by those systems which have been designed to support collaboration, and the concomitant need to manage document versioning (see Section 5.3.2). For instance, with the KMS system, users can add 'annotation items' to frames without necessarily altering the main content frames or their hierarchical structure[1]. Planned improvements to the NoteCards system offer another possible solution; the incorporation of History cards which will allow groups of material to be tied together and changes recorded[16].

6.8   Copyright and Royalties

The issue of copyright and the integrity of original works on electronic distribution systems is likely to become a major controversy with the new generation of interactive software. Works are potentially less protected in two senses: they may be corrupted; they may be copied without permission or payment of royalties.

Works may be corrupted in two senses also: the original may be annotated or edited, or fragments of the original may be used in other works in a sense that does not do justice to their original source, let alone accord payment of reproduction fees. The former possibility has always been possible with printed media. Objections to it when a copy of the work has been purchased by an individual are purely aesthetic. However, with publicly owned copies and collaborative works, strict social protocols and sanctions have developed. It is likely that such precedents will eventually be applied in law to protect owners of works from abuse of their property. The latter problem, plagiarism, has always existed to some extent, but it is aggravated by the fact that it may now be done rapidly on a far larger scale; fragments can be pasted into a new document in seconds. It may also be more difficult to prevent; it is easier to provide read-only systems and documents than to copy-protect them.

Various possibilities have been forwarded for the collection and distribution of royalties for accessing online information. These include charging by the chronological time unit, by CPU time used, by byte unit, by personal licence[13]. Among the more difficult issues to be resolved and then implemented are whether individuals should be allowed to take permanent copies of original works, and whether they should be charged on a one-off basis for access to a given item (and if so, how they will demonstrate that they have already paid).

Ted Nelson makes a strong case that precedents from current copyright law can be extended to resolve most of these issues[25]. However, there is considerable resistance by publishers at present to their materials being made available online. This is understandable; even without online distribution the ease with which electronic materials can be duplicated means that software piracy is a major problem. Alternatives such as shareware distribution have yet to be proven as effective; for instance, informal reports suggest that to date registration figures for products have been far lower in Europe than in the USA.

SUMMARY

There is a particularly wide potential for the implementation of hypermedia systems. However, it is advisable to assess systems in relation to specific criteria to achieve the optimal level of functionality.

Professional authors of hypermedia materials are likely to be generalists. Large, multimedia applications will additionally require specialists from outside the professions generally involved in software or publishing teams.

Default path structures should always be provided for unfamiliar users.

It is useful to distinguish navigation at the informational macro level from browsing at the micro level. These activities may be further broken down by purpose.

Hypermedia systems provide virtual environments for seamlessly interacting with information that is typically both heterogeneous in origins and relatively high-level in content. They also offer high-level means of manipulating the information and navigating through it; processes and techniques are implemented as virtual tools. Hypermedia tools may relate to navigating or browsing (see Figure 6.6).

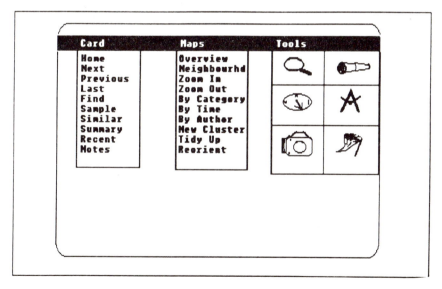

Figure 6.6 The hypermedia toolbox of the future?

The ability to modify materials or construct virtual documents may be desirable from a user's point of view; however, originals need to be safeguarded from malicious damage and other forms of corruption.

The issues of copyright and integrity of original works are likely to create major controversies with the arrival of large-scale interactive software systems. Increasing attention will be given to mechanisms for automatic 'pay-as-you-use' and 'roll-on' collection and distribution of royalties.

The online information media are still a very new. New rhetorics of presentation are developing, but have yet to become standardized. This issue is taken up in the next chapter.

REFERENCES

1.   Akscyn, R., McCracken, D. and Yoder, E. KMS: A distributed hypermedia system for managing knowledge in organizations. *Communications of the ACM*, **31 (7),** July 1988, pp. 820-835.

2.   Barden, R. Extending your home with an ITS: building a hypertext-based intelligent tutoring system. *Proceedings of Hypertext II*, University of York, 29-30 June 1989.

3.   Boyle, C. and Snell, J. Knowledge based navigation under hypertext. *Proceedings of Hypertext II*, University of York, 29-30 June 1989.

4.   Brockman, R. Exploring the connections between improved technology — workstation and desktop publishing and improved methodology — document databases. In: Barrett, E. (Ed.) *Text, ConText and HyperText*. Cambridge, MA: MIT Press, 1988.

5.   Canter, D., Rivers, R. and Storrs, G. Characterizing user navigation through complex data structures. *Behaviour and Information Technology*, **4 (2),** 1985, pp. 93-102.

6.   Chen, J., Ekberg, T. and Thompson, C. Querying an object-oriented hypermedia system. *Proceedings of Hypertext II*, University of York, June 29-30 1989.

7.   Cooke, P. and Williams, I. Design issues in large hypertext systems for technical documentation. In: McAleese, R. (Ed.) *Hypertext theory into practice*. Oxford: Intellect Books Limited, 1989.

8.   Conklin, J. and Begeman, M. gIBIS: a hypertext tool for exploratory policy discussion. *ACM Transactions on Office Information Systems*, **6 (4),** October 1988, pp. 303-331.

9.   Cove, J. and Walsh, B. Online text retrieval via browsing. *Information Processing and Management*, **24 (1)**, 1988, pp. 31-37.

10.   Doland, V. Hypermedia as an interpretive act. *Hypermedia*, **1 (1),** Spring 1989, pp. 6-19.

11.   Duncan, E. Structuring knowledge bases for designers of learning materials. *Hypermedia*, **1 (1)**, Spring 1989, pp. 20-33.

12.   Edwards, D. and Hardman L. 'Lost in hyperspace': cognitive mapping and navigation in a hypertext environment. In: McAleese, R. (Ed.) *Hypertext theory into practice*. Oxford: Intellect Books Limited, 1989.

13.   Foss, C. Tools for reading and browsing hypertext. *Information Processing and Management*, **25 (4)**, 1989, pp. 407-418.

14.   Hanson, R. Toward hypertext publishing. *Sigir Forum (ACM Press)*, **22 (1-2),** Fall/Winter 1987-88, pp. 9-27.

15.   Harland, S. Human factors engineering and interface development: a hypertext tool aiding prototyping activity. In: McAleese, R. (Ed.) *Hypertext theory into practice*. Oxford: Intellect Books Limited, 1989.

16.   Irish, P. and Trigg, R. Supporting collaboration in hypermedia: issues and experiences. In: Barrett, E. (Ed.), *The Society of Text*. Cambridge, MA: MIT Press, 1989.

17. James, G. Artificial intelligence and automated publishing systems. In: Barrett, E. (Ed.) *Text, ConText and HyperText.* Cambridge, MA: MIT Press, 1988.

18. Jones, M. and Myers, D. *Hands-on HyperCard.* NY: John Wiley and Sons, 1988.

19. Knopik, T. and Ryser, S. AI-methods for structuring hypertext-information. *Proceedings of Hypertext II,* University of York, June 29-30 1989.

20. Lewis, B. and Hodges, J. Shared books: collaborative publication management for an office information system. In: Allen, R. (Ed.) *Proceedings of the Conference on Office Information Systems,* March 23-25 1988, Palo Alto, California. *ACM SIGOIS Bulletin,* **9 (2-3),** April and July 1988, pp. 197-204.

21. McAleese, R. Navigation and browsing. In: McAleese, R. (Ed.) *Hypertext theory into practice,* Oxford: Intellect Books, 1989, pp. 6-44.

22. Marchionini, G. and Shneiderman, B. Finding facts *vs.* browsing knowledge in hypertext systems. *IEEE Computer,* **21 (1),** January 1988, pp. 70-80.

23. Monk. A. Getting to known locations in a hypertext. *Proceedings of Hypertext II,* University of York, 29-30 June 1989.

24. Monk, A., Walsh, P. and Dix, A. A comparison of hypertext, scrolling and folding as mechanisms for program browsing. In: Jones, D. and Winder, R. (Eds.) *People and Computers IV.* Cambridge University Press, pp. 421-435, 1988.

25. Nelson, T. *Literary Machines.* Swathmore, PA: Nelson (1981).

26. Salton, G. *Automatic Text Processing.* Addison-Wesley, 1989.

27. Salton, G. and Buckley, C. Term-weighting approaches in automatic text retrieval. *Information Processing and Management,* **24 (5),** 1988, pp. 513-523.

28. Seabrook, R. and Shneiderman, B. The user interface in a hypertext multiwindow program browser. *Interacting with Computers, The Interdisciplinary Journal of Human-Computer Interaction,* **1 (3),** December 1989, pp. 299-337.

29. Shneiderman, B. Reflections on authoring, editing and managing hypertext. In: Barrett, E. (Ed.), *The Society of Text.* Cambridge, MA: MIT Press, 1989.

30. Simpson, A. and McKnight, C. Navigation in hypertext. *Proceedings of Hypertext II,* University of York, June 29-30 1989.

31. Stotts, P. and Furuta, R. Petri-Net-based hypertext: document structure with browsing semantics. *ACM Transactions on Information Systems,* **7 (1),** January 1989, pp. 3-29.

32. Thompson, R. and Croft, W. Support for browsing in an intelligent text retrieval system. *International Journal of Man-Machine Studies,* **30 (6),** June 1989. pp. 639-668.

33. Trigg, R. Guided tours and tabletops: tools for communicating in a hypertext environment. *ACM Transactions on Office Systems,* **6 (4),** October 1988, pp. 398-414.

34. Van Dam, A. Hypertext '87 keynote address. *Communications of the ACM,* **31 (7),** July 1988, pp. 887-895.

35. Walker. J. Supporting document development with Concordia. *IEEE Computer,* **21 (1),** January 1988, pp. 48-59.

36. Walter, M. IRIS Intermedia: pushing the boundaries of hypertext. *The Seybold Report on Publishing Systems,* **18 (21),** August 1989, pp. 21-32.

37. Weyer, S. The design of a dynamic book for information search. *International Journal of Man-Machine Studies,* **17 (10),** July 1982, pp. 87-107.

38. Wright, P. and Lickorish, A. An empirical study of two navigation systems for two hypertexts. *Proceedings of Hypertext II,* University of York, June 29-30 1989.

7 Authoring Issues II — Style, Rhetoric and Methodology

7.1   Nodes and Links

7.1.1   Introduction: Organising Objects

One of the easiest traps to fall into when building a hypermedia application is in beginning without any idea of the desired result; the product of such efforts is likely to be unbalanced and confusing to use — it is often termed 'spaghetti' hypertext. To achieve a satisfactory organization of materials it is necessary to have a reasonable understanding of the relationships between their constituent objects. Normally it is necessary to strike a balance between the rigors of a strict, directed tree structure on the one hand, and at the other extreme the combinatorial explosion involved in connecting each object to all other objects. However, as well as the internal shape of the structure, authors should also consider the possible types of link involved, and the way boundaries are imposed on a collection of information.

7.1.2 Link Types, Link Cues

The directionality of links is an issue that is bound up with the overall structure chosen for a collection of hypermedia materials. However, as well as posing the debate as being about whether links should be one-way, or two-way, open or closed, it is possible to identify different schools of thought on the functional types of links a hypermedia system should support. Akscyn *et al*[1] argue for two basic sorts: tree items (structural elements) and annotations (associative). However, many hypermedia systems provide several other kinds of link, and may even allow users to define their own, arbitrary link types. Providing typed links may add to the investment in development but especially in larger knowledge bases it is likely to result in the most manageable of structures — particularly if links are presented consistently, e.g. graphical links always below their point of reference (see Figure 7.1).

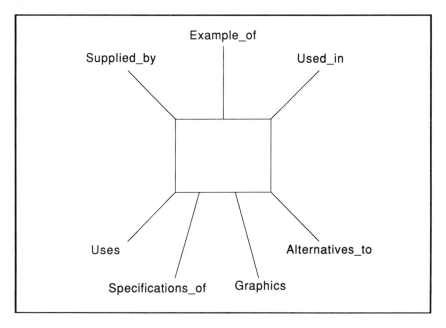

Figure 7.1 Some hypermedia systems support typed links between node objects.

In basic systems hypermedia 'links' are merely pointers to nodes or items. However, in more advanced systems links are attributes of nodes, or can be established automatically to all occurrences of a given attribute. Other systems designers have taken a step further and have made first order objects of the link structures themselves; in such cases links can be made to links. For example, Hanson, in proposing his LinkText publishing system, characterizes links as objects with three attributes or nodes themselves: from, to and type[19]. Note that systems which support typed links have strong similarities with the semantic net models described in Section 3.2. Such systems provide a valuable means of locating and grouping materials — each link type can be regarded as an attribute, and can be employed by cluster analysis techniques.

Another way in which links may be distinguished is in the level of granularity of the objects that can be retrieved from an access point. For instance, some systems allow links to reference a specific location or object in a document, (e.g. NoteCards, Guide, Hyperdoc, HyperCard) whilst others merely reference whole documents or frames (e.g. KMS). However, static dimensions are only part of the problem. An important consideration with dynamic, multimedia applications (using audio or video material, for instance) is the fact that links themselves need to be dynamic[8].

7.1.3 Problems with Goto

Goto is a programming language command that has a bad reputation; it breaks out of normal control structures provided by procedural languages. It has been variously described as unnecessary, confusing, and dangerous. However, it has a parallel in hypermedia, and indeed is one of the most common link types. In HyperCard, for instance, Goto is implemented as a string/field/card ID search utility. In Guide it is called a Reference button. It is used as a means of accessing a distant location, be it another node, document, or part of a document.

However, several studies have shown that users identify Goto facilities with the main cause of their disorientation, and that pop-up notes may be preferable wherever possible[22,26]. Materials that emphasize Goto-type navigation appear to have a heavier overhead than those that allow other forms of navigation. In fact, locating information appears to be the most problem-fraught area for users — understanding information, once found, is relatively straightforward[37]. As a possible alternative to replacement or Goto-style jump links, Stark offers evidence that expansion links (pop-up overlays — similar to embedded footnotes or glossary references) carry a lower cognitive overhead and are preferred by users[29].

7.1.4 Cards or Fragment Showers?

There are three fundamentally different ways in which hypermedia documents/materials can be broken up into nonsequential units. In the first, documents retain their linear structure, and can be conventionally read by scrolling and paging. However, embedded links allow nonsequential jumps to other sections or other documents. In the second, documents are divided into discrete chunks, either determined by the author or by the limitations of the screen display. These are commonly known as cards or chunks.

However, consider the 'Chunking Problem', (see Figure 7.2). Users may be seriously constrained by the author's predetermined divisions of material in that a particular chunk may be viewed in several different contexts, or arrived at via different routes. How can the author segment materials to best suit most users' perspectives? The third and most ambitious form of hypermedia is what Ted Nelson calls 'compound'[24]. Although the conventions of document-level division remain, the emphasis is on allowing users to combine 'fragment showers' of information into seamless, virtual documents consisting both of bytes which are native to the central document, and also bytes which are included *ad hoc* from other external sources.

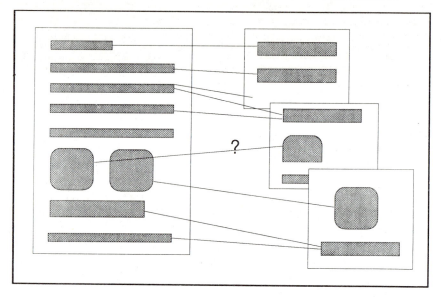

Figure 7.2 The Chunking Problem.

The granularity of nodes is a controversial issue. Purists such as Nelson insist that links should be between material at the micro-level, i.e. single terms and their underlying byte fragments. Most commercial systems have opted for a more pragmatic solution, and offer only general card-to-card/node or point-to-card/node links, as opposed to true point-to-point links. However, apart from restricting the freedom with which materials can be combined on the fly, a secondary problem with the simple chunk style of hypermedia is that links are static, in the sense that they persist to a given chunk or location no matter what happens to the material at the referenced chunk. In other words, there is no context-maintenance.

7.2 Structure

7.2.1 Hierarchical

Hierarchies and similar structures are closely related to the frame-based representations discussed in sub-section 3.2.1. At an implementational level, they are indeed normally represented as acyclic (one-way) directed graphs, e.g. KMS[1] or web-type digraphs in which the user has less concept of location in relation to a canonical structure (e.g. NoteCards). In the strictest form of hierarchy an object has only one link accessing it and is the only object accessing its own children (see Figure 7.3). Web structures will be discussed separately below. Tompa provides a holistic data model for hypertext databases as unrestricted graphs — emphasizing the usefulness of being able to keep structure separate from content[33].

Hierarchical or tree hypermedia can be particularly useful at a user's conceptual level by providing manageable structure in large documents or applications; at progressively higher levels in the hierarchy increasing abstraction occurs, and thus decreasing complexity. Specification of a level of granularity will be unambiguous. This is a common default structure in commercial hypermedia systems.

The rationale for hypermedia includes the minimizing of keystrokes. More powerful links are needed than those deterministically leading the user from one node to the next in a linear sequence, otherwise an application, however aesthetically elegant, is little more than a glorified magic lantern. As well as linear hierarchical links, most hypermedia applications call for links beyond neighboring or intermediate nodes to distant nodes. They also require links that are orthogonal to the main hierarchical axis; consider the inconvenience of needing to return to the root directory of a hierarchical operating system in order to be able to reach files in another directory's sub-directories. Consider also the inconvenience of having to browse through every address in an alphabetic desktop filebox to find, for example, Nigel Woodhead's.

A number of studies have addressed the question of how many intermediate nodes becomes prohibitive to users' browsing. Some programs (for instance HyperCard's Recent command) allow users to backtrack with ease through an audit trail, and this does appear to increase users' confidence. However, the number of simple items (let alone concepts or ideas) that an individual can hold in working memory is very small. Psychological studies suggest that seven is a reliable maximum [23], and physical limits of what can be displayed at one time may reduce this further.

In practice, most hypermedia authors limit themselves to a maximum of five explicit outlinks from any one node; above this, destinations become difficult to display concurrently, and the number of links begins to strain user's cognitive capacities. (It is not always easy to ensure that this limit is

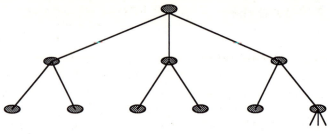

Strict hierarchy

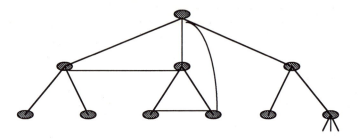

Compromised hierarchy

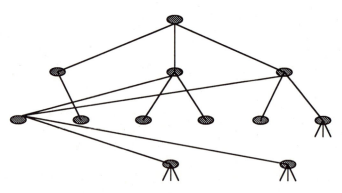

Overlapping hierarchies

Figure 7.3 Hierarchical structures are restricted forms of webs.

honored symmetrically — many nodes may coincide at a given node, and if all these paths are then available as backtrackable options, the user may become disoriented). Note also that as the breadth of the decision tree grows, the action of choosing a side-branching link may lead to users failing ever to reach the sub-topic they really wanted — unless they have sufficient navigating skills to backtrack, or loops return them to the requisite location. Familiar cues from print (such as visible sub-headings on the next linear page) will probably not be available.

7.2.2 Loops and Webs

However, potential problems do not end with single hierarchies. In hypermedia systems it is often also conceptually desirable to provide multiple hierarchies, each based around a particular attribute pattern or perceived purpose. An acyclic hierarchy is compromised as soon as multiple hierarchies are introduced; some of the hierarchies are likely to be steered in opposite directions, and thus the structure becomes cyclic, or loops. Some of these will conjoin or overlap at certain nodes to give users a choice of navigation strategy. However, there is an upper limit to the utility of link densities. The criterion is one of greatest use or meaningfulness — an application where every node was identically linked to every other node would be virtually unusable, and the combinatorial equation of N nodes by N — 1 would be prohibitive.

It is possible to construct a hierarchy in a top-down, bottom-up or both-ends-in manner, as anyone who has ever used an outliner will realize; the comparative ease with which any one of these methods is used depends on the support provided by a specific package. Thus a good hierarchical hypermedia application is a compromise, drawing on the available, domain-independent functionality of the hypermedia environment, and the specifically foreseen needs of the corpus of users for a subject domain; in the best cases users will be able to impose their own structures at run-time.

Authors or developers need to consider not only the epistemological, *a priori* structure they make explicit in information, but the way it will appear from the user's perspective or context at any one point. From an associative net point of view, the present position is always the head of the local hierarchy. Thus sufficient cues need to be provided to maintain a consistent, absolute sense of orientation in the information maze. At the most general level these cues should make apparent the location within the local document or object in relation to the entire collection of available materials. However, on the one hand the problem can be exacerbated if users are permitted to establish their own hierarchies, but on the other prohibiting this may seriously curtail the utility of an application (see sub-section 6.8).

The unconstrained web style of hypermedia architecture is exemplified by systems such as Intermedia[39] and Web Information Assistant.

7.2.3   The Framing Problem

The Framing Problem is similar to the Chunking Problem, but at a more macroscopic level[24]. Given a collection of chunks or nodes of information, there are potentially many more pieces of external information to which the collection could be linked. At some stage it is probably the author's task to impose a significant boundary between a collection and external materials, as in Figure 7.4. However, as in the Chunking Problem, it is difficult to please all users all of the time — an individual user's interests may lie at the intersection of the collection and another collection. The problem with real world sets is that they are 'fuzzy' — there are rarely hard and fast boundaries between delimiting one semantic category or family from another.

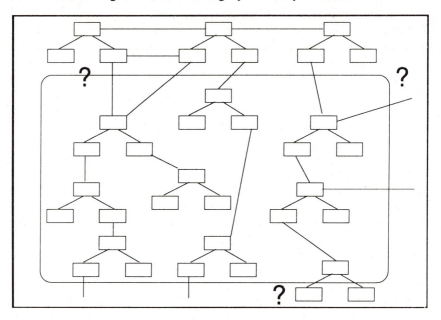

Figure 7.4   The Framing Problem.

The Framing Problem also exists for individual users faced with unmanageably large collections of information. Given a specific goal, much of the information in the author's 'canonical' collection is likely to be redundant, and somehow needs to be filtered out. If filtering or browsing tools are not provided, this task will have to be attempted manually. One means by which authors may reduce the user's potential Framing Problem is by structuring the information with typed links, as described in sub-section 7.1.1. If the types of links supported across collections is standardized, a seamless interface is available to those needing to consult a variety of sources.

7.3   Style and House Styles

7.3.1   A New Rhetoric

The main danger in *ad hoc* development of hypermedia materials is that there will be neither organizing standards across documents themselves nor across the interface to them. Apart from purely aesthetic considerations, or the desire for commercial, corporate identity, this oversight may be seriously detrimental to the ease of materials' use. Of course, a similar problem has always existed with printed materials, and seems to have been exacerbated with the arrival of desktop publishing software[7,31]. However, with computer-based media, the actual environment may be unfamiliar to users, and particular attention needs to be given not only to providing the right density of good guidance and cues, but to providing them in a uniform manner.

Many organizations already have house style manuals for printed materials; comprehensive guidelines to the permitted page layout designs, logos, typographic fonts, point size, and use of conventions such as italics and bold script, upper and lower case. Most professional text processing packages make provision for the creation of document templates incorporating such guidelines. Examples with particular hypermedia relevance include KMS schemas[1], InterLex formats[36] and Guide/Idex Shell Documents[13]. Guide provides default typographic styles for buttons (see Figure 7.5), but these are reconfigurable.

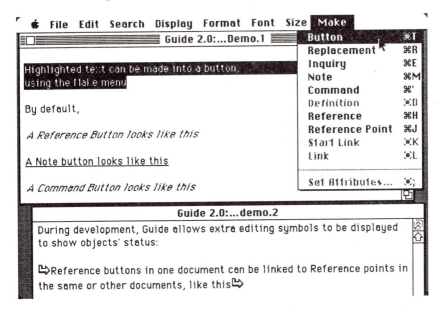

Figure 7.5   Guide's default typographic styles for text buttons.

In addition, there is currently a move towards supporting generic markup languages such as SGML and LaTeX[12],[25],[28]. These allow imported, marked up documents to be standardized against house style sheets, and the rapid alteration of these style sheets across documents. Object libraries are similar in purpose; for instance clip-art graphics and software code libraries both facilitate standardization across applications. Some hypermedia systems support both; HyperCard, for example provides extensive clip-art for buttons and icons (see Figure 7.6), and also direct access to HyperTalk scripts carried over from cutting and pasting objects.

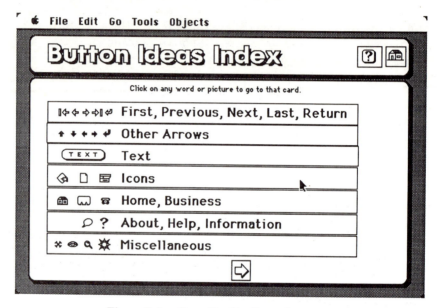

Figure 7.6   HyperCard's clip-art buttons.

Traditional structural style owes much to Aristotle's classical, linear model. Put simply, this has a beginning, a middle and an end (although Aristotle's writing also makes extensive use of non-linear and external references). Each of these sections has a specific kind of content. In the first comes the exposition or introduction of theme(s). In the second these are developed. In the final section the themes are integrated towards a result; French drama has a term for this, denouement, literally meaning unknotting or untangling of threads. Even the present text has three main sections: the first section introduces hypermedia in the context of other approaches; the second section discusses practical concerns for owners, authors and users; the final section reviews the main features of actual products. At a more granular, chapter level, each of these sections has a more or less tripartite structure.

The Aristotelian model has been very influential in the development of printed materials and the order of their contents, which can be described as narrative, and often chronologically linear. It has also influenced dynamic media such as drama — both for the stage and the screen. Despite the division of material into modules, be they acts or chapters, the structure remains overwhelmingly two-dimensional. However, the computer provides a vehicle which can so easily rearrange structure that emphasis of one canonical or 'best' structure is no longer necessary. In many cases it is desirable to have several, equally prominent structures, and each of these extra structures adds a dimension to the n-dimensional information space[38].

As well as structure and presentation of the materials, rhetoric can be applied to design of the system interface. Examples of such approaches include IBM's Systems Application Architecture/Common User Interface (and more recent guidelines for Presentation Manager applications), and Apple's Human Computer Interface Guidelines. IBM's CUA, for instance, proposes that all programs should be designed with a consistent interface, which has three major structural components progressing from top to bottom of the screen, as described in Figure 7.7:

- The Action Bar (e.g. command line pull-down menu titles)
- The Panel Body (the main input/output arena for information)
- The Function Key Area (details of dedicated keys, together with feedback as to recent actions or context)

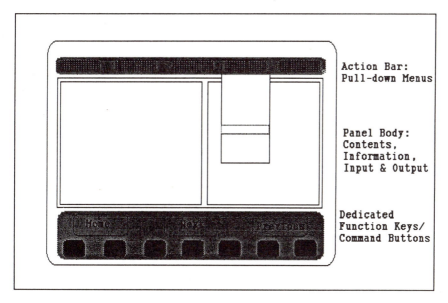

Figure 7.7 Application architecture standardization is likely to increase in the 1990s.

The purpose of such conventions is to reduce the cognitive overhead of new applications; users should be able to apply existing experience to applications which are themselves unfamiliar[17].

Another aspect of rhetoric is the skill with which an author discloses information. Identifiable techniques include:

- Gradual disclosure, where there is a smooth progression into finer, richer, more specific levels of detail

- Foreshadowing, where repeated references are given to a forthcoming item, in order to whet the audience's appetite

- Recapitulation, where prior topics are repeated for emphasis or to allow the audience to draw themes together.

The choice of these rhetorical devices needs to be considered in conjunction with the sort of user dialog issues discussed in the next chapter.

As a coda to this new rhetoric, we are now beginning to see a technology transfer back to printed materials — i.e. techniques developed in response to computerized hypermedia, but which can be partially implemented on paper. A good example of this is the 'qualified citation index' convention, as described by Duncan and McAleese[15]. Rather than merely specifying the authors and publication dates, references are also qualified with a grouping that hints at the specific nature of the findings or other relevant material. In effect this is analogous to typing a link in a semantic net or other online system. For instance, if such a convention had been used for the above reference, it would have appeared as: (Duncan and McAleese, 1982, %definition), and would be listed at the end of the chapter in an alphabetic subgroup along with other references of type 'definition'.

7.3.2 Metaphors

Listed below are some of the metaphors that have been suggested for and employed in hypermedia shells and applications to date, with examples of products employing the metaphor and relevant reference papers. Note that although often indicative of the data structure(s) employed by the system architecture, these virtual metaphors are not necessarily representative of all or only those structures which a given system is capable of supporting.

- Book/print[4,5,21]
- Library (Idex)
- Travel/Guided Tour[34]; (Glasgow On-line[3]); Hitch Hiker's Guide[2]
- Compass [6]

- Film (HyperCard; SuperCard;[34])
- Cards (HyperCard; SuperCard; NoteCards)
- Web (Intermedia[38]; Web Information Assistant)
- Annotation[37]

At the most generic level, these 'over-arching' metaphors seek to give users a concrete and familiar spatial and/or temporal meta-model. This is designed to help them in moving from any one location in an application to another, and in understanding the overall structure of the available information. These metaphors are in addition to the more abstract structural models described above. It is important to realize that the utility of a purely spatial (two-dimensional) metaphor seems to begin to break down as the size of the materials being studied increases — only the most abstract structure may be viewed graphically at the top level, for instance. Organization will be primarily by one attribute dimension, out of all the possible attributes in the information space[9].

Furthermore, as the number of sub-levels and views grows it is increasingly difficult to provide the user with a sense of consistent orientation. As Conklin[11] points out, information does not have a natural topography. Thus the hypermedia developer needs to employ an adequate, conceptual metaphor which can provide a smooth transition between displayable 'slices' in the multi-dimensional information space. It may be that a single metaphor will itself be inadequate for this. A hybrid model might be more useful, with different metaphors assuming prominence at different levels of granularity, within one overall framework such as the book[4]. However, consistency is also a vital consideration; too many metaphors and sudden changes from one to the other will increase the cognitive overhead of a system[20].

As an example of how one of these everyday metaphors can be consistently employed in an application, consider film. This powerful metaphor has been much underplayed in academic studies and commercial documentation,[35] although full credit to the HyperCard example stack authors, who include a variety of editing and animation scripts/objects. It seems likely that the film metaphor will achieve a deserved prominence with the shift from purely hypertext software toward truly dynamic hypermedia systems; film devices allow a breakaway from the linear chronological model.

Film devices can be applied to both the application building process e.g. editing tools[27], and in the effects of the final product the user encounters (dissolves, cutaways, etc.). Zoom ins and zoom outs can provide cues as to the relative movement across the granularity of an application. A montage could be used to present a flavor of the application to newcomers. Whereas most users might have difficulty in explicitly describing the nature of a flashback, panoramic shot, or cutaway, it is likely that they have unconsciously absorbed and understood its context and role from linear narratives of the film medium[14]. In other words users will recognize these device even if they cannot articulate their appropriateness. Empirical evidence pointing towards the utility of the film metaphor comes from a study by Vicente and Williges, who show that 'visual momentum' cues improve users' performance in orientation within a hierarchical file system[35].

Authors should consider in the contexts of their task domains which of the above metaphors are most centrally navigation metaphors, which emphasize browsing, which are uncommitted, and which may actually be ambiguous or confusing. Some metaphors may be specific to a knowledge domain, whilst others may be applicable to tasks such as navigation across a wide range of subjects. For instance, the Guided Tour implies navigation, but is often so constrained that the user may not be able to make the navigational choices desired, or may be offered minimal high-level navigational information. At worst, examples of this metaphor offer the user a series of modular options, each of which is so hard-wired that there is little opportunity to 'short-circuit' the tour — the emphasis is on linear browsing at the node level, according to the author's viewpoint. The Web is geared towards browsing, and the Compass is designed to provide consistent orientation.

One interesting qualification of the validity of functionally simple metaphors, such as those above, comes from Thomas and Norman[32]. These authors argue that an equally important design consideration is 'conversational competence' — systems need to be interactive in the sense that users' actions lead to clear feedback information. The issue of dialog design is taken up in the next chapter.

7.4 Prototyping and the Development Cycle

Hypermedia shells frequently lend themselves to prototyping applications and iterative problem solving[30]. As discussed in Chapter 1, several products which seem to be primarily applications development tools also have claims to being hypermedia shells. In a strictly conceptual sense, the one is independent of the other. However, in providing high-level CASE (computer-aided software engineering) facilities for structuring 'hypermedia' applications, shell developers offer rapid development speeds and the flexibility to implement other programs that may or may not emphasize hypermedia *per se*.

In the case of purely interpreted applications, the final run-time product will require at least the 'reader' version of the shell. It is likely to be relatively slower than an application that can be compiled to stand alone, and slower than a program developed with a conventional compiled language. On the other hand, the wide range of auxiliary features available in conjunction with the shell-bound application allow for greater ease of maintenance and modification.

However, it would be a mistake to begin the hypermedia development cycle with program design or coding without attention to the areas addressed by systems analysis and knowledge elicitation/engineering methodologies. Both seem relevant to hypermedia development in that the structure of information necessary goes beyond that of traditional data/information processing models[16]. Briefly, these methodologies allow developers to make the useful distinction between the physical (real-world) model, the logical or epistemological structure of information, and the (alternative) pragmatic or functional levels at which individuals may make use of materials. Developing a system is typically an iterative process of analysis, implementation, feedback and stepwise refinement. What is emphasised in hypermedia design is that this cycle should center around analysis of the user's tasks. Issues of user modeling and individual differences are further discussed in Chapter 8.

Prototyping has always been feasible with paper-based documents; in fact it is the editor rather than the user who approves or rejects draft documents in the traditional publishing cycle. However, the reader is rarely consulted, and hardly ever before the fact of publication. Any feedback is retrospective and can only be incorporated with the next edition; in practice, even this is unlikely to effect more than the smallest of changes, such as error correction. Once written and approved, for better or for worse, the published word is rarely revoked.

Even within the computer industry, usability/acceptance testing is still almost exclusively after the fact of production; there is rarely time allocated in the development cycle for major problems identified in feedback to be changed. However, there is a realization, particularly among some of the larger corporations, that documentation should start earlier, and play a more prominent role in the development cycle. IBM, for instance, regards information development as one of three equal areas in product development[17].

7.5 Producing Hypermedia Materials — a methodological approach

As has been emphasized throughout the text, it is a mistake to begin a hypermedia application without a definite plan of the desired overall structure of the information. In some cases this will be inherent in the information itself, but in other domains it will be more open to creative interpretation by the developers. A general methodological framework is available that encompasses both of the possible cases above. For instance, Trigg[34] suggests a simple three-stage, cyclical approach similar to those in use in conventional structured methodologies and AI knowledge elicitation:

- Capture-express
- Organize-analyze
- Retrieve-communicate.

This cycle is given explicit support in the NoteCards hypermedia system for Xerox workstations[18].

A similar three-stage approach is suggested by Carlson[10]. In her model, development of a 'smart' interface proceeds in parallel with development of the rhetoric and logical structure of the content materials. The first stage is to transform linear materials into a basic hirachical structure. At the next stage, the materials are given 'individual views', and usability is assessed. Finally, the interface is enhanced with a greater range of (intelligent) query mechanisms.

SUMMARY

Typed links are a tool for the management of complexity. Links may also access information at a variety of levels of granularity. 'Goto' links may be appealing to developers but can confuse users.

The Chunking Problem refers to the dilemma facing authors trying to decide how best to segment their material into card- or window-sized units.

Hierarchical structures provide clear levels of granularity, and clear views of information at a given level. However, simple hierarchies may be over-restrictive for a community of users with differing purposes, some of which will be orthogonal to the canonical hierarchy.

Loops and web structures accommodate more users but may exacerbate the problems of disorientation.

The Framing Problem is a macroscopic version of the Chunking Problem; how to delimit a collection of information from other neighbouring collections.

Standardizing links, interfaces and presentation templates permits easy integration of source materials and allows for easier familiarization with new applications.

Traditional rhetorics of content and structure can be usefully extended, but we are yet to see a consensus emerge.

Familiar media metaphors may provide useful navigation cues to users. Some are more suitable to some media, for instance dynamic or static materials, than others.

The hypermedia approach lends itself to prototyping. However, top-down planning of the main structure is still desirable to avoid 'spaghetti' hypermedia.

REFERENCES

1. Akscyn, R., McCracken, D. and Yoder, E. KMS: A distributed hypermedia system for managing knowledge in organizations. *Communications of the ACM, 31 (7),* July 1988, pp. 820-835.
2. Allinson, L. and Hammond, N. A learning support environment: The Hitch Hiker's Guide. In: McAleese, R. (Ed.), *Hypertext, theory into practice.* Oxford: Intellect Books, 1989.
3. Baird, P. and Percival M. Glasgow Online: Database development using Apple's HyperCard. In: McAleese, R. (Ed.), *Hypertext, theory into practice.* Oxford: Intellect Books, 1989.
4. Benest, I. A hypertext system with controlled hype. *Proceedings of Hypertext II,* University of York, 29-30 June 1989.
5. Benest, I., Morgan, G. and Smithurst, M. A humanized interface to an electronic library. In: Bullinger, H. and Shackel, B. (Eds.) *Human-Computer Interaction — INTERACT'87,* pp. 905-910, Elsevier Science Publishers (North-Holland), 1987.
6. Bernstein, M. The bookmark and the compass: orientation tools for hypertext users. *ACM SIGOIS Bulletin, 9 (4),* October 1988, pp. 34-45.
7. Brockman, R. Exploring the connections between improved technology — workstation and desktop publishing and improved methodology — document databases. In: Barrett, E. (Ed.) *Text, ConText and HyperText.* Cambridge, MA: MIT Press, 1988.
8. Brondmo, H. and Davenport, D. Creating and viewing the Elastic Charles — a hypermedia journal. *Proceedings of Hypertext II,* University of York, June 29-30 1989.
9. Caplinger, M. Graphical database browsing. In: Hewitt, C. and Zdonik, S. (Eds.) *Proceedings of the Third ACM SIGOIS Conference on Office Information Systems,* October 6-8 1986, Providence, Rhode Island, pp. 113-119. ACM Press.
10. Carlson, P. Hypertext: a way of incorporating user feedback into online documentation. In: Barrett, E. (Ed.) *Text, ConText and HyperText.* Cambridge MA: MIT Press, 1988.
11. Conklin, J. Hypertext: An introduction and survey. *Computer, 20 (9),* September 1987, pp. 17-41.
12. Coombs, J., Renear, A. and DeRose, S. Markup systems and the future of scholarly text processing. *Communications of the ACM,* November 1987, pp. 933-947.
13. Cooke, P. and Williams, I. Design issues in large hypertext systems for technical documentation. In: McAleese, R. (Ed.) *Hypertext theory into practice.* Oxford: Intellect Books Limited, 1989.
14. Dmytryk, E. *On Screen Writing.* Boston, London: Focal Press, 1985.
15. Duncan, E. and McAleese, R. Qualified citation indexing online? In: Williams, M. and Hogan, T. (Eds.) *National Online Meeting Proceedings.* Medford, NJ: Learned Information, 1982, pp. 77-85.
16. Forrester, M. and Reason, D. *The application of an "Intraface Model" to the design of hypertext systems.* (University of Kent, 1989, unpublished).
17. Grice, R. Online Information: what do people want? What do people need? In: Barrett, E. (Ed.), *The Society of Text.* Cambridge, MA: MIT Press, 1989.
18. Halasz, F. Moran, T. and Trigg, NoteCards in a nutshell. *Proceedings of the ACM CHI+GI 1987 Conference,* Toronto, Canada, April 5-9, 1987.
19. Hanson, R. Toward hypertext publishing. *Sigir Forum, 22 (1-2),* Fall/Winter, 1987-88, pp. 9-27.
20. Hardman, L. and Sharratt, B. User-centered hypertext design: the application

of HCI design principles and guidelines. *Proceedings of Hypertext II,* University of York, June 29-30 1989.

21.   Lewis, B. and Hodges, J. Shared books: collaborative publication management for an office information system. In: Allen, R. (Ed.) *Proceedings of the Conference on Office Information Systems,* March 23-25 1988, Palo Alto, California. *ACM SIGOIS Bulletin,* **9 (2-3),** April and July 1988, pp. 197-204.

22.   McKnight, C., Dillon, A. and Richardson, J. A comparison of linear and hypertext formats in information retrieval. *Proceedings of Hypertext II,* University of York, 29-30 June 1989.

23.   Miller, G. The magical number seven, plus or minus two: some limits on our capacity for processing information. *Psychological Review,* **60,** 1956, pp. 81-97.

24.   Nelson, T. (1981). *Literary Machines.* Swathmore, PA: Nelson.

25.   Niblett, T. and van Hoff, A. Structured hypertext documents via SGML. *Proceedings of Hypertext II,* University of York, 29-30 June 1989.

26.   Nielson, J. and Lyngbaek, U. Two field studies of hypermedia usability. *Proceedings of Hypertext II,* University of York, 29-30 June 1989.

27.   O'Connor, B. Access to moving image documents: background concepts and proposals for surrogates for film and video works. *Journal of Documentation,* **41 (4),** 1985, pp. 209-220.

28.   Rahtz, S., Carr, L. and Hall, W. Creating multimedia documents: hypertext-processing. *Proceedings of Hypertext II,* University of York, 29-30 June 1989.

29.   Stark. H. What do readers do to pop-ups, and pop-ups do to readers? *Proceedings of Hypertext II,* University of York, June 29-30 1989.

30.   Stefik, M., Foster, D., Bobrow, K., Kahn, K., Lanning, S. and Suchman, L. Beyond the chalkboard: using computers to support collaboration and problem solving in meetings. *Communications of the ACM,* **30 (1),** January 1987.

31.   Sullivan, P. Writers as total desktop publishers: developing a conceptual approach to training. In: Barrett, E. (Ed.) *Text, ConText and HyperText.* Cambridge, MA: MIT Press, 1988.

32.   Thomas, P. and Norman, M. Interacting with hypertext: functional simplicity without conversational competence. *Proceedings of Hypertext II,* University of York, June 29-30 1989.

33.   Tompa, F. A data model for flexible hypertext database systems. ACM Transactions on Information Systems, 7 (1), January 1989, pp. 85-100.

34.   Trigg, R. Guided tours and tabletops: tools for communicating in a hypertext environment. *ACM Transactions on Office Systems,* **6 (4),** October 1988, pp. 398-414.

35.   Vicente, K. and Williges, R. Accommodating individual differences in searching a hierarchical file system. *International Journal of Man-Machine Studies,* **29,** 1988, pp. 647-668.

36.   Walter, M. IRIS Intermedia: pushing the boundaries of hypertext. *The Seybold Report on Publishing Systems,* **18 (21),** August 1989, pp. 21-32.

37.   Weiss, E. Usability: stereotypes and traps. In: Barrett, E. (Ed.) *Text, ConText and HyperText.* Cambridge, MA: MIT Press, 1988.

38.   Wight, T. Annotation — a new metaphor for hypertext. *Proceedings of Hypertext II,* University of York, June 29-30 1989.

39.   Yankelovich, N., Haan, B., Meyrovitz, N. and Drucker, S. Intermedia: the concept and the construction of a seamless information environment. *IEEE Computer,* **21 (1),** January 1988, pp. 81-96.

8 User Issues — Hypermedia, HCI and Cognition

8.1 Introduction: Human Factors

This chapter discusses hypermedia from the perspective of the user's requirements. Hypermedia systems are potentially of great relevance to Human Computer Interaction (HCI) issues, for two main reasons. Firstly, because the integrated hypermedia paradigm is in itself a high-level, flexible representation that requires minimal familiarity for new users to be able to approach existing computer-based applications. Secondly, the model lends itself to easy and rapid prototyping which can be used by systems designers and researchers seeking optimal solutions in future applications[16,17]. However, conducting research in this area is likely to require an understanding of the basic concepts and methodologies of several disciplines:

experimental and cognitive psychology, ergonomics, computer, information and management science being among the most obvious.

As has been discussed in Chapter 3, hypermedia structures — and particularly those implementations which are broadly within the frame-based family of representations — are similar to functional level models of neurology and the higher-level cognitive models of human associative memory, which have also found favor in AI computational models. This chapter examines how such models can be related to computer-based research into human information processing.

8.2 Mental Models and Data Models

8.2.1 Model Building

Model building is a fundamental part of the hypothetico-deductive or analytic methodologies, which in turn are central to the above disciplines. It is probably useful, therefore, to distinguish the relevant abstract models proposed in connection with hypermedia systems and to discuss their actual use[16,17].

The user comes to a system with at least three models which are of relevance here. At the most general level there is his or her entire cognitive framework — comprising abilities, experience, attitudes, and expectations. Certain factors within this framework, such as spatial, logico-mathematical or verbal ability, can be quantified according to established psychometric scaling techniques.

More specifically, the user comes to a system with two sub-models: of the system itself (or of any other computer-based system with which he or she has had experience), and of his or her goals in relation to that system[11].

This latter dispositional model, or more strictly the range of models of the community of users, is what the system/application designer should seek to implement. This process is often referred to as 'accommodating' or 'affording' the users' interests. The designer needs to provide a conceptual model that the user will be able to accommodate. This may draw on the user's specific computer experience and also on more general cognitive abilities and experiences. In other words the functional emphasis of the system and the structure of any given application must be sufficient to support the community of users across a range of requirements that cannot be completely specified in advance.

The user model — that with which users interpret a hypermedia system — [11] and the dispositional model can be accommodated in one of two ways. Firstly, the task and the system can be redesigned so that they fall completely within the user's known cognitive capabilities. Alternatively, the system could provide sufficient meta-information (perhaps context-sensitive help) to 'bootstrap' the user through gaps in his or her knowledge[33].

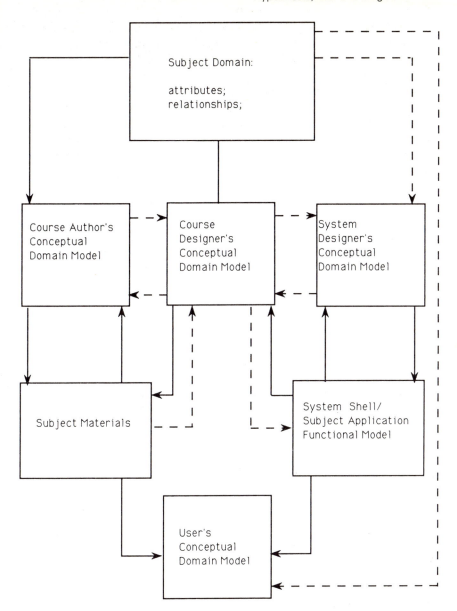

Figure 8.1 Development of hypermedia systems and materials, with regard to user feedback.

However, there are several fundamental problems entailed in either of these idealized solutions. How does the designer (or the system itself) assess what the users' relevant capabilities are? Can users be allowed to specify their own level of capability? How can the system be made sufficiently malleable? How can information and malleability be provided at an acceptable cost in increased cognitive overheads? (The cognitive overheads of task are taken to be a function of the following: information about the system's default functionality and how to customize it; the content and structural information of the application; the criteria of the task itself; see Figure 8.2.)

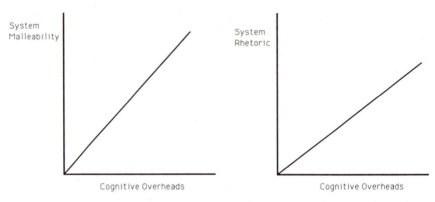

Figure 8.2 Cognitive overheads of hypermedia systems are increased by such factors as system malleability and system rhetoric.

In fact, the problem can be posed as one of reducing individual differences in performance — i.e. of reducing the advantage of talented and experienced users over unskilled, naive or infrequent users; this should occur by raising the performance of the latter group towards that of the former, rather than by producing a system with which both groups perform at some median, compromize level.

Several empirical studies have set out to investigate how individuals' general cognitive abilities affect performance in tasks relevant to hypermedia systems — such as searching hierarchical file systems — and to what extent enhancing the computer interface can improve performance. However, the evidence is not entirely consistent. There is certainly evidence that individuals with higher spatial ability perform better on navigation tasks than those with comparable computer exposure and low spatial ability. In a study of this kind using the Sun Help Viewer (a hierarchical hypermedia browser), Campagnoni and Ehrlich[5] show that for most non-professional users browsing strategies predominate (as opposed to analytical, indexing skills). Perceived task, application content and the design of the interface itself can all influence strategy and performance[5].

But educationalists also need to understand how hypermedia systems might affect the differential in performance between high and low spatial ability groups. On the one hand, Vicente and Williges show that providing a graphical interface with 'visual momentum' (cues similar to those found in film) does significantly improve performance by users with high and low spatial ability. This is qualified by the allied finding that the differential in performance by the two groups remains unaffected[33].

Several other studies have failed to show the same advantage of graphical over textual or symbolic search paradigms, or have even shown a disadvantage. For instance, Jones and Dumais found that naive computer users' performance with a graphical desktop/office metaphor dropped off rapidly as a function of the number of item locations to recall, soon falling significantly below that of users with the symbolic filing condition. Furthermore, subjects were unable efficiently to integrate spatial and symbolic information when both modes were available[19].

One possible qualification of the above study is that the task was specific to recall of location. Studies of the psychology of memory distinguish recall from recognition (prompted). The relative ease of recognition compared to recall in memory tasks is a well demonstrated psychological phenomenon[32]. Many hypermedia tasks seem to be better characterized as recognition tasks, or interactive recognition (general scanning and browsing as opposed to query formulation *per se).*

The disparity of findings between studies points towards the need for further research into the precise nature of spatial representations, and to what extent computer-based graphical models (generally two-dimensional, non-tactile, requiring very limited locomotor interaction) actually accommodate these.

As was been mentioned in Chapter 3, Berry and Broadbent advocate the development of intelligent systems with the capacity to construct individual, dynamic user models — especially with naive or infrequent users[4]. Forrester and Reason discuss similar criteria specific to the design of future hypermedia systems; it is likely that more flexible structural representations than those in use at present will be needed to accommodate a range of users[11]. At present there is only evidence for a default model; Marchionini provides evidence that high school students' default model of an information source is the printed encyclopedia, and furthermore, that they are able to employ this model effectively in developing skills with an electronic encyclopedia[25]. One of the possible dangers of using a simple, default metaphor is that it will limit the progress of users capable of employing more complex, subtle or efficient metaphors.

8.2.2 Cognitive Mapping and Hypergames

Cognitive mapping is a term used both by psychologists and by operations researchers. In the former discipline it has been investigated in relation to developmental and cross-cultural conceptions of causality, or of general navigational ability[11,20]. For instance, Gladwin[12] studies the use of cognitive maps for navigation by Oceanian islanders. In operational research, it has been used in a slightly more applied sense; for researching individual and group performance in organizational decision-making tasks. For instance, these have included commercial studies of group interaction[8] and historical analyses of political and military scenarios. Similar studies have been conducted using hypergame models. Like cognitive mapping, hypergame theory is a 'soft' OR technique; it seeks to represent ranked beliefs and preferences for competing/co-operating players in a cellular decision matrix. It has been used to analyze scenarios such as the Cuban Missile Crisis and the Fall of France[2,3]. Both are mentioned as examples in the present context because it would seem to be very straightforward to implement either approach within a (collaborative, interactive) hypermedia environment.

Cognitive maps represent concepts as nodes, linked by causal relationships. These relationships may be represented by simple positive and negative linkages. More commonly, they incorporate more complex types of links, for instance links expressing doubtful associations or null hypotheses, or inheritance relationships similar to those employed in semantic nets. For instance, a known positive cause and effect would be linked by a ' + ' arrow, a preventative or inhibitory cause by a '—' link, and a non-contributory cause by a null or '0' link. Efferent links are simply the aggregate of the afferent link weightings at a node. It is also possible to produce an aggregate representation of common concepts and linkages across users[7]. An example of a simple cognitive map representation is given in Figure 8.3.

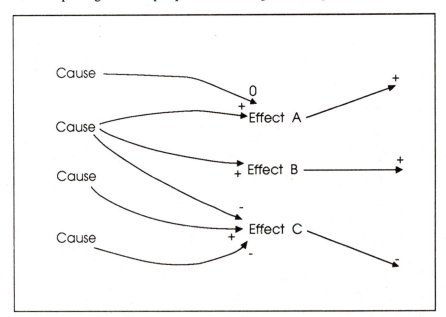

Figure 8.3 A cognitive map: efferent links are the aggregate of afferent links.

However, maps rarely go as far as allocating term weightings or Bayesian probabilities as used in inference nets[7] — the effect at a node in a user's map is simply the aggregate outcome of incident linkages. In other words, cognitive mapping is a technique that attempts to provide a 'soft' qualitative rather than a 'hard' quantitative solution; there is generally an acceptance of user's verbal statements of belief rather than any attempt to corroborate or correlate the information with quantitative psychometric measures. Thus cognitive maps form simplified representations — and thus have sometimes been criticized for being oversimplifications.

The term cognitive mapping has also found favor in the hypermedia literature, although it is unclear that it is being applied in the rigorous sense of one of the above disciplines. Rather it seems to be used in a weak sense to indicate any representational overview (often graphic) of knowledge in a computer-based system, or simply to describe an analogy to physical navigation according to environmental or topographic cues. Readers familiar with one of the more rigorous usages should treat the term's use in a hypermedia context with caution; hypermedia typically does not place so much emphasis on the nature of (causal) relationships between items in the map; mere close association or proximity may be entailed, or a link type based on an unintuitive attribute not normally used in human reasoning.

Klein and Cooper[22] conclude that cognitive mapping is a technique useful in three areas:

- Problem negotiation
- The teaching of decision-making skills
- The assessment of decision-making skills.

All three have direct application within a hypermedia framework — which can be used as a discussion or collaboration forum, a teaching and assessment vehicle. One of the major criticisms of cognitive mapping in the OR literature is that the maps are time-consuming to build, and difficult to validate with subjects because of their perceived complexity. A hypermedia solution, with multiple 'virtual' views would seem to bear the same relation to cognitive mapping that automated systems analysis tools bear to structured systems analysis methodologies, i.e. they can substantially reduce the tedious 'paper-crunching' of numerous redrafts.

The OR/psychological research into cognitive mapping and perception of causation also throws some light on the sorts of structure people seem to employ when dealing with complex decision matrices. Firstly, maps appear to be acyclic, i.e. there is a linear flow of perceived causal relationships from goal to outcome. Secondly, there are few indeterminate links in a map — maps are well resolved or 'balanced' rather than ambivalent. In other words, people tend not to make explicit the possible null hypotheses in a reasoning process. (Null hypotheses, i.e. that there is no causal connection between factors under consideration, are an essential part of formal hypothetico-deductive models). This bias may be a function of people's limited cognitive capacity to consider concepts concurrently, and possibly of their explicit awareness of this limit.

A similar phenomenon has been shown in estimates of the probability of hypotheses. Even professionals with a good theoretical knowledge of statistics tend to be biased against unlikely hypotheses. Alternatively, they may attempt to reduce subjective uncertainty by a bias towards the most salient hypothesis. This occurs even if the latter is also objectively unlikely; often there is inaccuracy to an alarming degree. Doyle provides a good overview of estimation errors[5]: Lichtenstein *et al.* show that subjects overestimated the odds of an event, rating it at 1,000,000 : 1 against an actual odds ration of only 10 : 1. Several studies have shown that physicians estimating subjective probability of unusual diseases tend to overestimate the odds, given some slight evidence, if they have a particular interest in the area[24]. Eddy reports that estimates of cancer given a positive mammogram were of 0.75 probability, against actual *a posteriori* probability of 0.075 — error by an order of magnitude. Doyle conclude that this seems to be due to a tendency to confuse the likelihood of a hypothesis given some evidence — P(HE) — with the converse relationship, that of the likelihood of the evidence given the validity of the hypothesis — P(EH).

Further relevant research into cognitive mapping shows how maps are developed in stages. Siegel and White[29] observe a four-stage process:

- Recognition of isolated, salient landmarks
- Routes between these landmarks
- Local network routes, or 'minimaps'
- Integrated minimaps or full survey maps.

Similarly, Weiss[34] characterizes four stages in users' relations with their systems by the kind of assistance they appear to require at each stage:

- Motivational
- Orientational ('elemental tutorial advice')
- Guidance ('demonstrations and advice on how to string the elements into functions')
- Reference (reinforcement, memory prompting materials)

These stages are similarly characterized by Herrstrom and Massey as overview, tutorial, procedural and reference[18]. The implication of these developmental models is that providing information purely at the reference level is grossly inadequate except for near-expert users. Edwards and Hardman believe that naive users of a hypermedia application can be confused by 'mixed structure' navigation possibilities[9].

There is also evidence to support a correlation between map-making as a general (spatial) ability and users' navigational efficiency in a hypermedia environment. Simpson and McKnight demonstrate that relatively good map-makers access fewer non-essential cards in a HyperCard-based question-answering task[30]. However, studies such as Gladwin's[12] show that cognitive maps may be based on many sorts of structure, not just the traditional Cartesian dimensions of Western graphical maps. There is scope for further study to discover whether *a priori* cognitive abilities in modes other than spatial ability are also correlated with navigational abilities.

The implications of mental modeling and cognitive mapping hyper-game studies for applications builders would seem to be threefold: users should be encouraged to learn one archetypal path or knowledge structure for a given domain before branching out (see also Section 6.4); users may benefit from a metaphor that echoes their own psychological models of causal/active relationships; certain users can be prompted to consider alternative 'less attractive' views in important decision-making situations.

8.2.3 Outline Densities and Idea Processing

Hypermedia documents differ from conventional documents or databases in that objects are discrete ideas — in a sense that has no direct equivalent in terms of a book's paragraphs or a database's records. They are typically dense in the sense that screens are 'busy', and there are several levels of information to consider at once. The density of links in relation to node content is likely to be greater than in most books, although less dense than that of a true semantic net (see sub-section 3.2.1). As mentioned in subsection 7.2.1, there is an upper limit to the amount of information that human users can deal with concurrently. However, this can be optimized, given an appropriate scratchpad or brainstorming tool.

Not only does hypermedia provide a means of browsing through the ideas of others, but it is also an environment for developing new idea structures [13]. Some systems are better designed for browsing existing materials than for outlining new ones. Potential users should be aware of these biases in selecting an appropriate system for their task. Examples of hypermedia systems particularly well suited to idea structuring include NoteCards, Intermedia, and Web Information Assistant, discussed in Section III.

8.3 Deciding on the Interface: Graphics, Text and Dialog

Readers in search of a general introduction to designing the human-computer interface are referred to Shneiderman[28]. Perhaps the major experimental finding to note in relation to hypermedia is the benefits to users of embedded (contextual) menu options as opposed to explicit (meta-level, and often arbitrary) menus[23]. If we characterize this difference as being parallel to that between microlevel and macrolevel cognitive processes, Forrester and Reason's criticism of the applicability of the traditional information processing metaphor may be relevant here[11]. They identify six conversational dialog forms which might be used as the basis for task-specific design criteria:

- Diagnostic conversation
- Interrogation
- Teacher-pupil
- Brain-storming or collaborative research
- Employer-employee discussion/negotiation
- Peer-peer open discussion

As mentioned above, a controversial issue in relation to choosing a system interface is the relative advantages and disadvantages produced by a graphic interface. Note that it is conceptually useful to separate those systems which support a graphic/iconic overview of information, and those which merely support embedded graphics.

Incorporating an extra medium such as graphic images, or video in an application may add considerably to the interest and comprehensibility of materials. Then there is the old paper-based maxim that a picture is worth a thousand words. However, it is worth bearing in mind that not all pictures are equal in terms of computerised storage. Bit-mapped graphics and digitized video are particularly expensive to store, although file compression algorithms have made impressive headway, and if available with your system they may be able to support fast, dynamic (de-)compression. Examples of systems which compress data in this way are HyperCard and Hyperdoc. On the other hand, it is often possible to achieve impressive 'graphical' results with character-based interfaces, using typographic cues, graphics character sets, screen painting, list boxes etc.

Another consideration specific to dynamic media such as video in hypermedia is the cost benefit ratio such information has in relation to static media [19]. Video requires extensive annotation if it is to be used in a true hypermedia fashion; perhaps subtitles will have to be added or a separate timeline cross-referenced transcript. At present there does not appear to be an adequate methodological approach to categorizing static graphic images, let alone dynamic image sequences. However, video/animation may be superior to other media in terms of paralinguistic description — there is no need in the former to interpret the unspoken aspects of a scene, such as gesture or physical relationship of people and objects.

Recent emphasis in HCI has been placed on the benefits of dialog styles of interaction; users have sophisticated models of dialog protocols which they can employ in a computerised context with minimal cross-training. Support for a dialog interface in hypermedia design is provided by Thomas and Norman[31], who argue for 'conversational competence' in systems as well as functionally simple interfaces. A good example of a system employing both is KMS[1], with context-sensitive mouse actions rather than intermediate menus, and which provides cursor feedback as to the consequences of possible actions. Basic guidelines for the implementation of dialogs are given by Hardman and Sharratt[15].

Whereas context-sensitive control of a system is a desirable feature, the actual content of information supplied at any one point should be as context-free as possible[13]. This is a sensible point to make in relation to any online system, but particularly relevant to hypermedia where the 'chunked nature' of information may result in users being unaware of the original (linear) context in which it was created. Each node should be as self-contained as possible, so that although external information is referenced it is normally only possible (and not necessary) to access it.

8.4 Tools for Trails II — Customized Tools for Users

A successful application requires integrated analyses of four distinct areas: product, user, task, and project[11,13]. In addition to the interface model chosen for the application, attention should be given to auxiliary tools that the user will need to accomplish his or her set of tasks. Furthermore, as well as providing users with tools to fit their needs, designers should ensure that users will realize that the tools exist, and that these tools will be of use. As was noted in the previous chapter, there is a continuum between those metaphors which are most appropriately seen as representations — the context in which tools are used — and those which are more explicitly manipulable tools[11].

The distinction between author and reader is also potentially unclear in hypermedia systems. In printed media, readers are normally restricted to annotating pages in longhand or to making separate reference notes. In hypermedia readers are often participative users — they have access to many of the same tools as the authors of original materials. It seems desirable to allow users to save customized copies of at least their own tool configurations, rather than requiring them to reconfigure their formats at each session. The sanctity or otherwise of original works is discussed below.

In some systems authors have more tools than users — for instance in the user level hierarchy of HyperCard, progressively more sets of tools are released at each level from Browsing to Authoring. However, this is not to imply that users' tools should be a restricted subset of authors' tools. Indeed, users will often have more first-hand need to use a tool than authors — for instance audit trails or backtracking aids. In the case of some domains it may be desirable to provide users with a general tool that they can use to customize specific applications. For instance, Monk suggests that one of the most useful tools to provide is a personalized browser, in which a map of an application is constructed on the basis of a user's most frequently visited nodes[26]. Thus the author is not forced to 'hardwire' a guided tour — which may be of interest only to a minority of users. This would be particularly valuable in cases where the author cannot foresee possible relationships between material in advance — for instance where new material is regularly added to the knowledge base.

8.5   How to Use a Hypermedia Application

This section describes the general strategies available to users rather than authors of hypermedia applications (although the distinction is often less clear than, for instance, between database administrators and database end users). Outlines for authoring hypermedia materials (for use by others) are given in Chapters 6 and 7.

When first presented with a hypermedia application, users need to familiarize themselves with both the structure and content. Their task will be made that much easier if the structure conforms to a standard rhetoric — for instance if there is an interactive table of contents, an overview or guided tour, and easily assimilated node and link types.

Naive users will also benefit from establishing the overall functionality of a system. The following questions are offered as introductory guidelines for 'consumer' users rather than experienced hypermedia producers.

Fourteen Ways to Get to Know a Hypermedia System

- What rhetorical devices indicate what actionable features?
- What search mechanisms are offered for text items?
- What level(s) of granularity are supported at the node and group level by the system and its applications?

- What level(s) of granularity are supported by tools for mapping and browsing?
- What tools or cues are provided to aid orientation?
- What range of link types are in use for any given application?
- Is it possible to navigate or view information according to a given link type or other attribute?
- What structure (such as hierarchy) is imposed on an application's contents?
- What are the explicit metaphors of the application?
- What is the breadth (variety) and depth (detail) of information in the application?
- Are user default preferences offered, e.g. for display?
- Is (context-sensitive) Help available?
- Is it possible to retrace a route through accessed information?
- Is it possible to save details of an interactive session for future use?

Hypermedia systems differ from most other software packages in the relative freedom of purpose they offer both users and developers — in terms of subject domain, representative media, and possible strategies for relating information. Hypermedia can support many methodologies but does not require any particular one. There is almost certain to be potential for authors and users from a given discipline to embed their own methodological approaches within a hypermedia framework. A standardized rhetoric may be desirable for presentation across applications, but this should not be confused with the kind of dogmatic approach characteristic of form in, for example, relational databases.

SUMMARY

Hypermedia interfaces are intrinsically high level; they facilitate rapid prototyping and hence have a particular relevance to HCI research.

There is a complex set of relationships between the conceptual models of designers and users, and the intermediate model of the computer interface.

Interfaces should be capable of supporting a community of users, possibly by dynamic assessment and adaptation.

Cognitive mapping techniques and hypermedia systems also have a symbiotic relationship. A good cognitive model will represent several layers of granularity and present users with null hypotheses which they might otherwise ignore.

It is not clear that a graphical/spatial metaphor alone is necessary or sufficient for hypermedia-type search tasks. A causal or other associative metaphor should also be considered. System metaphors should reflect demonstrated user models.

Dynamic media can uniquely represent some forms of information, but are also relatively expensive and laborious to implement.

Dialog design highlights the benefits of context-sensitivity and reduced keyboarding. Context-sensitive control of systems and graded access to further information are desirable; however, the information content at any one node should be as context-free as possible.

Unfamiliar users of systems/applications will benefit from a general awareness of available functionality.

There is rarely a clear distinction between authors and users. Hypermedia benefits from a standardized rhetoric, but does not require knowledge of or adherence to a dogmatic methodology.

REFERENCES

1. Akscyn, R., McCracken, D. and Yoder, E. KMS: A distributed hypermedia system for managing knowledge in organizations. *Communications of the ACM*, **31 (7)**, July 1988, pp. 820-835.

2. Bennett, P. and Dando, M. Complex strategic analysis: a hypergame study of the Fall of France. *Journal of the Operational Research Society*, **30 (1)**, January 1979, pp. 23-32.

3. Bennett, P. and Huxham, S. Hypergames and what they do: a soft 'OR' approach. *Journal of the Operational Research Society*, **33 (1)**, January 1982. pp. 41-50.

4. Berry, D. and Broadbent, D. Expert systems and the man-machine interface. Part Two: the user interface. *Expert Systems*, **4 (1)**, 1987, pp. 18-27.

5. Campagnoni, F. and Ehrlich, K. Information retrieval using a hypertext-based help system. *ACM Transactions on Information Systems*, **7 (3)**, July 1989 pp. 271-191.

6. Doyle, J. Probability problems in knowledge acquisition for expert systems. *Knowledge-Based Systems*, **1 (2)**, 1988, pp. 114-120.

7. Duda, R., Hart, P. and Nilsson, N. Subjective Bayesian methods for rule-based inference systems. In: *Proceedings 1976 National Computer Conference*, AFIPS Press, 1976.

8. Eden, C. and Jones, S. Publish or perish? — A case study. Journal of the Operational Research Society, 31, 1980, pp. 131-139.

9. Edwards, D. and Hardman L. 'Lost in hyperspace': cognitive mapping and navigation in a hypertext environment. In: McAleese, R. (Ed.) *Hypertext theory into practice*. Oxford: Intellect Books Limited, 1989.

10. Egan, D. and Gomez, L. Assaying, isolating and accommodating individual differences in learning a complex skill. In: Dillon, R. (Ed.) *Individual Differences in Cognition*, **Vol. 2**, pp. 173-217. NY: Academic Press, 1985.

11. Forrester, M. and Reason, D. *The application of an ''Intraface Model'' to the design of hypertext systems.* (University of Kent, 1989, unpublished).

12. Gladwin, T. *East is a Big Bird*. Cambridge, MA: Harvard University Press, 1970.

13. Grice, R. Online Information: what do people want? What do people need? In: Barrett, E. (Ed.), *The Society of Text.* Cambridge, MA: MIT Press, 1989.
14. Halasz, F. Moran, T. and Trigg, NoteCards in a nutshell. *Proceedings of the ACM CHI+GI 1987 Conference,* Toronto, Canada, April 5-9, 1987.
15. Hardman, L. and Sharratt, B. User-centered hypertext design: the application of HCI design principles and guidelines. *Proceedings of Hypertext II,* University of York, June 29-30 1989.
16. Harland, S. Human factors engineering and interface development: a hypertext tool aiding prototyping activity. In: McAleese, R. (Ed.) *Hypertext theory into practice.* Oxford: Intellect Books Limited, 1989.
17. Hartson, H. and Hix, D. Toward empirically derived methodologies and tools for human-computer interface development. *International Journal of Man-Machine Studies,* 31, 1989, pp. 477-494.
18. Herrstrom, D. and Massey, D. Hypertext in context. In: Barrett, E. (Ed.), *The Society of Text.* Cambridge, MA: MIT Press, 1989.
19. Hodges, M., Davis, B. and Sasnett, R. Investigations in multimedia design documentation. In: Barrett, E. (Ed.), *The Society of Text.* Cambridge, MA: MIT Press, 1989.
20. Johnson-Laird, P. *Mental Models,* Cambridge: Cambridge University Press, 1983.
21. Jones, W. and Dumais, S. The spatial metaphor for user interfaces: experimental tests of reference by location versus name. *ACM Transactions on Office Information Systems,* 4 (1), January 1986, pp. 42-63.
22. Klein, J. and Cooper, D. Cognitive maps of decision-makers in a complex game. *Journal of the Operational Research Society,* 33 (1), January 1982 pp. 63-72.
23. Koved, L. and Shneiderman, B. Embedded menus: selecting items in context. *Communications of the ACM,* 29 (4), April 1986, 312-318.
24. Lichtenstein, S., Fischoff, B. and Phillips, L. Calibration of probabilities: the state of the art to 1980. In: Kahneman, D., Slovic, P. and Tversky, A. (Eds.) *Judgement Under Uncertainty: Heuristics and Biases.* Cambridge University Press, 1982, pp. 306-334.
25. Marchionini, G. Making the transition from print to electronic encyclopedias: adaptation of mental models. *International Journal of Man-Machine Studies,* 30 (6), June 1989, pp. 591-618.
26. Monk, A. The Personal Browser: a tool for directed navigation in hypertext systems. Interacting with Computers, *The Interdisciplinary Journal of Human-Computer Interaction,* 1 (2), August 1989, pp. 191-196.
27. Oatley, K. Inference, navigation and cognitive maps. In: In Johnson-Laird, P. and Wason, P. (Eds.) *Thinking: readings in cognitive science,* Cambridge University Press, 1977.
28. Shneiderman, B. *Designing the User Interface: Strategies for Effective Human Computer Interaction.* Reading, MA: Addison-Wesley, 1987.
29. Siegel, R. and White, T. The development of spatial representations of large-scale environments. In: Reese, H. (Ed.) *Advances in Child Development and Behaviour,* 10, NY: Academic Press, 1975.
30. Simpson, A. and McKnight, C. Navigation in hypertext. *Proceedings of Hypertext II,* University of York, June 29-30 1989.
31. Thomas, P. and Norman, M. Interacting with hypertext: functional simplicity without conversational competence. *Proceedings of Hypertext II,* University of York, June 29-30 1989.
32. Tulving, E. and Thompson, D. Encoding specificity and retrieval processes in episodic memory. *Psychological Review,* 80, 1973, pp. 352-373.

33. Vicente, K. and Williges, R. Accommodating individual differences in searching a hierarchical file system. *International Journal of Man-Machine Studies, 29,* 1988, pp. 647-668.

34. Weiss, E. Usability: stereotypes and traps. In: Barrett, E. (Ed.) *Text, ConText and HyperText.* Cambridge, MA: MIT Press, 1988.

Section III

Commercial Packages

Introduction

The following listings and reviews give a flavor of each product and the variety of the hypermedia market in general. They are not meant to be procedural, 'how-to' introductions, but rather they are designed to be indications of the sort of possibilities each system favours, drawing on ideas developed in Section I. Where good third-party documentation exists with respect to a program, references are given. At time of press there was relatively limited third-party documentation about IBM-compatible hypermedia software; most of the existing user manuals are for Macintosh software, with publishers waiting to be convinced of a developing market for PC-based hypermedia. Another reason for the relative lack of auxiliary manuals may be a function of the software itself; many hypermedia implementations for the PC are relatively simple, relying on external programs to provide much of the functionality supported internally by Macintosh programs such as HyperCard.

In each sub-section, several archetypal products are examined in greater depth. Space prohibits equal attention to all programs, and the length of review is not necessarily an indication of a product's superior suitability for an individual application. Many of the suppliers quoted will be happy to provide demonstration disks or promotional literature on request.

9 Hypermedia on the IBM PC

9.1 Text-based Programs

HyperBook

HyperBook is a joint development by the software company, Logotron, and Longman, the publishing house. The latter is planning to launch a major series of low-priced texts including technical reports, to be read using the HyperBook reader. However, HyperBook can also be purchased as a full authoring system that can also be used by third-party developers to create their own applications. Several search modes can be instigated at once, including text string and Boolean criteria. A useful feature is integrated text compression.

Both the HyperBook reader and authoring system are relatively low-priced packages, well worth considering for the creation and distribution of reports, and other text-intensive materials.

Supplier:
Logotron Ltd. Dales Brewery, Gwydir Street, Cambridge, CB1 2LJ. Tel: 0223 323656.

HyperInfo

This program from Information Learning Systems Ltd. and Softia is a memory resident adjunct to other software. Specifically, HyperInfo is designed for producing context-sensitive Help applications, activated by words, phrases, or partial text strings from the host environment. HyperInfo is card-oriented; highlighted text buttons link to other cards, each of which may be indexed with up to 50 synonyms. In addition there is a hierarchical structure to cards in an application. The Recent option allows users to retrace their steps through accessed cards.

The HyperInfo development system is modular, and is available as a full authoring system, or as a compiler and run-time library. These will work in conjunction with material produced by any word processor. HyperInfo employs the cursor direction keys rather than a mouse interface. Cards are presented as simple line boxes. Colors of text and card background can be reconfigured from a palette. Key functions can also be redefined. A particularly useful feature is the ability to drag cards around the screen using the cursor keys under NumLock — after all, the system is designed to produce Help cards to be overlaid on material from other programs. Applications can also be automatically merged, thus supporting possible collaborative development projects.

HyperInfo is relatively expensive, but its speed and configurability may justify this to the developers of specialist online Help applications. Above average support can be expected from the supplier, ICUC, which specializes in CBT and related consultancy. Future developments planned include HYPERIMAGE, a full hypermedia system with graphics capability, and an OS/2 version.

Supplier:
ICUC Ltd, Queensway House, Hatfield, Herts, AL10 0NS. Tel: 07072 68068. Information Learning Systems, 18 The Buchan, Camberley, Surrey, GU15 3XB. Tel: 0276 683711.

HyperPAD

HyperPAD, from Brightbill-Roberts, aims to emulate many of the basic features of Apple's HyperCard. Instead of a card metaphor it proposes pads, and instead of the Home Card, the Home Pad. And, of course, it has its own object-oriented application development language, PADtalk, which has the advantage of being compiled rather than interpreted. It also allows the creation of external commands and functions in C or Assembler. The

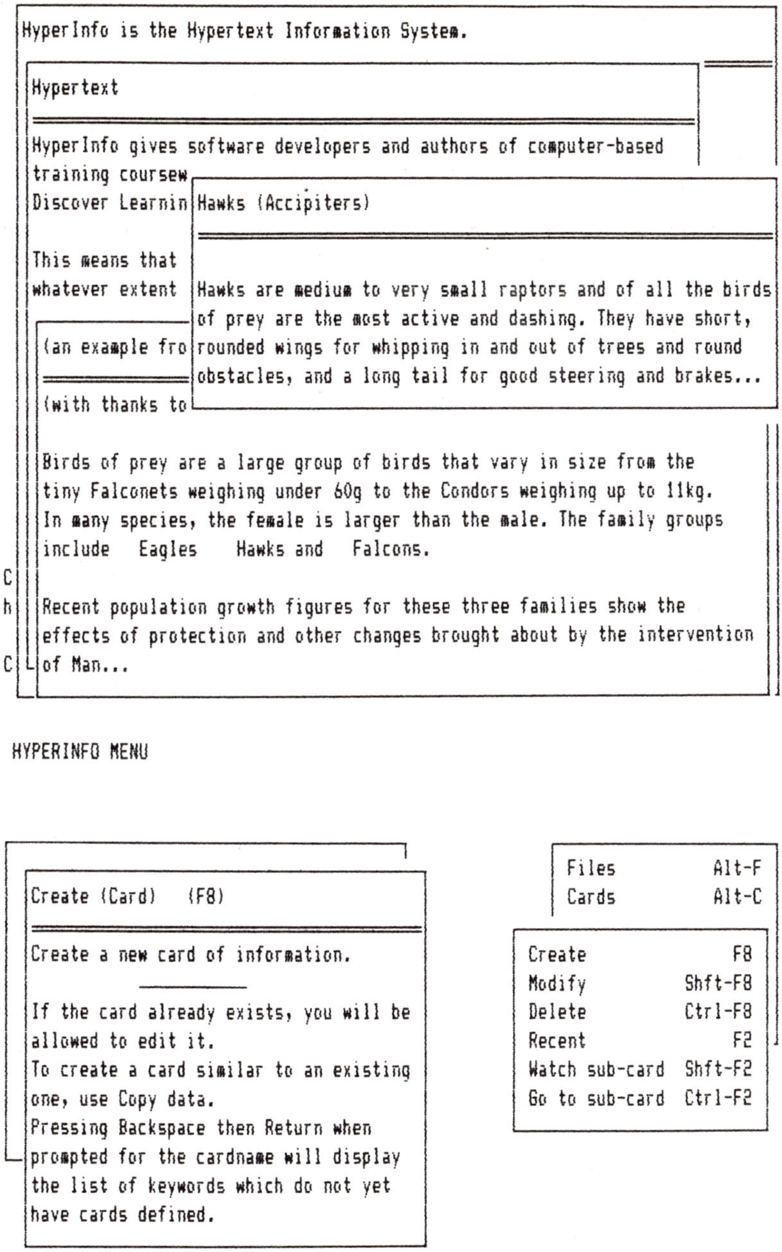

HyperInfo is the Hypertext Information System.

Hypertext

HyperInfo gives software developers and authors of computer-based
training coursew
Discover Learnin | Hawks (Accipiters)

This means that
whatever extent | Hawks are medium to very small raptors and of all the birds
of prey are the most active and dashing. They have short,
(an example fro | rounded wings for whipping in and out of trees and round
obstacles, and a long tail for good steering and brakes...
(with thanks to

Birds of prey are a large group of birds that vary in size from the
tiny Falconets weighing under 60g to the Condors weighing up to 11kg.
In many species, the female is larger than the male. The family groups
include   Eagles   Hawks and   Falcons.

Recent population growth figures for these three families show the
effects of protection and other changes brought about by the intervention
of Man...

HYPERINFO MENU

Create (Card)   (F8)

Create a new card of information.

If the card already exists, you will be
allowed to edit it.
To create a card similar to an existing
one, use Copy data.
Pressing Backspace then Return when
prompted for the cardname will display
the list of keywords which do not yet
have cards defined.

| Files | Alt-F |
| Cards | Alt-C |

Create	F8
Modify	Shft-F8
Delete	Ctrl-F8
Recent	F2
Watch sub-card	Shft-F2
Go to sub-card	Ctrl-F2

Figure 9.1 Hyperinfo cards and development menus.

interface has a series of pull-down menus — somewhere between the feel of MS-Windows and HyperCard, and supports both MS-compatible mouse and cursor keys. HyperPAD can be run as a memory-resident addition to other programs, or as their front end and launch pad (occupying a minimum of 2k); Lotus 1-2-3 and dBASE IV data formats are among those explicitly supported.

Unlike HyperCard, however — and indeed unlike a number of its hypermedia/application management rivals on the PC market — HyperPAD does not support graphics. Its interface is completely character-based — although it is possible to build text boxes or menus with the screen paint tools. This may be of advantage to prospective purchasers with only basic screen configurations (although text mode is supported for EGA and VGA screens).

Developing a HyperPAD application is very simple. Editing supports cut and paste operations on objects, which carry their own attributes and scripts, as with HyperCard. As for HyperPAD's claims to hypertext status — it can create both hierarchical and cross-reference links to materials, although it is not possible to create links within programs such as Lotus 1-2-3 and dBASE *per se*. HyperPAD is probably best thought of as a relatively inexpensive means to create Help and CBT applications.[2,13,14]

Supplier:
Software Paradise, 2 Clive Chambers, Clive St, Caerphilly, Mid Glamorgan, CF8 1GE. Tel: 0222 882334.
or
Brightbill-Roberts, 120 East Washington St, Suite 421, Syracuse, New York 13202. Tel: (0101) 315 474 3000.

HyperShell

This inexpensive program has much of the functionality of some of its main rivals, and is in use by a number of corporate clients. As it is available as shareware, it is discussed in the Shellware Appendix.

HyperTies

This system was originally developed for the Sun workstation at the University of Maryland. The commercial PC version employs cursor keys rather than a mouse. It is included here as a text-based system in that the PC version does not allow for linked graphics. See also Chapter 11, on workstation hypermedia.

Supplier:
Cognetics Corporation, 55 Princeton-Highstown Road, Princeton Junction, NJ 08550. Tel: 609 799 5005.
or
University of Maryland, College Park, Maryland, USA.

MemoryMate

MemoryMate is a simple, memory-resident, free text database and hypertext utility. It can be used to search, index and structure information, which is organized into record cards. Although it requires only around 80K of RAM. MemoryMate can manage a database of up to 32 Mb. Hypertext buttons are defined via a menu, and can reference record cards from their own or an external database file. For *ad hoc* queries, MemoryMate automatically indexes each term in a record, providing for rapid free text searching. It also has basic timeline specification facilities — it is possible to search by creation date, and to specify records created before or after a specific date.

Extra features of MemoryMate include hotkeys, file import/export, as well as cut and paste facilities. Users can also generate simple form templates to standardize presentation. In relation to the database power it provides, MemoryMate is remarkably low priced, and easy to use. It is designed primarily for producing memory-resident Help applications — managing a large reference manual, perhaps — but could also be used as a stand-alone program or simple project manager.

Supplier:
Domark, Ferry House, 51/57 Lacy Road, London, SW15 1PR. Tel: 081 780 2222.

Microsoft OS/2 QuickHelp/Helpmake

QuickHelp can be used to produce context-sensitive Help screens to be used in conjunction with applications running under the OS/2 operation system. Supplied with the OS/2 Presentation Manager Toolkit, QuickHelp comes with context sensitive user information for operating system users. However, the Helpmake compiler allows developers to build their own text databases, overlaid with hyperlinks. It allows string search, and backtrackable audit trails, but restricts applications to 23 topics. QuickHelp's main limitation appears to be that it is not possible to alter open files, thus real-time indexing — referencing other files from within the open file — would be difficult if not impossible.

Supplier:
Microsoft (bundled with OS/2 PM Toolkit).

Asymetrix ToolBook

ToolBook is one of the first of a new generation of object-oriented applications for Microsoft's Windows 3.0. It makes full use of Dynamic Link Library (.DLL) technology — code modules that are paged in and out of memory under Windows' improved memory management. ToolBook is primarily designed for users who want to develop their own interactive applications, such as specialist financial and multimedia interfaces, and context-sensitive glossaries or help systems.

ToolBook encourages use of most of the accepted hypermedia structuring metaphors — such as the interactive map, text and graphics cards, buttons and backtracking. It complements, and is well complemented by, generic Windows features, such as window scrolling and tiling, as well as text search. It has its own scripting language — much along the lines of Apple's HyperTalk. — allowing high-level implementation of simple animation, device drivers, and so on. To make use of this, you need to buy the developers' version. This is not to underestimate the run-time version currently being bundled with Windows 3.0, as it goes well beyond most demonstration programs in the field. One fully functional ToolBook application is supplied as well — DayBook, a useful diary/personal organizer. The other introductory materials are not fully-rounded enough to be very interesting to experienced hypermedia users, and they seem to perform slowly, even on a fast 386-based machine. However, they give a flavour of what will be possible with ToolBook and other Windows 3.0 applications. Although ToolBook and its applications are unlikely to out-perform or compete directly with Windows C developers, ToolBook is probably a much easier and faster route for prototyping.

Supplier:

US Tel: 1-800-624-8999, ext. 299E

Asymetrix Corporation, 110-110th Ave NE, Suite 717, Bellevue, WA, 98004 USA

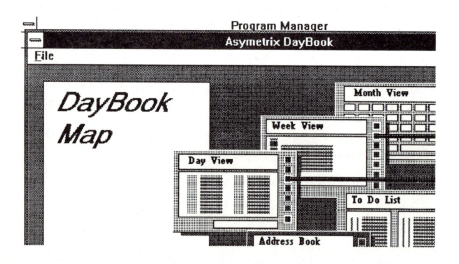

Fig 9.2 Examples of cards from the Toolbook personal organiser.

9.2   Project Management Programs

Lotus Agenda

Lotus Development's Agenda is really in a class of its own in relation to other commercial software. In terms of functionality it is a hybrid product, marketed as a personal information manager. However, it has definite affinities with hypertext, and incorporates sophisticated AI natural language parsing techniques for matching items with categories.

Agenda has a hierarchical emphasis. Items (records up to 350 words) are assigned to categories, which can be accessed in turn by views. Items can be cross-referenced by more than one category, but are economically located at one memory address and accessed via multiple pointers. Views can be defined to show compressed category titles, or expanded to show items, and notes behind items. Categories can also be nested as in an outliner, to a depth of 12 levels.

At its most basic, Agenda can be used as a scratchpad or brainstorming tool; *ad hoc* notes can be given structure, and as an application grows the user can begin to rely on a powerful set of tools such as auto-completion of entries, and auto-assignment to categories or views. Agenda also allows the user to filter items, by three degrees of fuzzy matchmaking: complete, partial or slight. These can utilize Agenda's preset views and default concepts — of dates, for instance. Alternatively, the user can define synonym-category relations, which may themselves have a hierarchical priority. At its most fuzzy, Agenda is capable of interpreting and categorizing items in a startlingly liberal manner.

Although Agenda does not support hypertext-style reference buttons, the flexibility provided by views allows users to create multiple structures between sets of information. With these it would be quite feasible to create a multi-dimensional document, or reference a set of notes. Agenda's main disadvantage is that it is so subtle and versatile that it may be difficult to master rapidly.

Agenda is a rich and powerful tool, reasonably priced in the middle range of project management software. It is available in DOS and OS/2 versions. Users who require multi-user support under OS/2 may find that their needs are better served by Lotus' forthcoming Notes program, which is rumoured to be conceptually similar to Agenda in its ability to link heterogeneous information sources.

The second supplier listed below is a management consultant who will provide reasonably priced support to hotline members, as well as training schemes and applications templates.

Supplier:
Lotus Development, Consort House, Victoria Street, Windsor, Berks, SL4 1EX. Tel: 0753 840281.
or

Time/system, 40 West Street, Marlow, Buckinghamshire, SL7 2NB. Tel: 06284 76071.

AskSam 4

AskSam 4 is a product of Seaside Software Perry, Florida, and is distributed in the UK by In Touch Computer Solutions. Although not marketed as a pure hypertext system it is included here as an example of a text-oriented database. It could equally be used for project management (and includes a phone dialler, which Agenda does not). Its best features are its flexibility, and its potential to manage very large text databases. Its worst feature is that it is relatively difficult to learn; all askSam's search and report generation operations rely on its own idiosyncratic query language rather than a predominately menu-driven interface. Furthermore, it does not have the kind of preset views offered by Agenda. These drawbacks are offset to some extent by the provision of context-sensitive help.

Nodes in the askSam database can be free-form text blocks, structured text fields, or hybrids. These are grouped into files, only one of which can be handled at a time. AskSam allows the user to define templates for search patterns, but these operate at the text or field levels rather than over data types, which do not exist. There are also Boolean operators and vicinity qualifiers within the query language. Basic hypertext facilities are provided for using words in records as the means to access files or invoke programs.

AskSam 4 is a medium price range product. It is fast, powerful and has a wide potential applicability — for card-indexes, project management, or document indexing. Database novices will require considerable familiarization with this product, however.

Supplier:
In Touch Computer Solutions, Fairfield House, Brynhyfryd, Caerphilly, CF8 2QQ. Tel: 0222 882334.

Web Information Assistant

Web Information Assistant is a product of Octave Associates. It runs under the Digital Research GEM desktop environment, versions 2 or 3 (supplied at nominal extra cost with Web). Originally created as an inhouse tool for project support, the potential of Web is much greater. Web provides sophisticated facilities for building multiple 'views' of hypertext applications, which are defined as threads of linked 'frame' nodes; the same frame of text and/or interpreted commands can be linked to several threads, and this is how webs are created. In contrast to most hypertext implementations there are no embedded text 'buttons' as such. Instead, thread links are listed in a 'thread-margin' from where the user can access other webs and, albeit indirectly, their related nodes. This apparent primacy of the thread/web takes a little getting used to; some users may find it not too dissimilar to using a network database. However, it is more powerful than this; for instance it is possible to have several webs open at any one time and displayed in separate windows. Views of a web can also be filtered by attributes. This follows on from the frame implementation — each file/frame/web has a title and further possible attributes — such as date and time, for instance.

Once familiar with Web, developing text-based applications with it will be rewarding. Using the Build Threads option it is very easy to create automatic links to every instance of a text string (and perhaps to save this collection of instances as a new web). There is also an auto-edit facility; using this means that editing a particular item on a web automatically results in its being edited everywhere else that it appears, thus maintaining consistency.

Web requires a minimum of 512k and runs on PC-compatibles and PS/2s. It supports all major graphics modes, and is much improved with a mouse. As well as an information manager, Web can be used as a front end to other software, or to provide an alternative structure to a DOS directory of files[16]. Its flexibility and manipulative power are impressive. Its features are well-planned, and if not as flashy or plentiful as those of Agenda, they are probably easier to learn. However, Web has several idiosyncrasies that may be less attractive: it requires GEM, which is hardly the state-of-the-art standard in desktop environments; its documentation has a hurried feel to it and some of the jargon terms (such as DogEar) are less than intuitive. Overall, Web is very reasonably priced at the lower-middle end of the PC hypertext market.
Supplier:
Octave Associates, Graphic House, 21 Normandy Street, Alton, Hampshire, GU34 1DD. Tel: 0420 89515.

9.3   Graphics Emphasis Programs

Guide and Idex

Guide was originally developed at the University of Kent[1], but the commercial version is now produced by Office Workstations Limited, Edinburgh, which also supplys Idex. It is a contender for market leader of PC-based hypermedia; the version for the Macintosh has a very similar feel (see Chapter 10).

The original product, Guide, is now available for both the IBM PC/AT and the Apple Macintosh[10]. Idex, its 'industrial-strength' offspring, is currently available for PC networks (probably served by a DEC VAX minicomputer or similar). Both Guide 3.0 and Idex in their PC versions require MS-Windows 2.03 or above; OS/2 versions are due to be launched in the near future.

To take a metaphor from the developers, if Guide has the functionality of a bookcase, Idex has that of a library, with management and categorization tools supplied. Both products fall into the general-purpose hypermedia category. Documents or 'Guidelines' (implemented as scrolling Windows) can support both hierarchical and non-hierarchical link structures, which can themselves be triggered by several 'button' types[5,6,8,9].

Guide Buttons:

Replacement buttons are analogous to nested or hierarchical links, whilst reference buttons are analogous to non-hierarchical 'Goto' links. The latter are essentially item-to-item rather than the item-to-document references implemented in some other programs. This means you could have one button referencing the introduction of a long document, and another referencing the bibliography. Expansion buttons are pop-up notes that appear for the duration of a mouse-click.

Buttons are defined as embedded text items, or as graphic items. Text buttons are then denoted by means of default or user-defined typographic styles — bold, italic, underlined, etc. These styles are then more or less exclusively available to the button creation routines; a consistent implementation of a hypertext rhetoric if not a very imaginative one. In addition, the mouse cursor changes shape distinctively when it is over one of these active text buttons, or a comparable graphic button. For instance, when over an expansion button the cursor changes to a cross-hair, and when over a reference button it becomes a hollow arrow. Figure 6.1 shows the default appearance of button text styles, and their corresponding cursor types.

Buttons are created in a two-stage process — by specifying the items at start and finish points, using mouse highlighting and the Make menu. It is possible to begin with either end of the link you want to create, although it is slightly easier to begin with the target point. It is also possible to create multiple links to one item, except with an expansion button, which has a unique provenance hidden behind it until actioned.

Commands:

Command buttons allow access to the Definitions window, where Guide's internal scripting language can be used to launch external programs or to drive peripherals such as video storage devices and modems via an interpreter. In fact, as well as using the supplied Launch and Serial port interpreters, it is possible to develop bespoke interpreters to mediate more specialised tasks such as linking Guide with an external application via a DDE (prototype under development by OWL). An Interpreter Development Kit, including C and assembler source code for sample interpreters, is available at nominal cost from OWL for Macintosh or Windows developers. (Interpreters are implemented as a Windows Executable Library).

Guide's scripting language is relatively basic (compared, for instance to Apple's HyperTalk or to Agenda's or FrameWork's macro languages). A sample command definition to open an Excel worksheet and import data might be worded as follows:

```
launch
run/windows/excel/excel.exe
initiate excel sheet1
request sheet1 r1c1
terminate sheet1
```

Text and Graphics:
Rather than supplying its own extended range of text and graphics tools, Guide makes use of standard Windows facilities. Although it is possible to edit text in Guide, it is probably easier to create a document with an external word processor and import it, (Windows Write and ASCII formats supported) as you might do when using a desktop publishing program such as Aldus PageMaker.

Guide can import most Windows Metafile graphic formats (e.g. Windows Draw, PC Paintbrush). These can be cut and pasted to Guide by means of the standard Windows clipboard, and can then be scaled or cropped internally. This can be rather a clumsy process — imported graphics files cannot be physically segmented within Guide, although it is possible to create multiple buttons on graphics as 'invisibles'. However, IBM France markets Guide with augmented graphics-editing facilities under the name of Hyper-soft, and the Macintosh version comes with a Scribbler utility that functions as a simple drawing toolbox. Developers of hypermedia applications with potentially large amounts of graphic material may find that Guide is a less practical environment than some of its competitors (e.g. Hyperdoc, HyperCard) which compress graphics files.

Navigation:
Guide does not maintain a graphic overview of active materials like, for instance NoteCards. However, like HyperCard, it allows two forms of backtracking via icons: back to the start of the original document, or back through a trail of up to 32 recent actions. Text searching is also supported, although only in a forwards direction from the user's current position.

The Inquiry function allows the author to group expansion buttons, together with related text and graphics so that when any button in the group is actioned, all other items in the group are replaced with whatever is hidden behind the actioned expansion button. This reduces the complexity of the resulting screen, (and removes conflicting choices for further action). In other words, it is a deterministic structural feature, directing the user along a path of the author's choosing.

Other Authoring facilities:
Guide is controlled via a menu command line, or via shortcuts — using the CTRL button and command initials. Some of the more notable options include:

Find:
Guide can perform standard text searches, although these are limited to the current active Window.

Freeze:
The Freeze option effectively disables button actions, allowing the author to edit the actual button text or graphic.

Show Symbols:
This is useful during debugging, providing extra visual cues as to the identity and type of buttons, and is illustrated in the next chapter.

Glossary:
The Glossary is a sort of internal clipboard for items such as buttons and definitions which authors are likely to re-use. With a little dexterity it is possible to semi-automate the creation of buttons in a dynamic context. The Glossary is also a way of easily duplicating notes used repeatedly by several expansion buttons.

Documentation:
All documentation (tutorial and reference/Help material) to Guide is supplied as a conventional printed manual, and in slightly truncated form as online, hypermedia Guidelines.

Support:
Guide and Idex are well supported by OWL from Edinburgh, and by the sister company OWL International in the US. Because of the particularly individual requirements of hypermedia projects, this kind of support is invaluable for large projects, and OWL has considerable expertise in providing corporate solutions. In addition, there are a number of modular interpreters under development which may be obtained by negotiation.

Reader Facilities:
OWL make special provision for read-only distribution by marketing a Guide Reader/Envelope shell. This is relatively cheap, and uses little memory, giving the integrated package a distinct advantage over systems that require all users to have a fully paid-up copy of the development shell.

The Guidance development version allows authors to create context-sensitive Help applications, and not only for use with Guidelines, within Guide; for instance, Aldus has employed it as the engine providing Help in PageMaker.

General Comments:
Guide is a hypermedia workhorse with potential for demanding corporate documentation projects as well as elegant educational materials. It has been

well thought out — the flexibility of methods for building buttons enhances rather than complicates use. Windows users will be able to familiarize themselves rapidly with Guide's facilities[11,15,17]. It provides a substantial addition to Windows' functionality — the ability to manage applications at macro- and micro-levels, and to combine a variety of data formats in a structured manner (although extended memory is likely to be needed with more than one Windows application loaded at a time, and certainly if you wish to use Guide in parallel with Excel or PageMaker). Organizations with PCs and Macintoshes will be able to run Guide in both environments.

Idex

Idex is very similar to Guide in the basic hypermedia facilities it provides, and in its general appearance. However, it supports networking and provides system level administrative facilities over and above the levels of control Guide provides to the single author and reader. These include the kind of security features that might be expected of a conventional DBMS, and document lifecycle/status auditing. Documents can be allocated types, and departmentalized according to users' needs. What is really interesting, considering the Windows-based origins of Guide and Idex, is that this structuring is done according to the high-level library metaphor rather than a hierarchical file/directory model *per se*. This gives Idex an extra level of transparency that concentrates the user's attention on the contents of materials rather than their location.

Users of Idex can also experiment with the use of SGML (Standard Generalized Markup Language) to create structural markup. Idex can use markup codes internally to generate consistent buttons against style templates or Glossary items.

As mentioned above, Idex can interpret SGML to format imported materials. It uses a structured database metaphor to organize collections of documents (libraries), and a more free-form hypermedia model for interpreting each document's internal structure. Documents are typically large objects, such as reference manuals. Within each of these the hypertext structure conforms to the logical, hierarchical structures of chapters or sections. Idex also supports user-defined search templates, which can be used to filter information according to standard requirements. These can be extended with Boolean criteria. Eventually it is hoped to replace the proprietary database with a standard SQL-type protocol, to coincide with upgrading to OS/2[3].

A useful distinction made by Idex is that between window format, and page format templates — the former allows information (including bit-mapped graphics) to be displayed dynamically according to the available window dimensions, the latter can be used on any document that requires printing.

Currently Idex conforms to the Systems Application Architecture

(SAA) standard, but it is likely to move towards a server architecture in the OS/2 version.

Summary:
These products are to be seriously considered at all levels of entry into the hypermedia arena. Short of a Unix-based workstation system, there is little competition at the corporate end of the market, particularly for those committed to IBM-compatibles and Microsoft Windows/OS/2.

Supplier:
Office Workstations Limited, Rosebank House, 144 Broughton Road, Edinburgh, EH7 4LE. Tel: 031 557 5720.
or
OWL International, Inc. 14218 Northeast 21st St, Bellevue, WA 98007. Tel: (0101) 800 344 9737.

Hyperdoc

Hyperdoc is a French hypermedia product from GECI International. It has been developed with a particular emphasis on facilities for the electronics, electrical engineering and advanced technology sector — particularly for users producing large reference works such as aircraft maintenance manuals.

Hyperdoc is implemented as a group of C modules, and the program runs in its own Metawindows environment. Though the manufacturer claims these modules can be easily ported to most machines and adapted to most peripheral devices, UK marketing is currently aimed at the PC market. Data files are stored in a 'neutral' format, compatible with any operating system; graphics are independent of any particular standard and are automatically displayed to available screen resolution without distortion. Furthermore, graphics can be easily rescaled, and with the proprietary add-on hardware card both static and video images (plus digitized sound tracks) can be dynamically compressed and decompressed. Up to 16 video images can be displayed at once, at what is effectively better than television quality resolution, (though only one image can be active), and both the speed and ratio of compression are impressive.

Flexibility:
Hyperdoc also has its own interpreted macro language; this is relatively simple (52 verb/statements) yet it allows users to create sophisticated applications without the need to resort to altering the modules at the source code level. Among the more notable of these macro facilities are menu definition, external program access, user input, error checking, conditional statements and scientific mathematical functions. This is to be extended in the near future with full SGML-compatibility for document markup and display.

The Hyperdoc interface makes full use of a two-button mouse, with reduced keyboard commands. A simple graphical audit trail is available, as well as secondary pop-up menus from which users can, for example, reconfigure screen colors, resize and move object windows. Function keys can also be redefined using the macro language. Online help is also provided. The graphics and text editors are menu-driven and superior to those of other PC-compatible hypermedia products.

Once materials have been assembled they can be imported and suitable links attached. Hyperdoc's links can be defined from areas of a graphic or from text, to other graphics or text locations. Up to 10 documents or other objects can be displayed on the screen at any one time. Hyperdoc's 'Glossaries' allow commonly used macros to be saved; thus the semi-automated creation of links between objects is possible. The developers have concentrated on database compatibility with dBASE III, from which files can be directly imported. Hyperdoc can also import scanned and other graphic images (.DXF, .PCX, .TIFF formats). It allows users to create simple graphics internally and to add color touches to their scanned images.

Hyperdoc also provides a choice of symbols with which developers can design applications as flow charts, or fault trees for problem diagnosis. Using the mouse or cursor keys, the user can then access context-sensitive information; these make Hyperdoc a strong competitor to rule-based expert diagnosis systems; Hyperdoc might be more appropriate than a conventional expert system in cases where diagnosis is particularly serendipitous, or visually driven. It would be equally amenable to large CBT projects. Hyperdoc can also be used as an electronic mail front end, and includes simple security management facilities.

In summary, Hyperdoc is a serious hypermedia tool for large applications; as such it is relatively expensive, though far less so than some of its indirect competitors running on UNIX workstations. However, for users outside a workstation environment, the range of facilities, flexibility and general high standard of the specification make it a very worthwhile consideration. Most PC/AT hardware configurations are supported; Hyperdoc requires a mere 640K RAM, so that the only 'extras' most users will need to consider are peripherals such as scanner and video card. The supplier also provides all forms of support and maintenance. Versions for OS/2 and possibly for UNIX are currently planned. For DOS users, Hyperdoc version 2.0 will include major extensions to the hypertext search facilities, as well as the ability to define entire objects as hotspots or buttons.

Supplier:

Mohacs International Limited, Hanover House, 76 Coombe Road, Kingston-on-Thames, Surrey, KT2 7AH. Tel: 081 541 1877.

LinkWay

LinkWay is a product of International Business Machines Corporation. It has been specifically developed for authoring educational multimedia materials, including CD-ROM and video-disk. LinkWay supports text and color graphics (up to 256 colors) in all the IBM modes, although with an emphasis on VGA/MCGA (a PS/2-compatible machine and mouse are also required).

Applications:
LinkWay's applications are called folders, each of which consists of pages containing objects. These objects can include text, fields, buttons and pictures. To create an application a new folder is opened from the command line menu. Both text editing and paint facilities are provided with the program; materials can be created internally, or imported as ASCII text. LinkWay also comes with an image grabber utility, and facilities to specify screen graphics modes[12]. The basic text fonts are somewhat garish, in fact the text medium seems to have been implemented as a relatively low priority. Greater attention seems to have been given to the graphics facilities — for instance, static images may be sequenced by means of the auxiliary animation program to provide quite convincing visual effects. Add-on cards extend LinkWay's range of media to cover digitized speech, music and video sequences.

Once objects have been assembled, they can be structured using LinkWay's own basic, 40-statement authoring language; scripts written with these statements can be pasted into pop-up boxes attached to objects, where they can be easily located for future editing. The main environment allows authors to create highly flexible applications. However, it is also possible to restrict users to read-only facilities.

LinkWay has been launched at a very competitive low-end price which belies its overall power and sophistication.

Supplier:
IBM UK Ltd., Academic Systems Marketing, P.O. Box 41, Northern Road, Portsmouth, Hants, PO6 3AU. Tel: 0705 323088/370911.
or
IBM Atlanta, USA. Tel: (0101) 404 238 3000.
Local IBM dealerships.

Matrix Layout 2.0

Layout 2.0, from Matrix Software, is an advanced CASE (computer-aided software engineering) tool with hypermedia features. Stand-alone applications can be created directly from flowchart diagrams. Alternatively, Layout can use these diagrams to produce externally compilable code in a variety of language implementations. Layout's applications employ a card-based, multi-windowing metaphor; cards can contain buttons, fields, dialog boxes, etc. Sophisticated functions and procedures, including scientific maths, are added from Layout's code library via the simple, menu-driven interface. It supports both mouse and keyboard commands. All Layout's modules can be accessed from the icon-driven desktop, which in turn can be run directly from DOS, or from MS-Windows.

Layout is supplied with several modular applications, to be used in conjunction with the main development environment (and actually created with it). The auxiliary Paint program provides graphics tools, color, and scanner support. Helpmaker allows developers to create context-sensitive Help applications (such as the supplied online Layout reference guide). There is also a selection of desk accessories, and a font library. Layout has an extendable, open architecture — facilities for purposes such as telecommunications and advanced graphics can be created as 'Black Boxes.' Layout also supports material from dBASE II, III and III+, and a variety of external graphics formats.

Layout 2.0 is a versatile prototyping tool, for experienced or novice programmers alike. Priced at the lower-middle range of the hypermedia market, it offers very good value for money. Free support from the telephone hotline is an added bonus.

Supplier:
Matrix Software Technology, Matrix House, Derriford Business Park, Derriford, Plymouth, PL6 5QZ. Tel: 0752 796363/100 Freefone Matrix Software.
or
Matrix Software/Europe, Geldenaakseban 476, B3030 Leuven, Belgium. Tel: 016 202064.

9.4   Expert Systems Hybrids

KnowledgePro

KnowledgePro is an expert system shell from Knowledge Garden Inc. The basic KnowledgePro application unit is a topic — which could be a parameter value, a hypermedia graphics window, a menu or a document; in fact an object at any level of granularity. Hypertext/hypermedia functionality has been added in response to the common problem users have with querying expert system applications. Hypermedia objects are created like other topics using KnowledgePro's flexible, high-level application development language (which is much more user-friendly than, for instance, askSam's query language). Topics support hierarchical attribute inheritance, and this is the default structure for KnowledgePro's implementation of hypermedia. For example, a hypertext phrase search that fails to find a match at the local level will go to higher levels in the hierarchy, allowing for economical storage of common explanations or comments.

The KnowledgePro environment includes a simple WordStar-style editor with which to build topics. To create purely hypermedia knowledge bases with KnowledgePro it is only necessary to learn the basics of the development language; Knowledge Garden claim users can begin with only six of the 120 command terms. Basic query facilities include Boolean and relational operators, and there is also a full range of mathematical functions. However, in addition to these standard database features, there is a great deal of potential AI functionality to be added by more ambitious developers. This includes both forward and backward chaining rules, and simple natural language facilities.

KnowledgePro is predominantly a character-based system. However, interactive graphics can be used within its hypermedia applications. Support is provided for all the major screen modes, but obviously graphics will require a graphics card/screen. PC Paintbrush (.PCX) files can be imported using the Graphics Toolkit and used, for instance, to create icons, backgrounds or buttons. Like text phrases, these can be used in conjunction with a mouse or keyboard commands.

Database, and Interactive VideoDisk Toolkits are also available as extras with KnowledgePro. These provide access to files from dBase III and Lotus 1-2-3, and to interactive laser disk players, respectively. Another optional accessory is KnowledgeMaker, an induction engine for deriving rules from sets of data. In addition, a number of third-party applications that can be used with the KnowledgePro run-time library or the actual system are available through shareware suppliers. These include TextPro, which extends the hypermedia facilities provided by KnowledgePro itself. Applications can be distributed free of royalties.

KnowledgePro is fairly memory-intensive (and seems to require at least 640K, without any other memory-resident applications). It is also relatively slow on anything less than a 386-based machine, particularly for graphics applications. However, overall it compares favourably in its range of facilities and ease of use with other medium-priced expert system shells[4]. A recent development is the release of a MS Windows-compatible version with improved support for graphical applications[7].
Supplier:
Intellisoft (UK) Ltd, 77A Packhorse Road, Gerrards Cross, Bucks, SL9 8PQ. Tel: 0753 889972.

Intelligence/Compiler

Similar to KnowledgePro, this expert system shell with hypertext functionality has a slightly more object-oriented flavour. It can be used to produce free run-time versions of applications.

Intelligence/Compiler is an upper-middle price-range shell, offering reasonable value for money.
Supplier:
Far Communications, 5 Harcourt Estate, Kibworth, Leics, LE8 0NE. Tel: 0533 796166.

VP-Expert 2

This expert system shell provides basic hypertext access to ASCII documents, and a simple interactive graphics capability. It also supports audit trails — a consultation's logic sequence can be recorded and displayed as a text or graphic tree. VP-Expert includes an induction engine, with which it is possible to create rules from examples found in external data files — Lotus 1-2-3, Symphony, and dBase (II, III and III +) formats are all supported. In fact its range of features is as extensive as some shells costing several times as much.

VP-Expert is marketed at the lower end of the expert system price range, and would be good value even if it was only used for its hypertext facilities.

Supplier:
Paperback Software UK Ltd, The Widford Old Rectory, London Road, Chelmsford, Essex, CM2, 8TE. Tel: 0245 265071.

REFERENCES

1. Brown, P. Interactive documentation. *Software — Practice and Experience,* **16 (3),** March 1986, pp. 291-299.
2. Collingbourne, H. Rants and raves. *Computer Shopper,* August 1989, pp. 103, 106.
3. Cooke, P. and Williams, I. Design issues in large hypertext systems for technical documentation. In: McAleese, R. (Ed.) *Hypertext theory into practice.* Oxford: Intellect Books Limited, 1989.
4. Eager, A., Whitehorn, M. Forsyth, R. and Powell, M. Expert Systems. *PC Magazine,* May 1989, pp. 54-73.
5. Edwards, D. and Hardmanm L. 'Lost in hyperspace': cognitive mapping and navigation in a hypertext environment. In: McAleese, R. (Ed.) *Hypertext theory into practice.* Oxford: Intellect Books Limited, 1989.
6. Franklin, C. Hypertext defined and applied. *Online,* **13 (3),** May 1989, pp. 37-49.
7. Franklin, C. KnowledgePro: hypertext meets expert systems. *Database,* **12 (6),** pp. 71-76.
8. Harland, S. Human factors engineering and interface development: a hypertext tool aiding prototyping activity. In: McAleese, R. (Ed.) *Hypertext theory into practice.* Oxford: Intellect Books Limited, 1989.
9. Hershey, W. Guide. *Byte,* **12 (11),** October 1987, pp. 244-246.
10. Kinnell, S. Comparing HyperCard and Guide. *Database,* **11 (3),** June 1988, pp. 49-54.
11. Kinnell, S. Hypertext on the PC: Guide, Version 2.0. *Database,* **12 (4),** August 1989, pp. 62-64.
12. Northwood, J. Links to the past? *Personal Computing (UK),* March 1990, pp.110-112.
13. Rheinhart, A. Desktop manager with hypertext power. *BYTE,* **14 (7),** July 1989, pp. 90, 92.
14. Stepno, B. A HyperCard for the PC. *BYTE,* **14 (9),** September 1989, pp. 189-190, 192.
15. Tebbutt, D. Screentest: Guide. *Personal Computer World,* June 1988.

16. Tebbutt, D. Screentest: Web. *Personal Computer World*, October 1989.
17. Wesley, M. A guide to Guide. *MacUser*, January 1988, pp. 126-132.

10 Hypermedia on the Apple Macintosh

10.1 Product Reviews

References

10.1 Product Reviews

Guide

Guide, from Office Workstations Limited, is available for the Macintosh as well as the IBM PC. Its appearance and facilities on both machines are very similar, except that in the Mac version the interface is directly to the Macintosh desktop, as opposed to MS Windows on the PC. The Mac version also provides a Scribbler accessory with which to create simple graphics from within Guide. (On the UK PC version these have to be created with an external graphics package and imported). Unlike HyperCard, below, Guide can be used to create stand-alone applications (such as hypertext versions of books) for third party distribution[7]. The button menus are simple to learn and make for very rapid development. Figure 10.1 demonstrates Guide's Show Symbols option for developers. For further details refer to Chapter 9.

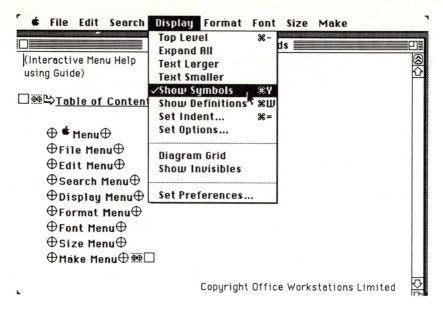

Figure 10.1 Guide's show symbols option is useful during development of materials.

HyperCard

HyperCard, from Apple Computer Inc. is an extremely notable program for a number of reasons. Launched in 1987, it is by far and away the most successful hypermedia program launched to date. The fact that HyperCard offered Macintosh programming facilities to complete novices, the fact that it was bundled free with new Macintosh computers, and its general purpose applicability, have resulted in a user base of over a million[5,8,9,10,11]. It has broken ground for other hypermedia programs, provoking a huge amount of attention in the press and enthusiasm from users in many different professions. A large number of 'StackWare' applications are available at low cost from third-party developers, supporting a range of specialised interests that until now has not been served by commercial software[1,3]; Appendix. HyperCard has been used to produce applications from catalogs to expert systems[4].

HyperCard uses the standard Macintosh desktop and toolbox metaphors across its applications, which gives it a familiar 'look and feel'. Applications are structured as cards in 'Stacks' (the document, folder or file level). However, although HyperCard supports integration of many different media, there is some doubt as to what extent it is first and foremost a hypermedia program in terms of the link structures and search tools it provides. Only one card at a time can be displayed by the current 1.2.1 version, although apparently there are plans to extend this facility in future releases to bring HyperCard back into line with its clones. The current, limited implementation is in contrast to the dynamic 'fragment shower' ideal of hypertext models such as Ted Nelson's — though to be fair, HyperCard is far from alone on failing to live up to this ideal.

Some commentators have preferred the terms 'relational file manager' or personal organizer to hypermedia for describing HyperCard. Indeed, it comes supplied with a set of simple office management utilities — demonstrating the sorts of tool that can be easily built. But it would be a mistake to conclude that this is where its capabilities end. It goes beyond the relational database in that it integrates graphics and other more structured or heterogeneous data in one environment; HyperCard is probably best seen as an augmentation to a tabular database or spreadsheet, rather than a direct rival. In addition, HyperCard goes well beyond the automated office; it has proved to be an almost unequalled application prototyping tool for the Macintosh. In fact, on machines with extended memory it can be used as a generic front end with which to manage, integrate and even extend conventional software — from word processors and spreadsheets to programming languages and project managers. Given at least 2Mb of RAM, HyperCard can be used in conjunction with the Macintosh MultiFinder to give virtual multi-tasking capabilities.

HyperTalk

HyperTalk is HyperCard's own application development language[13]. In form it is a high-level, block-structured language, seemingly with features similar to those of Pascal, and to those of the object-oriented language Smalltalk, and indeed to natural language (English). Its syntax is notable for the large amount of overloading it employs for its operators or keywords (see subsection 2.3.2), so that there is a relatively small kernel of terms that users need to learn. It is particularly tolerant of user-defined terms, so that a typical HyperTalk script is closer to a natural language statement than a procedure written in a conventional third generation language such as Pascal. Despite this ease of use it is moderately powerful — including a range of mathematical functions that can be used, for instance, to create sophisticated simulations or spreadsheet applications. An example of a short script that launches Microsoft Word would be:

```
One MouseUp
open ''microsoft word''
End MouseUp
```

As well as allowing authors to define HyperTalk scripts that subsist behind objects, HyperCard provides a useful shortcut; authors can also enter script commands directly at any time via the pop-up Message Box. In summary, HyperTalk is a versatile language suitable both for entry-level and competent programmers. It provides the easiest way to begin programming on a machine which was previously notoriously difficult to program.

User Levels:
HyperCard defines several distinct user levels, which can be set from the
Home Card. In order of increasing power these are:

● Browsing: This is HyperCard's read-only level; browsing users
cannot add material to fields, nor change cards' appearance, either
temporarily or permanently. However, they have access to basic card
browsing options, as illustrated in Figure 10.2.

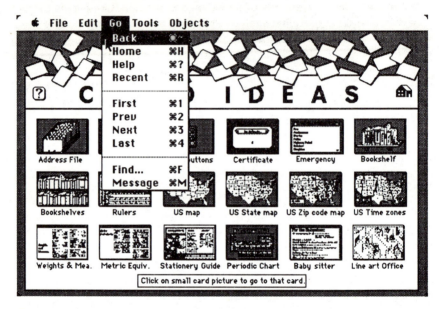

Figure 10.2 HyperCard's Go menu offers a variety of ways to browse cards.

● Typing: At the typing level, users can add or change text in
HyperCard's fields.

● Painting: At this level, HyperCard releases access to its painting
toolbox. In addition, users can use the copy, cut and paste functions to
customize cards with imported material. Paint objects are implemented as low-resolution bit-mapped graphics.

● Authoring: Authors can begin to create their own card buttons and
fields, and to establish simple card-to-card links. However, the
underlying HyperTalk scripts remain transparent.

● Scripting: HyperCard's full functionality is released at the scripting
level, via HyperTalk and all the tools from lower user levels.

At each progressive level of expertise, increasing facilities of control and extra tools are made available. At the highest level, Scripting, HyperCard's programming language, HyperTalk, is directly accessible. It is very easy to begin 'scripting' with HyperTalk, which gives direct access to all the objects in HyperCard (see Figure 10.3). However, it is not necessary to learn HyperTalk to be able to create simple, personalized application stacks. One level that does not exist, but would be extremely useful, is an intermediate browse/create temporary card option. This would allow users much greater flexibility in using protected materials; at present it is not possible to permit the addition of new cards without also permitting the removal of existing material. Such an option would retain a stack's copyright integrity, but allow users a more interactive role than merely changing field contents, as in the present Typing level.

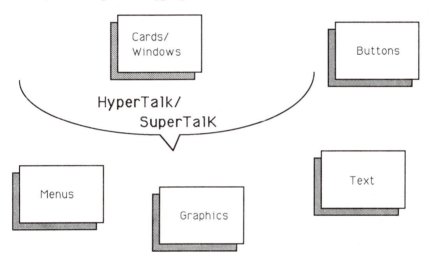

Figure 10.3 HyperTalk is a powerful structured language.

As described above, HyperCard is internally extendable in that the user can define new terms and operators. HyperCard can also be linked with external modules of code called XCMDs and XFCNs (external commands and external functions). These can be written and compiled in C or Pascal and may provide opportunities to get round the limitations of using a strictly interpreted language[2].

The Card Metaphor:
One of HyperCard's most serious limitations to date has been that it can only display one card (the size of a standard Macintosh screen) at a time. On the other hand, material on a card is not restricted to the visible area — up to 16 A4 sheets can be accessed using the scroll bars, although there are almost certainly better ways of structuring material. Cards are divided into two layers — the background and foreground — both of which can contain other

objects. The fact that fields are separate entities, and that HyperCard's objects may be composites of these, may lead to difficulties in altering scripts; deleting information in a field may have no effect on an accompanying button, unlike Guide, for instance, where buttons cannot exist as empty fields.

HyperObjects:

Stacks, cards, backgrounds, buttons and fields are all objects, in the sense that they have default properties with parameters which can be manipulated with HyperTalk. Furthermore, HyperTalk means that HyperCard itself can be tailored according to needs — by means of scripts. And because HyperTalk is highly tolerant of overloading, and is not strictly typed, objects and scripts tend to be highly re-usable.

HyperCard's object structure is divided up into layers, or 'local fences'. By default, control in an application falls through these until suitable parameter values or operator definitions are found, until HyperCard itself is reached if necessary. Figure 10.4 summarizes HyperCard's implementation of inheritance.

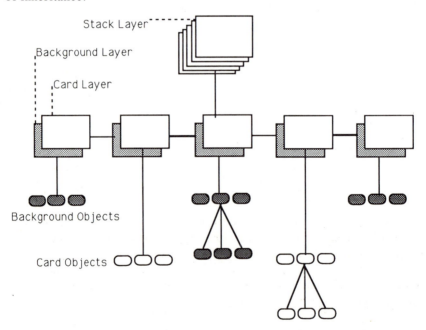

Figure 10.4 Inheritance and parameter passing between objects in HyperCard.

However, herein lies a major problem for programming aesthetes. Although HyperCard is in one sense an object-oriented environment, and supports 'clean control structures through message passing (passing parameter values and commands between objects' scripts), in practice the ideal seems rarely to be achieved. The ease with which new users can begin to write their own scripts, and the lack of support for high-level debugging with which they are provided, often leads to the use of a large number of global flags — values available to all and sundry. In conventional structured programming this is regarded as very bad style. However, the use of globals even in quite professional StackWare products is quite startling.

Maintaining or altering a HyperCard application can also be more difficult than one would expect. HyperCard does not support versioning, and its auto-save feature can rapidly overwrite working stacks with bug-filled duplicates. Once written, it is difficult to alter an individual script, or indeed to discover the precise problem it is encountering, apart from the terse information provided by the standard error messages.

A further problem with HyperTalk is that (at least at the time of going to press) it is a purely interpreted language, needing the memory-intensive HyperCard environment at run-time to start an application stack. In common with interpreted languages in general, it suffers from a problem of speed; applications which involve computation — particularly 'number-crunching' — are typically sluggish, and HyperCard's limited garbage collection sometimes leads to the frustrating experience, after minutes of awaiting a result, of exhausted working memory.

However, HyperTalk seems set to continue to develop, and to achieve a common development standard with its emerging clones. For instance, SuperCard's implementation, SuperTalk is in fact a compilable superset to HyperTalk (see Figure 10.5). Apple has recently announced the formation of a HyperTalk Language Committee, together with Silicon Beach (SuperCard/ SuperTalk) and other Macintosh developers. Apple is also willing to supply HyperCard's file format protocols to interested third party developers, in an effort to maintain data compatibility between applications. Thus familiarity with one of these products will probably permit a user to rapidly transfer to another environment, should he or she need to find more suitable facilities. It is also likely that an increasing number of serious third-party software applications will appear on the Macintosh with a HyperCard front end — Oracle Corporation's recent HyperSQL (a front end to the world's leading relational database) being a case in point.

Navigating and Browsing:
There are several ways of finding your way around a HyperCard stack. Cards are defined in relation to each other and to the Home Card; by default the user can move to the next card created in a linear sequence, or by buttons to more distant cards. The Find option (via a menu or through the use of the term 'find' in a script) will search for text strings — field contents or object names. The Recent option provides a card with miniatures of the most recently accessed 42 cards, any of which can be directly accessed (see Figure 6.2). In addition, the Home Card icon is always available to return the user to the top of a stack. There is also the Go menu (see Figure 10.2) that can be used at any time to access a specific, known location.

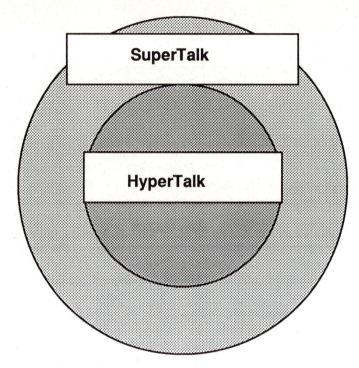

Figure 10.5   HyperTalk has been challenged and extended by SuperTalk.

Support:
Apple does not provide the kind of telephone support policy with HyperCard
that some other hypermedia suppliers offer — after all, for most users it is a
free product bundled with the computer. However, most Apple dealers have
some degree of expertise in HyperCard applications, and users may be able to
develop a useful relationship on an individual basis. However, there is a
second major channel through which HyperCard information is dissemi-
nated; its huge installed user base means there are dozens of local user
groups, regularly advertised through the computer press and on bulletin
boards.

In addition, the StackWare culture is itself an invaluable source of
information — each application is potentially the provenance of new card,
button and script ideas, many of which are easy to reverse engineer even if
they cannot be directly copied. Furthermore, Apple's long-term commitment
to extensive product development means that HyperCard is likely to become
more popular, with an even greater market for third-party user manuals;
several are listed in the bibliography and are of an unusually high standard.

HyperCard users in search of advice can turn to the following sources:

- Local Apple dealers
- User groups
- Bulletin boards
- StackWare sources
- Third-party user manuals.

Supplier:
Apple Computer UK Limited, Eastman Way, Hemel Hempstead, Herts, HP2 7HQ. Tel: 0442 60244.
Local Apple Centre dealers.

Intermedia 3.0

Intermedia has been developed over a number of years on Unix-based workstations at Brown University's Institute for Research in Information in Scholarship[18]. Version 3.0 is now available as a commercial package for the Mac II under the A/UX operating system (Apple's implementation of Unix), and requires between 4Mb and 8Mb of RAM[16] per client terminal. The A/UX server requires 40Mb to 80Mb depending on ancillary applications.

Intermedia implements hypertext via a web metaphor, displayed within a Macintosh/Smalltalk-type windowing desktop. Its program environment allows for consistency between the set of application tools via an object-oriented framework. These applications include InterText (a text editor), InterVal (a timeline editor), InterDraw (a graphics editor), InterPix (a viewer for scanned images) and InterSpect (an 3-D image examiner); all conform to Macintosh/MS-Windows development criteria. In addition, an effort has been made to provide a common function interface across them, and to allow the creation of uniform style property sheets and style palettes.

Intermedia links are objects in their own right, with destination properties; an unusual property of Intermedia links is that they can have several destinations. Moreover, links are bidirectional, point-to-point, and as object properties they are automatically carried over with their owners, from cut and paste operations. (Targets can be at any level of granularity from document size to insertion point). Links are indicated by means of icons near to their owners[18].

Documents and graphics are displayed in scrolling windows. At the desktop icon level, Intermedia separates documents from application tools, which are grouped in their own window. Several optional applications are available, including the InterLex dictionary ands Houghton Mifflin's American Heritage Dictionary.

There are several ways to navigate and browse in Intermedia. Intermedia can display dynamic local networks of links graphically, via the Map view. In addition, the Path View maintains an iconized audit trail of users' interactions. Search operations such as keyword search operate over an entire web 'context', but not between webs, or on link attributes. Using the InterLex dictionary it is also possible to conduct very powerful 'context searches on a word's associated terms[16]

Intermedia supports concurrent interaction by users across a network, as does KMS, but not to KMS' level of 'optimistic concurrency' (i.e. where two users can access and edit the same document at the same time); however, Intermedia includes the possibility that several users will create links in a web to common documents at the same time. There are three levels of access rights across tools and documents: read, write, and annotation, determined by password security.

Intermedia allows users to integrate all the standard hypermedia: text, graphics, video, etc. However, although running on a Mac II, because of the non-standard A/UX operating system it is not possible to integrate it with standard Macintosh software. On the other hand, data can be imported from these programs. Walter[16] advocates the eventual implementation of a hypermedia facility at the level of the operating system.

Intermedia and associated applications have been marketed in the US, at a very low price, by IRIS — a non-profit organization (no UK supplier details were available at the time of going to press). They offer serious hypermedia developers facilities unrivaled for their power and flexibility. The only drawback seems to be the expensive machine configuration needed to run them.

Supplier:
Brown University, Institute for Research and Information in Scholarship (IRIS), P.O. Box 1946, Providence, RI 02912. Tel: (401) 863 2001.
or
Apple Computer Programmers' and Developers' Association.

SuperCard

SuperCard, from Silicon Beach, is a recent product that owes much to HyperCard, but also advances the field significantly in several key resource areas[14,15,16]. In fact, there is similarity to the point of one-way compatibility; HyperCard stacks and HyperTalk objects can be imported directly into SuperCard, and extended with SuperTalk. SuperCard supports a greater range of data formats than HyperCard for importing material created with other programs, although version 1.0 appears to have some minor bugs in this area, particularly with import from HyperCard. SuperTalk is an extended version of HyperTalk, supporting such features as color graphics, and sophisticated animation. Graphics can be bit-mapped, a la HyperCard, or object-oriented — and the useful AutoTrace tool can convert the former to the latter. Buttons are more flexible than in HyperCard — for instance it is possible to define an irregular, freehand graphic as a button. It is easy to attach scripts to any SuperCard object. Cards each have their own palette of a maximum of 256 colors stored as a color look-up table (CLUT); and there are management facilities to overcome possible CLUT clashes.

SuperCard's applications are called Projects. Each Project can display a number of Windows concurrently on the screen — thus providing an intermediate layer of organisation between the application and its individual cards. Moreover, Windows from a number of Projects can be open at one time, i.e. it is possible to develop multi-window, multi-tasking applications[7]. Projects are created and best manipulated in SuperCard's auxiliary editor suite, SuperEdit. This provides separate Script Editor frames for each object's script, and the Overview window keeps an inventory of all the Windows, objects etc. in the current Project (see Figure 10.6). The Script Editor menus contain all the SuperTalk terms, allowing users to create scripts solely with the mouse.

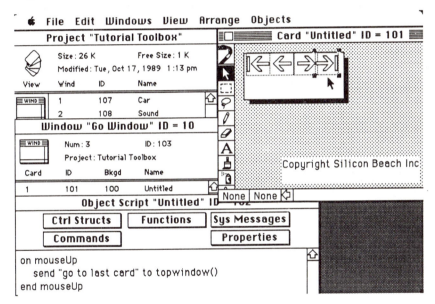

Figure 10.6 Developers have access to multiple Windows with SuperCard and SuperEdit.

SuperCard's performance, on less than a Macintosh II, is relatively slow[12]. Users also require System 6.0 or higher. SuperCard is more memory-intensive than HyperCard, requiring at least 1024K of RAM to run applications. SuperEdit requires 750K or 1500K for monochrome or color editing respectively. It is possible to create stand-alone applications which may require rather less memory, depending on size and features. These applications may be distributed free of royalties. However, having the editing facilities separate to the main environment means that debugging may be more time-consuming than in HyperCard. On the other hand, the user has more control over versioning than in HyperCard, with the choice of Save or

Save As. Careful attention to saving is important — to safeguard work, but also to make sure that versions are managed sensibly and vital files not overwritten with new bug-filled copies.

Support and Documentation:
SuperCard comes with an extensive user manual and a SuperTalk language manual. However, free technical support is available to registered users by telephone during office hours, or by mail. It is very possible that novice users will need to make extensive use of this — the documentation is inadequately referenced and sometimes unbalanced in the detail given to a topic. User groups are forming in the US, together with online services via the major bulletin boards such as CompuServe.
Supplier:
Silicon Beach Software, Inc., P.O. Box 261430 or 9770 Carroll Center Rd., Suite J, San Diego, CA 92126. Tel: (0101) 619 695 6956.
UK Supplier:
The MacSerious Company, Tel: 041 332 5622.
or
Persona-TMC, Tel: 0372 729611.

Recent Arrivals:

Plus

This German product, from Format Software, features extensions to HyperCard similar to those of SuperCard: Plus can import stacks, add simple color, and multiple windows. It also has 'object-oriented' drawing tools. The Find option is more sophisticated than HyperCard's, allowing the user to index files for rapid searching. It is not possible to create stand-alone applications, but the run-time version is supplied for free distribution. An English version is available.
Supplier;
Olduvai, Florida. Tel: (0101) 305 665 4665.
Softline, Tel: 081 642 4242.

ArchiText

ArchiText is a product of Brainpower Inc. It features a number of facilities not found in other Macintosh programs[6]. The most notable of these is the ability to create multiple maps (each with a different 'view') of the links between document nodes. Furthermore the links themselves are explicitly directed (uni- or bidirectional arrows). Unlike HyperCard, the ArchiText interface consists of three windows: one for the current document, one for maps and one for nodes. However, the most important and distinctive feature of ArchiText is its ability to maintain semi-automated maps of documents.

However, links are only supported between documents, and ArchiText lacks a programming language facility.

Supplier:
Brainpower Inc., 24009 Ventura Boulevard, Suite 250, Calabasas, ČA 91302, USA. Tel. (0101) 818 884 6911.

Business Filevision

Business Filevision is successor to Filevision — arguably the first DBMS for microcomputers to implement any true form of hypertext link. The present version combines object-oriented graphics and a flat text database in a neat, conceptually simple environment. The emphasis is on links from graphical objects — so that applications in need of/allowing visual categorization will be well served. There are powerful report generation facilities, but no programming language.

Supplier:
Marvelin Corporation, 3420 Ocean Park Boulevard, Suite 3020, Santa Monica, CA 90405. Tel: (0101) 205 450 6813.

REFERENCES

1. Beattie, R. Apple talk. *PC User* (UK) February 14-27 1990, p 157.
2. Bond, G. *XCMDs for HyperCard*. MIS Press, Inc., 1988
3. Ertel, M. A tour of the stacks. HyperCard for libraries. *Online,* **13 (1),** January 1989, pp. 45-53.
4. Evans, R. Expert systems and HyperCard. *BYTE,* **15, (1),** January, 1990 pp. 317-324.
5. Franklin, C. Hypertext defined and applied. *Online,* **13 (3),** May 1989, pp. 37-49.
6. Franklin, C. Mapping hypertext structures with ArchiText. *Database,* **12 (4),** August 1989, pp. 50-61.
7. Gartshore, P. Multi-window environments for hypermedia systems. *Computing,* 15 March 1990, pp. 43-44.
8. Goodman, D. *The Complete HyperCard Handbook*. NY: Bantam, 2nd edition 1988.
9. Jones, M. and Myers, D. *Hands-on HyperCard*. NY: John Wiley and Sons, 1988.
10. Kinnell, S. Comparing HyperCard and Guide. Database, 11 (3) June 1988, pp. 49-54.
11. Kitza, W. *Inside HyperCard*. NY: Addison-Wesley, 1988.
12. Lasky, R. How Super is SuperCard? *BYTE,* **14 (10),** October 1989, pp. 217-218, 220.
13. Poole, L. *HyperTalk*. Microsoft Press, 1988.
14. Stefanac, S. On beyond HyperCard. *MacWorld (UK)*, July 1989, pp. 12-14.
15. Stefanac, S. SuperCard 1.0. *MacWorld (UK)*, October 1989, pp. 125, 129, 133.
16. Walter, M. IRIS Intermedia: pushing the boundaries of hypertext. *The Seybold Report on Publishing Systems,* **18 (21),** August 1989, pp. 21-32.

17.   Williams, G. First impressions: HyperCard. *BYTE,* **12 (14),** December, 1987, pp. 109-117.
18.   Yankelovich, N., Haan, B., Meyrovitz, N. and Drucker, S. Intermedia: The concept and the construction of a seamless information environment. *IEEE Computer,* **21 (1),** January 1988, pp. 81-96.

11 Workstation Hypermedia

11.1   Introduction

Many of the products described below have developed directly out of experimental, in-house and academic systems. One important feature typical of these systems is networking support, rare with the PC and Macintosh systems described in the previous two chapters.

11.2   Product Reviews

FrameMaker

FrameMaker is a product of Frame Technology/ICL, designed for advanced document generation (primarily for producing paper-based materials). However, it also has potential for online document distribution systems, and computer-based training. It combines artificial intelligence frame techniques with secondary hypertext link facilities. FrameMaker presents 'WYSIWYG' document layouts, and the high resolution workstation screens required make it particularly suited to mixed media — text plus graphics[17]. Thus one of the major areas in which it is being used is in documenting industrial production and CAD systems.

Among FrameMaker's more notable features are: object-oriented graphics recognition capability; PostScript compatibility; style templates; X-Windows support; support for a variety of data formats such as spread-sheets and databases, via the Live Links utility; intelligent mathematics; a Read-only mode; MIF, FrameMaker's own application interface language; hypertext. The context-sensitive help supplied is itself an example of FrameMaker's hypertext capabilities. More strictly this is a hypermedia capability — links can be defined from graphics as well. Pop-up, Goto and executable links are all possible.

The commercial version of FrameMaker has been implemented by ICL on Sun workstations, but is also available in a DEC version.
Supplier:
Frontline, Tel: 0706 351466.

HyperTies

Hyperties has existed for several years as a research system, but commercial packages are available for both Sun workstations and PC-compatibles[12,13]. It supports both text and graphics. Items are displayed in non-scrolling frames; links are denoted by highlighted text.
Supplier:
University of Maryland, Dept. of Computer Science and Human Computer Interaction College Park, Maryland, MD 20742. Tel: (301) 454 4255.

Intermedia 3.0

Intermedia has been developed over a number of years on Unix-based workstations at Brown University's Institute for Research in Information in Scholarship[19]. Version 3.0 is now available as a commercial package for the Mac II with extended memory under the A/UX operating system, and is discussed in the Macintosh hypermedia section[18].

KMS

Knowledge Management System is the commercial version of an earlier system, ZOG, developed at Carnegie-Mellon University. It is frame-based rather that node-based, and supports two link types — hierarchical and cross-referential, which are distinguished to aid browsing. Frames are organised into task-related hierarchies. As well as 'tree item' frames, KMS allows the creation of annotation items. However, links are one-way, and to whole frames rather than to smaller items. Links are implemented as properties of frames rather than objects in their own right. Navigation is via backtracking, Goto or Home commands.

KMS emphasises rapid text-search and indexing facilities, with no graphical browsing (although graphic items are supported). Very rapid access times have been a development priority — one of the most famous ZOG applications is with the US Navy; the 20,000-frame management information system onboard the nuclear-powered USS Carl Vinson is claimed to be the largest online hypermedia database in the world[15].

Great emphasis has been placed on the design philosophy behind ZOG/ KMS, particularly with regard to its interface[9]. To facilitate speed of interaction, there is a 'risc' (reduced instruction set of commands) interface based on context-sensitive actions with a three-button mouse. It is claimed that 90% of users' interaction can be accomplished with single point-and-click operations[1]. New developments include fuzzy search criteria, and extended schemas or templates for frame standardisation. KMS can also be extended by means of a flexible, high-level development language.

Other KMS features include: versioning support for applications with long life-cycles; system management and distribution security. KMS is a relatively expensive product.

Supplier:
Scribe Systems Incorporated, Commerce Court, Suite 240, 4 Station Square, Pittsburgh, PA 15219. Tel: (412) 281 5959.

NoteCards

NoteCards, from Xerox Palo Alto Research Center (PARC), has been developed over the last six years from an experimental system into an internationally marketed commercial package. Written in Xerox Lisp, NoteCards runs under the Unix operating system on both Sun and Xerox workstations. It is described as a unified environment for information structuring, particularly for idea structuring, and recently supporting collaborative projects[14].

The basic metaphor is of index cards, managed within a FileBox, which can be seen more generally as a case of a windowing/desktop environment. Other basic NoteCards objects are the links, which carry user-defined types and are explicitly bi-directional, and Browsers, which are structural notecards providing system-maintained (but user manipulable) local maps of a network of other notecards. Links are shown as icons, and are point-to-card, i.e. they address a whole notecard rather than, say, a particular part of a card. The fact that links are typed allows the user to view, order, and alter a collection of cards according to multi-attribute taxonomic informa-tion[4,6,7,8]). Meta-information about a network of notecards and their FileBox owners is stored in NoteFiles, which are themselves private entities with regard to other NoteFiles. FileBoxes can be nested, allowing hierarchical division between application levels.

NoteCards supports text, graphics, external programs and animations, as well as video. In addition, it can be easily integrated with other Lisp-based packages. NoteCards' Lisp programmer's interface allows its range of over 100 system functions to be customized; there is also high-level support for parameter customization by non-programmers, and for the addition of extra functionality.

Navigation is generally by means of the Browser cards, although limited search facilities (e.g. string search) are also available. The feeling is very much of object-oriented programming, of objects in a semantic net. The spatial emphasis on navigation and object manipulation is well thought out — a number of cards can be displayed at any one time, and resized as necessary. An attempt has been made to provide navigation information to users by means of link types; the level of detail specified in the overview Browser is fairly inflexible, and typically brief — although some hypermedia commentators would argue that the latter is no bad thing. However, additional browsing aids have been implemented recently; Summary and History Trees allow users to maintain trails through materials they access, and to annotate them[5].

In addition to simple annotation facilities, collaborative support is now provided by features such as History Cards (edit and audit information) and Message Cards (meta-discussion details). NoteCards is an extremely versatile environment for all kinds of multi-user information management[7]. It is also at the expensive extreme of the market.

Supplier:
Artificial Intelligence Limited, Greycaine Road, Watford, Herts, WD2 4JP. Tel: 0923 247707.
or
Xerox Palo Alto Research Center, Intelligent Systems Laboratory, 3333 Coyote Hill Road, Palo Alto, CA 94304. Tel: (415) 494 4000.

Xanadu

In a sense there are two Xanadus: the concept, and more recently the commercial implementation of the basics of this concept. The unusual aspect of this is that the concept has been public knowledge for decades.

Project Xanadu is one of the longest established, and conceptually ambitious of hypermedia systems (under development by Ted Nelson and team for nearly 30 years). Originally an academic project, Xanadu's prototype storage engine has been available to third-party developers for several years. A major commercial launch of the system is due in 1990, to be followed in due course by an integrated publishing system.

The driving paradigm behind Xanadu is of a two-level document and byte based system. User-level virtual documents are created by 'inclusions' of bytes, resulting in 'fragment showers' from actual documents in the storage system. Pointer structures are primarily to the actual byte addresses rather than to macro level points or 'spans' in the document, but this 'back end' complexity is transparent to the user, and all linking is apparently seamless. This addressing system allows for reduced if not unique storage. Providing addressing at the byte level allows links at all levels of granularity — in Nelson's terminology the three broad categories are: point-to-point; point-to-span; span-to-span (span being a block of text or similar).

An important feature in respect of transclusions is version control — users must be able to view the original document, and then all its overlays of annotations and citations, together with annotations of annotations, etc. — a vast tree of alternative versions that requires a subtle but powerful classification system. Nelson also envisages the need for explicit link types to reduce complexity. These will be extensible in a high-level language — so that users can define their own[10]. There will also be a need for a query language along the lines of that described in Literary Machines[11].

The ambitions of the Xanadu designers are to provide a universal data structure and storage base for global electronic publishing in all media. This includes the automatic collection and distribution of royalties for used bytes. Great attention has been given to the mathematical feasibility of the classificatory system, which has been developed as a system of 'forking numbers', divided into four major fields of Server, User, Document and Contents. This is necessary because of the potentially vast size of the Xanadu database(s); as size increases the classificatory system's access times must increase by a loglike function rather than a square root function, to allow more or less instantaneous access.

A prototype front end has been available on Sun workstations to prospective developers for several years. Early 1990 sees the launch of the Xanadu document server for single users and LANs, to be followed later in the year by the multi-server storage and delivery program. Xanadu Operating Company hopes to have the automatic royalty service implemented in 1991, and to begin public-access open hypertext publishing in 1992.

The eventual aims of Project Xanadu are to provide a common interface for many hardware front ends and operating systems, and to a community of 'co-operative' software applications. In other words, the Xanadu server program is a system level facility — interface applications will be left to third party developers. Nelson foresees an eventual international network of franchized, public access terminal stations, rather like hi-tech libraries. This attention to the rigorous implementation of Nelson's hyper-media data model, as well as to the infrastructure in which the Xanadu system will operate makes the project particularly worthy of future attention.

Supplier:

Xanadu Operating Company, 550 California Street, Palo Alto, CA 94306. Tel: (415) 856-4112.

or

Autodesk, Inc., 2320 Marinship Way, Sausalito, CA 94965. Tel: (415) 332-2344.

11.3 Experimental and In-house Systems

The following hypermedia systems have been developed as academic, in-house or experimental projects. They are unlikely to be marketed in Europe in the near future, but further information may possibly be obtained from addresses quoted in the bibliographical source papers below. They are included here as examples of systems with relatively long development cycles and ambitious goals — as indicators of the direction commercial packages may follow into the 1990s.

Concordia

This system runs on Symbolics workstations and has been in use in-house at Symbolics since 1983; it is now also used by external software developers. It is an extension of the bundled Genera applications development environment, but designed specifically to address the problems faced in documentation of large, long life-cycle technical projects[16]. More specifically it is a database management system for use in conjunction with the bundled Genera Document Examiner front end. It provides support for individual phases of documentation, including object-oriented graphics, generic markup (Postscript), version, collaboration and distribution management facilities. Links can be viewed from or to records in the database, or structured as a graph. The developers claim Concordia particularly facilitates rapid prototyping as well as document debugging and restructuring.

Supplier:
Symbolics Inc., 11 Cambridge Center, Cambridge, MA 02142, USA.

gIBIS

gIBIS stands for graphical Issue Based Information Systems, and is an implementation of Horst and Rittel's IBIS methodology. It has been developed at the MCC/Software Technology Project to run on the Sun workstation. gIBIS supports conversational collaboration in the design process, but can also be used for brainstorming by individuals[2].

The mouse-based gIBIS interface is based around a four-window screen. This presents a graphical browser, a structured index, a control panel and a node inspection window. Nodes are of three types: Issue, Position and Argument. The browser is unusual in that it simultaneously provides both local and general views of the node network, at different resolutions. The network itself is structured with nine link types, such as Responds-to, Refers-to and Objects-to[3]. New links are created via templates and can be linked and moved graphically. gIBIS also supports the inheritance of body features from subnets. Primary links are hierarchically structured, but secondary links allow non-hierarchical links to other parts of the network. Other features are Query-by-example and online Help.

TEXTNET

Randall Trigg's Textnet approach has been implemented as the TEXTNET system. Written in Lisp, it runs under UNIX on a DEC VAX 11/780. It employs two types of node: 'chunk' or text content nodes, and 'toc' or table of contents nodes. The authors describe it as a semantic net implementation of hypertext[15]. Tocs can be used to organize hierarchical structures (directed acyclic graphs), whilst non-hierarchical graphs can be created using TEXTNET's typed links (more than 80 have been developed).

TEXTNET's interface is menu-based and multi-windowing. The system supports default paths for users and can be used for collaboration and annotation[3]. The variety of links and possibilities for structural organisation make it ideally suited to a community of users with differing goals. Further improvements are planned including link facilities to links themselves, as well as user modeling.

REFERENCES

1. Akscyn, R., McCracken, D. and Yoder, E. KMS: A distributed hypermedia system for managing knowledge in organizations. *Communications of the ACM*, **31 (7)**, July 1988, pp. 820-835.
2. Begeman, M. and Conklin, J. The right tool for the right job. *BYTE*, **13 (10)**, October 1988, pp. 255-266.
3. Conklin, J. Hypertext: An introduction and survey. *Computer*, **20 (9)**, September 1987, pp. 17-41.
4. Duncan, E. (1989a) A faceted approach to hypertext? In: McAleese, R. (Ed.) *Hypertext theory into practice*. Oxford: Intellect Books Limited, 1989.
5. Foss, C. Tools for reading and browsing hypertext. *Information Processing and Management*, **25 (4)**, 1989, pp. 407-418.
6. Halasz, F. Reflections on NoteCards: Seven issues for the next generation of hypermedia systems. *Communications of the ACM*, **31 (7)**, July 1988, pp. 836-852.
7. Halasz, F. Moran, T. and Trigg, NoteCards in a nutshell. *Proceedings of the ACM CHI + GI 1987 Conference*, Toronto, Canada, April 5-9, 1987.
8. Irish, P. and Trigg, R. Supporting collaboration in hypermedia: issues and experiences. In: Barrett, E. (Ed.), *The Society of Text*. Cambridge, MA: MIT Press, 1989.
9. McCracken, D. and Akscyn, R. Experiences with the ZOG human-computer interface. *International Journal of Man-Machine Studies*, **21 (2)**, August 1984, pp. 293-310.
10. Nelson, T. *Literary Machines*. Swathmore, PA: Nelson (1981).
1. Nelson, T. Managing immense storage. *BYTE*, January 1988, pp. 225-238.
12. Shneiderman, B. Reflections on authoring, editing and managing hypertext. In: Barrett, E. (Ed.), *The Society of Text*. Cambridge, MA: MIT Press, 1989.
13. Shneiderman, B. and Morariu, J. *The interactive encyclopedia system (TIES)*. Dept. of Computer Science, University of Maryland, College Park, Maryland, June, 1986.
14. Trigg, R., Suchman, L. and Halasz, F. Supporting Collaboration in NoteCards. *Proceedings of the Conference on Computer Supported Cooperative Work*, Austin, TX, December 3-5 1986.

15. Trigg, R. and Weiser, M. TEXTNET: a network-based approach to text handling. *ACM Transactions on Office Information Systems,* **4 (1),** January 1986. pp. 1-23.

16. Walker. J. Supporting document development with Concordia. *IEEE Computer,* **21 (1),** January 1988, pp. 48-59.

17. Walker, M. Framed documents. *Desktop Publishing Today,* **4 (5),** May 1989. pp. 36-37.

18. Walter, M. IRIS Intermedia: pushing the boundaries of hypertext. *The Seybold Report on Publishing Systems,* **18 (21),** August 1989, pp. 21-32.

19. Yankelovich, N., Haan, B., Meyrovitz, N. and Drucker, S. Intermedia: The concept and the construction of a seamless information environment. *IEEE Computer,* **21 (1),** January 1988, pp. 81-96.

Appendices: ShareWare and ShellWare

A note about ShareWare:

ShareWare disks are supplied on a try-before-you-buy basis; a nominal charge covers initial disk copying by the distributor, and the user is then free to experiment with the product for an evaluation period — normally a month. Continued personal or commercial use after this period requires registration under international Copyright laws. ShareWare distribution allows developers to reach a wide potential market without the huge costs involved in conventional marketing. As such, the cost of registering products is typically low; registered users receive the latest product versions, and often printed documentation.

Appendix 1: IBM-PC and Compatibles

The following program demonstration/evaluation systems (some with limited functionality) are available from several Public Domain and ShareWare sources, including:
The Public Domain Software Library, Winscombe House, Beacon Road, Crowborough, Sussex, TN6 1UL. Tel: 0892 663298.
PC Independent User Group, The Computer Centre, 87 High Street, Tonbridge, Kent, TN9 1RX.

KnowledgePro

This expert system shell with hypermedia facilities is available with limited functionality as shareware. The system is discussed in Chapter 9 on IBM-PC hypermedia.
Supplier:
Knowledge Garden Inc.
or
Intellisoft (UK) Ltd, 77A Packhorse Road, Gerrards Cross, Bucks SL9 8PQ. Tel: 0753 889972.
or
ShareWare distributors.

TextPro

TextPro expands on KnowledgePro's implementation of hypermedia by providing explicit hierarchical structure to applications, thus allowing documents to be folded away or expanded in depth. It can be used as a stand-alone program with the KnowledgePro run-time, or within the full KnowledgePro system. As with KnowledgePro, there may be problems of speed. Figure A.1 shows a typical TextPro/KnowledgePro screen.

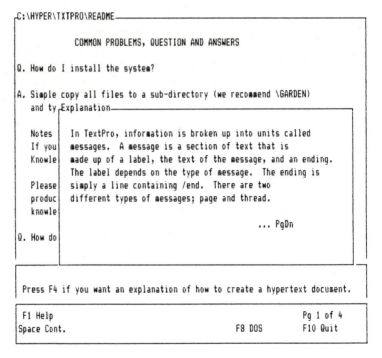

Figure A.1   Embedded text buttons provide links in KnowledgePro and TextPro.

Supplier:
ShareWare distributors.

Black Magic

This hypermedia product supports both WYSIWYG text and bit-mapped, interactive graphics, although the current shareware version does not print graphics. It has been marketed as a sophisticated word processor, and is supplied as a document development system plus reader version and disk documentation. The interface utilizes both mouse and keyboard functions.

Black Magic documents can contain Reference, Replacement and pop-up Note links. Text search and simple backtracking are provided, as well as a reference mapping facility. This displays the levels and reference branches of a document graphically, together with samples of text at selected locations. Direct access to these locations is also supported. Other facilities include a screen grab utility for importing graphics, and Bookmarks for faster loading to specific points in a document. In fact speed may be a limiting factor for some users — particularly for loading large documents and refreshing graphics screens. However, for developing structured documents — particularly educational materials — it may provide an interesting alternative to an outliner.

Supplier:
NTERGAID, 2490 Black Rock Turnpike, Suite 337, Fairfield, CT 06430.
or
ShareWare distributors.

PC-Hypertext

The origins of this program are closely linked with the hierarchical outliner MaxThink, and the network-based outliner, Houdini. The interface on early shareware versions is exclusively driven by the cursor direction keys and menus (no mouse support), but mouse support for graphics is provided in the latest version. PC-Hypertext primarily uses ASCII text files with simple < angle-bracketed > buttons (see Figure A.2); it also supports a growing range of other formats, including Houdini and .PCX files. Basic backtracking (last three steps), and text search facilities are available. Documents can also be structured into tables of contents, networks, and hierarchies — and dynamic flow charting is provided in the new version. DOS and external program calls can be initiated via embedded buttons — and PC-Hypertext now allows the user to specify whether the program is memory-resident or deinstalled.

MaxThink can also supply application building tools: a marker, splitter, checker, classifier, tree builder and verifier. With these it is possible very rapidly to assemble large ASCII-based hypertexts; extensive disk examples and advice are supplied and are well worth browsing through. Although less sophisticated in appearance than some of it WYSIWYG competitors, this program is fast, powerful and registration is very reasonably priced.

Supplier:
N. Larson, MaxThink, 44 Rincon Road, Kensington, CA 94707. Tel: (0101) 415 428 0104.
or
ShareWare distributors.

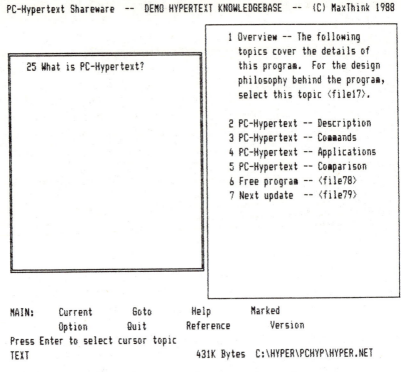

```
PC-Hypertext Shareware  --  DEMO HYPERTEXT KNOWLEDGEBASE  --  (C) MaxThink 1988
```

```
                                      1 Overview -- The following
                                        topics cover the details of
      25 What is PC-Hypertext?           this program. For the design
                                        philosophy behind the program,
                                        select this topic <file17>.

                                      2 PC-Hypertext -- Description
                                      3 PC-Hypertext -- Commands
                                      4 PC-Hypertext -- Applications
                                      5 PC-Hypertext -- Comparison
                                      6 Free program -- <file78>
                                      7 Next update  -- <file79>
```

```
MAIN:    Current      Goto      Help        Marked
         Option       Quit      Reference   Version
Press Enter to select cursor topic
TEXT                              431K Bytes  C:\HYPER\PCHYP\HYPER.NET
```

Figure A.2 Overview of ASCII files in PC-Hypertext.

HyperShell

This inexpensive program from Text Technology has many of the features of some of its more expensive commercial rivals. A fully functional system is available as ShareWare.

HyperShell is a frames-based implementation of hypertext (one frame represents a subject). It has claims to being an intelligent system in that with its scripting facility it is possible for developers to incorporate conditional flow of control, and context-sensitivity (as exemplified in the online Help provided). The scripting language is closer to assembler than a block structured language like HyperTalk, but allows programmers great freedom to implement new features. The system comprises a Runtime Browser (requires only 42K), an editor and a syntax/cross reference checking utility for debugging applications. The menu-based interface supports several mouse formats, and a variety of reference types (see Figure A.3).

HyperShell documents (or hyperfiles) consist of structured frames. These can be initially accessed from tables of contents, or embedded links. HyperShell also provides sequential backtracking through visited frames, and frame marking. The 'Select Back' option leads to a 'dynamic menu' of frames that have been accessed — a facility similar to HyperCard's Recent screen. Other features include pop-up notes, simple text string search and 'auto-referencing'; the latter highlights occurrences of keywords on the fly in normal text files, allowing the user to select them and thus access external reference materials. The forthcoming release will provide greatly extended features, including file compression and interactive graphics.

HyperShell is relatively fast, powerful and well designed. It is remarkably low-priced, and well worth considering for large academic or commercial applications, as well as personal use.

Supplier:
Text Technology, 66 Kennedy Avenue, Macclesfield, Cheshire, SK10 3DE. Tel: 0625 31357.

Educational users can obtain the system for evaluation via the JANET network from the PD archive at Lancaster.

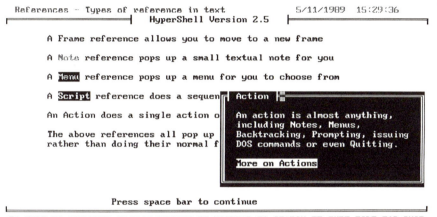

Figure A.3 Reference types in HyperShell.

Appendix 2:   Macintosh ShellWare

We now seem to be entering a virtual second generation of application software designed for use with Apple's HyperCard; early StackWare (ShellWare for Hypercard) is typically domain-specific, or provides small auxiliary tools for use with other applications. More recently, 'professional' developers have begun to accept HyperCard as a prototyping platform, or as a serious market. As well as stacks, there are commercial resources implemented as XCMDs or XFCNs — external code modules which HyperCard can access. Sophisticated tools such as inference engines, database front ends, music studios and intelligent tutoring shells are now available, often in the public domain, or as ShareWare.

StackWare

General Distributors:

ApplePhone Bulletin System, 60 Tenby Drive, Luton, Bedfordshire, LU4 9BL. Data line (HyperCard bulletin board): 0582 584134 (300, 1200 and 1200/75 baud)

EDUCORP Computer Services, *742 Genevieve, Suite D, Solana Beach, CA 92075, USA. Tel: (0101) 800 843-9497.*

Details through Apple dealers and UK contact:

Trans Latum International, Carmel Road, Carmel, Holywell, Clywd. Tel: 0352 710276. (PD, ShareWare and StackWare for Macintosh)

Heizer Software (Stack Exchange), 1941 Oak Park Boulevard, Suite 30, Pleasant Hill, CA 94523, USA. Tel: (0101) 415 943-7667 for catalogue.

(PD, ShareWare and StackWare for Macintosh — Heizer runs Stack Exchange, with over a hundred utilities available at nominal cost; enquire about overseas orders.)

HyperCard Educational Application Developers Group (HEAD), The Anchorage, George Road, Brightlingsea, Essex, CO7 0NE.

MacTel, 15 Elm Tree Avenue, West Bridgeford, Nottingham, NG2 7JU. Tel: 0602 455444.

Data line (HyperCard bulletin board): 0602 810237

MacUser Magazine Regular shareware page features a variety of low-cost StackWare disks.

Most Apple dealers also have a range of commercial stacks, and names of local contacts, or contact:

Apple Computer, 6 Roundwood Avenue, Stockley, Park, Uxbridge, Middlesex.

Product Stacks:

Many of the publishers below have plans to release further stacks in the near future and welcome general enquiries.

Business Class (Travel information/atlas, by Danny Goodman, HyperCard's author/designer). *Mediagenics, Blake House, Manor Farm Road, Reading, Berks, RG2 0JN. Tel: 0734 311666.*

Focal Point/Focal Point II (General business/personal organizer; as per Business Class).

HITS (HyperCard Intelligent Training System — under development by Logica at time of going to press; may be available free to educational developers in the near future). Enquiries to: *Logica Cambridge Ltd, Betjeman House, 104 Hills Rd, Cambridge, CB2 1LQ. Tel: 0223 66343.*

HyperKRS (HyperCard stack for knowledge retrieval. Includes indexer and search engine). *Pergamon Compact Solution, Irwin House, 118 Southwark St. London SE1 0SW. Tel: 071 928 1404.*

HyperMIDI (Midi deck front end). *ApplePhone, as above.*

HyperNews 1.2 (Newsletter). *ApplePhone.*

HyperQuiz (Tutorial/test shell). *EDUCORP.*

Hyper*SQL (Oracle Corporation's market leading relational database has been launched on the Mac with HyperCard and SuperCard front ends. Impressive, relatively expensive). *Oracle Centre, Ring Road, Bracknell, Berks. Tel: 0800 678222.*

HyperTalk Tutor. (Hands-on tutorial, for those who find the books heavy going). *ApplePhone.*

HyperX (US Public Domain inference engine). *Millenium Software, 1970 South Coast Highway, Laguna Beach, CA 92651, USA.*

MacRecorder, plus HyperSound (Resources to digitize sound, edit and make stacks). *Farallon Computing, Gomark Ltd, 10 Hurlingham Business Park, London SW6 3DU. Tel: 071 731 7930.*

Reports (Write reports as stacks). *Mediagenics Blake House, Manor Farm Road, Reading, Berks, RG2 OJN. Tel: 0734 311666.*

ScriptExpert (Another HyperTalk tutorial). *MacLine, Wren House, Sutton Court Road, Sutton, Surrey, SM1 4TL.* Tel: 081 643 4626.

ShellWare Bibliography

Brown, P. All hyped up. *MacUser,* 36, June 1989, pp. 51-53, 55.

Buyers' Guide — Hypertext and Hypermedia. *MacUser (UK)* 12 Jan 1989, pp. 43-44.

Hammond, C. First of the stackware. *Practical Computing,* April 1988, pp. 29-32.

Goodman, D. *The Complete HyperCard Handbook.* New York: Bantam, 2nd edition 1988.

Jones, M. and Myers, D. *Hands-on HyperCard.* New York: John Wiley and Sons, 1988.

Glossary

AI Artificial intelligence; branch of psychology and computer science that seeks to represent aspects of reasoning and symbolic representation in machine-based models.

Algorithm Formal, language-independent procedure guaranteed to converge on a correct or optimal problem solution.

Application Specific-purpose program or material, as opposed to a general system.

BLOB Binary Large OBject Data type used in multimedia databases — text or binary data is stored in logical regions or relational-style columns.

Backtracking The process of retracing the user's trail through a series of previously visited nodes or locations. Some systems backtrack on chronological sequence, or maintain a map of a limited number of recently visited nodes.

Bookmark A marker inserted in a file/document to facilitate return navigation.

Boolean Logical set representation that allows statements to be combined by use of operators such as AND, OR and NOT. Often used to construct search criteria.

Browsing Strategy used in following path through information nodes; may be with specific or general purpose.

Browser Virtual tool, often graphical, to aid user's perception of an aspect or abstract view of information.

Button An iconic representation of a procedure or option that can be activated by means of a mouse or keystrokes.

CAD Computer-aided Design. CAD systems typically employ object-oriented techniques, representing objects as vectorized or other mathematical descriptions rather than bit-mapped images.

CAI/CBT Computer-aided instruction; Computer-based training.

CASE Computer-aided software engineering. Tools approach to creating software without the need for explicit programming language knowledge; code is typically generated from menus or diagrams.

CD-ROM Compact optical disk, read-only memory. Large capacity storage medium, particularly useful for graphic information. CD-ROMs are one form of the larger class of digital technology optical disk storage media.

Canonical Regular, accepted or original version (of a document); a 'deep' representation, underlying all possible 'surface' structures, such as overlays, commentaries, personalised versions etc.

Cognition Thought processes, generally macrolevel as opposed to neurobiological.

Cognitive mapping Psychological capacity to relate concepts symbolically or spatially; 'soft' methodology in Management Science for representing this ability.

Compiled Describes program code that has been parsed and translated from source code into machine-readable object code which can often be executed as a stand-alone program, as opposed to interpreted code which is read from source at run-time.

Connectionism Artificial intelligence approach using micro-level structures (software or hardware) that mimic some aspects of neurological information processing such as firing weights, mutual excitation and inhibition.

Context Possible protocol for managing collaborative media systems (Delisle and Schwartz).

DDE Dynamic Data Exchange; program designed to allow real-time data exchange between other programs and files.

DDBS Distributed database system; Information is stored at a variety of physical locations which are linked via network communications technology.

DVI Digital Video Interactive; the IBM/Intel joint technology for digitized video data (de)-compression. Enables compression of files to one per cent of original size, with decompression in real time on a PC equipped with the custom DVI custom chips and software.

Declarative Style of programming/query language in which required data or actions are described rather than procedurally specified.

Desktop Common software metaphor for graphically representing information in frames within nested windows and files or folders.

Dialectic Pertaining to logic or discourse.

Epistemology The study of knowledge — its origins and methods.

Ergonomics The study of efficiency in human working practices.

Expert System An application or shell environment employing various decision-making techniques of artificial intelligence.

Filter Pattern mask/matcher as used in general database approaches to return only data meeting a given set of criteria.

Fisheye Browser Viewing tool in which the most local or relevant nodes/information/objects are given disproportionate emphasis in terms of relative size, color, textual characteristics, etc.

FOPL First order predicate logic — formal logic representation capable of describing instances and properties and simple theorem resolution, but inadequate for metalevel issues of greater generality. The logic language PROLOG has much in common with FOPL, although most implementations lack true theorem resolution capability.

Frame Class of knowledge representational formalisms in psychology and artificial intelligence, including semantic nets, schemata and scripts, and object-oriented approaches. Frames consist of attributes or slots which can be instantiated by default or specified values. Frames are often linked by special hierarchical or network slots to form more complex representational structures.

Granularity Discrete level of detail or abstraction in a view or information node. Granularity is a central concept in hierarchically organized hypermedia, and also in some other knowledge-based paradigms such as the blackboard architecture style of expert system.

HCI Human Computer Interaction (or interface — formerly/also known as Man-Machine Interaction). Discipline involving cognitive and ergonomic psychological research into optimal computerized solutions for human users.

Heuristic A systematic algorithm, strategy, or guideline used in problem solving to reduce intractable complexity and produce an acceptable if not optimal solution.

Hyper- Prefix denoting the quality of being beyond, or excessive.

Hyperdocument Sometimes used to denote the entire corpus of documents available on a workstation or network.

Hypermedia Generic class of, or approach to computer-based materials linked by non-linear structures. The term is variously applied as a subset of or synonym to interactive multimedia.

Hypertext Subset of hypermedia, dealing exclusively with textual materials. Sometimes used as a noun, for a single application.

Icon Graphic representation of a tool or application that can be activated with a mouse or keystrokes, for instance, a button or analog control panel.

Inheritance Process in hierarchical systems e.g. frames/object-oriented representations whereby nodes lower in the structure acquire properties or methods of those above them.

Interpreted Describes code that is read from source at run-time, as opposed to compiled.

Inverted File Sorted database index of terms/items against addresses/ locations. Typically used for rapid access, especially with relatively static databases.

IPSE Integrated Project Support Environment; project management software that implements the techniques of formal management science techniques such as PERT or CPM.

KBS Knowledge-based or expert system; program based on a database of knowledge, often interpreted by a set of rules which operate according to context. Sometimes also known as IKBS — intelligent knowledge-based system.

Link Structure/syntax of a hypermedia system. These may be implicit, or explicit objects with defined types. Generally from and to a node.

LISP Artificial intelligence programming/query language in which the primary data structure is the list.

Map Generally a two-dimensional, graphical representation of nodes and links at or between levels of granularity in a knowledge base.

Media Channels, materials or technological systems by means of which information is stored and distributed.

Metaphor Representation of one object or process by another, e.g. of the operating system interface by a desktop and folders or set of windows and icons.

Multimedia A synonym of hypermedia and interactive technology approaches. The term interactive multimedia is strictly a superset to hypermedia, in that not all interactive multimedia support hypermedia cross-referencing.

Multi-tasking Capacity to run more than one program concurrently, or virtually concurrently.

NL/Natural language An everyday human language, spoken or written, as opposed to a logical or mathematical representational formalism, or a programming language.

Navigation Use of abstract features, structure or other tools and cues for orientation in relation to the available knowledge.

Nodes The semantic microfeatures of a hypermedia system; for instance an item of text or a graphical object. Connected by links, in a variety of possible structures.

OS/2 Microsoft's Operating System 2 for IBM's PS/2 computers and compatibles.

Object-oriented An approach to database and programming language design, similar to frame-based methods; based on autonomous objects possessing attributes and procedural methods, communicating via messages, and often hierarchically related.

Path/Trail A series of linked nodes — may be default (predetermined by application author) or user-defined.

Postscript Page description language.

PROLOG PROgramming in LOGic; a 'fifth generation' or AI language with declarative, symbolic representation features similar to those of the first order predicate calculus.

Parsing Analysis of sentence structure and components.

Prototype Working model derived by iterative cycles of an analytic methodology, with the purpose of gaining feedback and closing on an optimal solution.

Query Language High-level formalism such as SQL used to interrogate a database.

ROM Read Only Memory — procedures are preprogrammed into the hardware of a chip, which cannot be overwritten.

Read Only/Reader/Envelope system Low-cost version of a shell development system, with stripped down functionality; allows users to read materials and use basic tools, but neither to alter them nor to develop their own.

Relational database Characterized by: set-style relations between data entities; structured query language and other high level management facilities, allowing virtual views of given relations, regardless of actual organization of tables.

Rhetoric The art of eloquence, effective or stylish communication. Used specifically for the conventions of style and cueing in hypermedia materials.

SGML Standard Generalised Markup Language; used for text formatting and structural description. Similar formatting tools include TEX and Scribe.

SQL Structured Query Language

Scripting User level or activity, employing a high-level application development language such as HyperCard's HyperTalk.

Semantics Meaning of words or other information, as opposed to its syntax or structure.

Semantic Net Model of concept association derived from psychological models of human memory; nodes with semantic content exist within a structure (often hierarchical) by links indicating the nature of the relationship.

Shell General-purpose software environment or set of tools, often commercial.

ShellWare Third-party software, to be used with the above, or its run-time library/reader version.

Smalltalk Object-oriented programming system; code objects are hierarchically structured into classes and can possess or inherit procedural methods.

Spatial ability Cognitive index of intelligence, contrasted with, for instance, lexical or mathematical ability.

Stack Used in the context of this book solely to mean a desk-level folder or file of cards in Apple Macintosh software such as HyperCard, rather than its more general computing use i.e. a machine-level portion of memory.

StackWare ShellWare or third-party software specifically for use in conjunction with Apple Computer's HyperCard.

Term Weight Indexing Approach in which content identifiers or attribute terms are represented with relative numerical weightings. These are then used to reduce the number of items typically retrieved by search criteria, and to increase the likelihood of their relevance.

Timeline A path or directed pattern of links in a hypermedia document or database, determined by chronological sequence.

Tools High-level, virtual representations of processes or techniques as explicitly manipulable objects

Users The word users is preferred to readers, as implying a more active mode of interaction with the application.

Virtual Apparent, in effect. What the end user perceives, as opposed to a possibly different underlying implementation.

WIMP Windows, Icons, Mouse, Pop-up menus; interface approach as exemplified by many Macintosh and Presentation Manager applications, and also common in hypermedia.

WYSIWYG 'What you see is what you get': a high resolution screen display permits accurate representation of typographic styles, formatting, etc.

Window A virtual screen within the main display screen; often multiple.

XCMDs and XFCNs External commands, external functions. Code modules written in C or Pascal which can be used to provide HyperCard with additional resources.

Bibliography

Note: several useful compendia of articles have been published recently in special editions of journals. Among the best are:

BYTE, **13 (10), October 1988**

BYTE, **15 (2), February 1990**

Communications of the ACM, **31 (7), July 1988**

The only journals to date to deal exclusively with the field are:

HyperLink Magazine, Publishers Guild, Inc., PO Box 7723, Eugene, Oregon
      97401, USA.

Hypermedia, Taylor Graham Publishing, 500 Chesham House, 150 Regent
      Street, London, W1R 5FA, UK.

Interactive Multimedia, Sigma Press, 1 South Oak Lane, Wilmslow,
      Cheshire, SK9 6AR, UK.

European readers wishing to study Bush's seminal article *As We May Think,* originally published in 1945 in *Atlantic Monthly,* may find it easier to get hold of Ted Nelson's *Literary Machines* (a masterpiece in its own right), or *CD ROM, The New Papyrus* (Microsoft Press) which both include a reprint. Ted Nelson's influential book can be obtained from:

    Mindful Press,
    3220 Bridgeway #295,
    Sausalito, CA 94965.
    Price: $25 plus $5 for overseas orders.

Annotated Bibliographies:

Readers in search of additional and annotated bibliographical material, with slightly different emphases, should consult the following:

Franklin, C. An annotated hypertext bibliography. Online, **12 (2),** March
    1988, pp. 42-46.

Franklin, C. A bibliography on hypertext and hypermedia with selected
    annotations. *Database,* **13 (1),** February 1990, pp. 24-32, and
    Database, **13 (2),** April 1990.

Hawkins, D. Applications of artificial intelligence (AI) and expert systems
    for online searching. *Online,* **12 (1),** January 1988, pp. 31-43.

Nielson, J. Hypertext Bibliography. *Hypermedia,* **1 (1),** Spring 1989,
    pp. 74-91.

Articles, Books, and Papers:

Akscyn, R., McCracken, D. and Yoder, E. KMS: A distributed hypermedia system for managing knowledge in organizations. *Communications of the ACM,* **31 (7),** July 1988, pp. 820-835.

Allinson, L. and Hammond, N. A learning support environment: The Hitch Hiker's Guide. In: McAleese, R. (Ed.), *Hypertext, theory into practice.* Oxford: Intellect Books, 1989.

Anderson, J. *Human Associative Memory.* Washington, DC: Winston, 1973.

Anderson, J. A spreading activation theory of memory. *Journal of Verbal Learning and Verbal Memory,* **22 (3),** 1983.

Baird, P. and Percival M. Glasgow Online: Database development using Apple's HyperCard. In: McAleese, R. (Ed.), *Hypertext, theory into practice.* Oxford: Intellect Books, 1989.

Barden, R. Extending your home with an ITS: building a hypertext-based intelligent tutoring system. *Proceedings of Hypertext II,* University of York, 29-30 June 1989.

Barden, R. Using hypertext in building intelligent training systems. *Interactive Learning International,* **5,** 1989, pp. 109-115.

Barrett, E. (Ed.), *Text, ConText and HyperText.* Cambridge, MA: MIT Press, 1988.

Barrett, E. Textual intervention, collaboration, and the online environment. In: Barrett, E. (Ed.), *The Society of Text.* Cambridge, MA: MIT Press, 1989.

Bartlett, F. *Remembering, a study in experimental and social psychology,* Cambridge University Press, 1932.

Beattie, R. Apple talk. *PC User* (UK) February 14-27 1990, p 157.

Begeman, M. and Conklin, J. The right tool for the right job. *BYTE,* **13 (10),** October 1988, pp. 255-266.

Benest, I. A hypertext system with controlled hype. *Proceedings of Hypertext II,* University of York, 29-30 June 1989.

Benest, I., Morgan, G. and Smithurst, M. A humanized interface to an electronic library. In: Bullinger, H. and Shackel, B. (Eds.) *Human-Computer Interaction — INTERACT'87.* Elsevier Science Publishers (North-Holland), 1987, pp. 905-910.

Bennett, P. and Dando, M. Complex strategic analysis: a hypergame study of the Fall of France. *Journal of the Operational Research Society,* **30 (1),** January 1979, pp. 23-32.

Bennett, P. and Huxham, S. Hypergames and what they do: a soft ''OR'' approach. *Journal of the Operational Research Society,* **33 (1),** January 1982. pp. 41-50.

Bernstein, M. The bookmark and the compass: orientation tools for hypertext users. *ACM SIGOIS Bulletin,* **9 (4),** October 1988, pp. 34-45.

Berry, D. and Broadbent, D. Expert systems and the man-machine interface. Part Two: the user interface. *Expert Systems,* **4 (1),** 1987, pp. 18-27.

Bertino, E., Gibbs, S. and Rabitti, F. document processing strategies: cost evaluation and heuristics. In: Allen, R. (Ed.) *Proceedings of the Conference on Office Information Systems,* March 23-25 1988, Palo Alto, California. *ACM SIGOIS Bulletin,* **9 (2-3),** April and July 1988, pp. 169-181.

Bond, G. *XCMDs for HyperCard.* MIS Press, Inc., 1988

Boyle, C. and Snell, J. Knowledge based navigation under hypertext. *Proceedings of Hypertext II,* University of York, 29-30 June 1989.

Brockman, R. Exploring the connections between improved technology — workstation and desktop publishing and improved methodology — document databases. In: Barrett, E. (Ed.) *Text, ConText and HyperText.* Cambridge, MA: MIT Press, 1988.

Brockman, R., Horton, W. and Brook, K. From database to hypertext via electronic publishing: an information odyssey. In: Barrett, E. (Ed.), *The Society of Text.* Cambridge, MA: MIT Press, 1989.

Brondmo, H. and Davenport, D. Creating and viewing the Elastic Charles — a hypermedia journal. *Proceedings of Hypertext II,* University of York, June 29-30 1989.

Brown, P. Interactive documentation. *Software — Practice and Experience,* **16 (3),** March 1986, pp. 291-299.

Brown, P. All hyped up. *MacUser,* **36,** June 1989, pp. 51-53, 55.

Bryan, M. *SGML, an author's guide to the Standard Generalized Markup Language.* Addison-Wesley, 1988.

Bunnell, D. Hypervisions. *MacWorld (UK),* **4 (3)** 1987, pp. 21, 24, 28, 30.

Bunnell, D. The challenge of hypermedia. *MacWorld (UK),* **4 (11),** 1987 pp. 17, 21, 23.

Bush, V. As we may think. *Atlantic Monthly* **176 (1),** July 1945, pp. 101-108 (see note above).

Campagnoni, F. and Ehrlich, K. Information retrieval using a hypertext-based help system. *ACM Transactions on Information Systems,* **7 (3),** July 1989 pp. 271-191.

Canter, D., Rivers, R. and Storrs, G. Characterizing user navigation through complex data structures. *Behaviour and Information Technology,* **4 (2),** 1985, pp. 93-102.

Carlson, P. Hypertext: a way of incorporating user feedback into online documentation. In: Barrett, E. (Ed.) *Text, ConText and HyperText.* Cambridge, MA: MIT Press, 1988.

Carlson, P. Hypertext and intelligent interfaces for text retrieval. In: Barrett, E. (Ed.), *The Society of Text.* Cambridge, MA: MIT Press, 1989.

Carroll, J. and Aaronson, A. Learning by doing with simulated intelligent Help. In: Barrett, E. (Ed.), *The Society of Text.* Cambridge, MA: MIT Press, 1989.

Caplinger, M. Graphical database browsing. In: Hewitt, C. and Zdonik, S. (Eds.) *Proceedings of the Third ACM SIGOIS Conference on Office Information Systems,* October 6-8 1986, Providence, Rhode Island, pp. 113-119. ACM Press.

Cawkell, T. From Memex to MediaMaker. *The Electronic Library,* **7 (5),** October 1989, pp. 278-286.

Ceri, S. and Pelagatti, G. *Distributed Databases.* NY: McGraw-Hill, 1984.

Checkland, M. *Systems Thinking, Systems Practice.* John Wiley, 1981.

Chen, J., Ekberg, T. and Thompson, C. Querying an object-oriented hypermedia system. *Proceedings of Hypertext II,* University of York, June 29-30 1989.

Chomsky, N. *Aspects of the Theory of Syntax.* Cambridge, MA: MIT Press, 1965.

Christodoulakis, S. and Graham, S. Browsing within time-driven multimedia documents. In: Allen, R. (Ed.) *Proceedings of the Conference on Office Information Systems,* March 23-25 1988, Palo Alto, California. *ACM SIGOIS Bulletin,* **9 (2-3),** April and July 1988, pp. 219-227.

Codd, E. A relational model of data for large, shared data banks. *Communications of the ACM,* **13 (6),** June 1970, pp. 377-382.

Colbourn, C. and Cockerton-Turner, T. Using hypertext for educational 'Help' facilities. *Proceedings of Hypertext II,* University of York, June 29-30 1989.

Collingbourne, H. Rants and raves. *Computer Shopper,* August 1989, pp. 103, 106.

Conklin, J. Hypertext: an introduction and survey. *Computer,* **20 (9),** September 1987, pp. 17-41.

Conklin, J. and Begeman, M. gIBIS: a hypertext tool for exploratory policy discussion. *ACM Transactions on Office Information Systems,* **6 (4),** October 1988, pp. 303-331.

Cook, R. Desktop video studio. *BYTE,* **15 (2),** February 1990, pp. 229-234.

Cooke, P. and Williams, I. Design issues in large hypertext systems for technical documentation. In: McAleese, R. (Ed.) *Hypertext theory into practice.* Oxford: Intellect Books Limited, 1989.

Coombs, J. Renear, A. and DeRose, S. Markup systems and the future of scholarly text processing. *Communications of the ACM,* November 1987, pp. 933-947.

Cove, J. and Walsh, B. Online text retrieval via browsing. *Information Processing and Management,* **24 (1),** 1988, pp. 31-37.

Dallas, K. Windows works it out. *PC User (UK),* **119, 8-21** November 1989, pp. 104-113.

Date, C. *An Introduction to Database Systems, Volume 1.* Reading, MA: Addison-Wesley, Fourth Edition, 1986.

Date, C. *Relational Databases: selected writings.* Reading, MA: Addison-Wesley, 1986.

Delisle, N. and Schwartz, M. Contexts — a partitioning concept for hypertext. *ACM Transactions on Office Information Systems,* **5 (2),** April 1987, pp. 168-186.

Dmytryk, E. *On Screen Writing.* Boston, London: Focal Press, 1985.

Doland, V. Hypermedia as an interpretive act. *Hypermedia 1* **(1),** Spring 1989, pp. 6-19.

Duda, R., Hart, P. and Nilsson, N. Subjective Bayesian methods for rule-based inference systems. In: *Proceedings 1976 National Computer Conference,* AFIPS Press, 1976.

Duncan, E. A faceted approach to hypertext? In: McAleese, R. (Ed.) *Hypertext theory into practice.* Oxford: Intellect Books Limited, 1989.

Duncan, E. Structuring knowledge bases for designers of learning materials. *Hypermedia,* **1 (1),** Spring 1989, pp. 20-33.

Duncan, E. and McAleese, R. Qualified citation indexing online? In: Williams, M. and Hogan, T. (Eds.) *National Online Meeting Proceedings. Medford, NJ: Learned Information,* 1982, pp. 77-85.

Eager, A., Whitehorn, M. Forsyth, R. and Powell, M. Expert Systems. *PC Magazine (UK),* May 1989, pp. 54-73.

Eden, C. and Jones, S. Publish or perish? — A case study. *Journal of the Operational Research Society,* **31,** 1980, pp. 131-139.

Edwards, D. and Hardman L. 'Lost in hyperspace': cognitive mapping and navigation in a hypertext environment. In: McAleese, R. (Ed.) *Hypertext theory into practice.* Oxford: Intellect Books Limited, 1989.

Egan, D. and Gomez, L. Assaying, isolating and accommodating individual differences in learning a complex skill. In: Dillon, R. (Ed.) *Individual Differences in Cognition, Vol. 2,* pp. 173-217. NY: Academic Press, 1985.

Eirund, H. and Kreplin, K. Knowledge based document classification supporting integrated document handling. In: Allen, R. (Ed.) *Proceedings of the Conference on Office Information Systems,* March 23-25 1988, Palo Alto, California. *ACM SIGOIS Bulletin,* **9 (2-3),** April and July 1988, pp. 189-196.

Engelbart, D. A conceptual framework for the augmentation of man's intellect. In: *Vistas in Information Handling,* Vol. 1, London: Spartan Books, 1963.

Ertel, M. A tour of the stacks. HyperCard for libraries. *Online,* **13 (1),** January 1989, pp. 45-53.

Evans, R. Expert systems and HyperCard. *BYTE,* **15, (1),** January, 1990 pp. 317-324.

Feiner, S. Seeing the forest for the trees: hierarchical display of hypertext structure. In: Allen, R. (Ed.) *Proceedings of the Conference on Office Information Systems,* March 23-25 1988, Palo Alto, California. *ACM SIGOIS Bulletin,* **9 (2-3),** April and July 1988, pp. 205-212.

Fiderio, J. A grand vision. *BYTE,* **13 (10),** October 1988, pp. 237-244.

Fletton, N. A hypertext approach to browsing and documenting software. *Proceedings of Hypertext II,* University of York, June 29-30 1989.

Foss, C. Tools for reading and browsing hypertext. *Information Processing and Management,* **25 (4),** 1989, pp. 407-418.

Forrester, M. and Reason, D. *The application of an "Intraface Model" to the design of hypertext systems.* (University of Kent, 1989, unpublished).

Franklin, C. An Annotated hypertext bibliography. *Online,* **12 (2),** March 1988, pp. 42-46.

Franklin, C. The hypermedia library. *Database,* **11 (3),** June 1988, pp. 43-48.

Franklin, C. Hypertext defined and applied. *Online,* **13 (3),** May 1989, pp. 37-49.

Franklin, C. Mapping hypertext structures with ArchiText. *Database,* **12 (4),** August 1989, pp. 50-61.

Franklin, C. KnowledgePro: hypertext meets expert systems. *Database,* **12 (6),** pp. 71-76.

Franklin, C. A bibliography on hypertext and hypermedia with selected annotations. *Database,* **13 (1),** February 1990, pp. 24-32, and *Database* **13 (2),** April 1990.

Frisse, M. Searching for information in a hypertext medical handbook. *Communications of the ACM,* **31 (7),** July 1988, pp. 880-886.

Frisse, M. From text to hypertext. *BYTE,* **13 (10),** October 1988, pp. 247-253.

Furuta, R. and Stotts, P. Separating hypertext content from structure in Trellis. *Proceedings of Hypertext II,* University of York, June 29-30 1989.

Gale, W. (Ed.) *AI and Statistics.* Addison-Wesley, 1986.

Gallant, S. Connectionist expert systems. *Communications of the ACM,* **31 (2),** February, 1988 pp. 152-169.

Garg. P. Abstraction mechanisms in hypertext. *Communications of the ACM,* **31 (7),** July 1988, pp. 862-70, 879.

Gartshore, P. Hypertext as a programming environment for the authoring and production of interactive videodisc training packages. *Proceedings of Hypertext II,* University of York, June 29-30 1989.

Gartshore, P. Multi-window environments for hypermedia systems. *Computing,* 15 March 1990, pp. 43-44.

Gladwin, T. *East is a Big Bird.* Cambridge, MA: Harvard University Press, 1970.

Goodman, D. *The Complete HyperCard Handbook.* NY: Bantam, 2nd edition 1988.

Grice, R. Information development is a part of product development — not an afterthought. In: Barrett, E. (Ed.) *Text, ConText and HyperText.* Cambridge, MA: MIT Press, 1988.

Grice, R. Online Information: what do people want? What do people need? In: Barrett, E. (Ed.), *The Society of Text.* Cambridge, MA: MIT Press, 1989.

Hainebach, R. Focus on full text. Interview. *Information World Review,* February 1990, pp. 20-21.

Hahn, U. and Riemer, U. Automatic generation of hypertext knowledge bases. In: Allen, R. (Ed.) *Proceedings of the Conference on Office Information Systems,* March 23-25 1988, Palo Alto, California. *ACM SIGOIS Bulletin,* **9 (2-3),** April and July 1988, pp. 182-188.

Halasz, F. Reflections on NoteCards: Seven issues for the next generation of hypermedia systems. *Communications of the ACM,* **31 (7),** July 1988, pp. 836-852.

Halasz, F. Moran, T. and Trigg, NoteCards in a nutshell. *Proceedings of the ACM CHI + GI 1987 Conference,* Toronto, Canada, April 5-9, 1987.

Hammond, C. First of the stackware. *Practical Computing,* April 1988, pp. 29-32.

Handy, C. *Understanding Organisations.* Penguin, 1976.

Hanson, R. Toward hypertext publishing. *Sigir Forum (ACM Press),* **22 (1-2),** Fall/Winter 1987-88, pp. 9-27.

Hardman, L. Hypertext tips: experiences in developing a hypertext tutorial. In: (Eds.) Jones, D. and Winder, R. *People and Computers,* **IV.** Cambridge: CUP, 1988, pp. 437-451.

Hardman, L. Evaluating the usability of the Glasgow Online hypertext. *Hypermedia* **1 (1),** Spring 1989, pp. 34-63.

Hardman, L. and Sharratt, B. User-centered hypertext design: the application of HCI design principles and guidelines. *Proceedings of Hypertext II,* University of York, June 29-30 1989.

Harland, S. Human factors engineering and interface development: a hypertext tool aiding prototyping activity. In: McAleese, R. (Ed.) *Hypertext: theory into practice.* Oxford: Intellect Books Limited, 1989.

Hartson, H. and Hix, D. Toward empirically derived methodologies and tools for human-computer interface development. *International Journal of Man-Machine Studies,* **31,** 1989, pp. 477-494.

Haselkorn, M. The future of ''writing'' for the computer industry. In: Barrett, E. (Ed.) *Text, ConText and HyperText.* Cambridge, MA: MIT Press, 1988.

Hawkins, D. Applications of artificial intelligence (AI) and expert systems for online searching. *Online,* **12 (1),** January 1988, pp. 31-43.

Hawkins, D. Levy, L. and Montgomery, K. Knowledge Gateways: the building blocks. *Information Processing and Management,* **24 (4),** 1988, pp. 458-468.

Herrstrom, D. and Massey, D. Hypertext in context. In: Barrett, E. (Ed.), *The Society of Text.* Cambridge, MA: MIT Press, 1989.

Hershey, W. Ideas Processors. *BYTE,* June 1985. p. 337.

Hershey, W. Guide. *BYTE,* **12 (11),** October 1987, pp. 244-246.

Hintzman, D. MINERVA 2: A simulation model of human memory. *Behaviour Research Methods, Instruments & Computers,* **16 (2),** pp. 96-101.

Hintzman, D. 'Schema abstraction' in a multiple-trace memory model. *Psychological Review,* **93,** pp. 411-28.

Hodges, M., Davis, B. and Sasnett, R. Investigations in multimedia design documentation. In: Barrett, E. (Ed.), *The Society of Text.* Cambridge, MA: MIT Press, 1989.

Howell. G. Hypertext meets interactive fiction. *Proceedings of Hypertext II,* University of York, June 29-30 1989.

Irish, P. and Trigg, R. Supporting collaboration in hypermedia: issues and experiences. In: Barrett, E. (Ed.), *The Society of Text.* Cambridge, MA: MIT Press, 1989. James, G. Artificial intelligence and automated publishing systems. In: Barrett, E. (Ed.) *Text, ConText and HyperText.* Cambridge, MA: MIT Press, 1988.

Johnson-Laird, P. *Mental Models.* Cambridge: Cambridge University Press, 1983.

Johnson-Laird, P. In: Johnson-Laird, P. and Wason, P. (Eds.) *Thinking: readings in cognitive science,* Cambridge University Press, 1977.

Jonassen, D. Semantic networking approaches to structuring hypertext. *Proceedings of Hypertext II,* University of York, June 29-30 1989.

Jones, W. How do we distinguish the hyper from the hype in non-linear text? In: Bullinger, H. and Schackel, B. (Eds.) *Human-Computer Interaction — INTERACT'87.* Elsevier Science Publishers B.V. (North-Holland), 1987.

Jones, W. and Dumais, S. The spatial metaphor for user interfaces: experimental tests of reference by location versus name. *ACM Transactions on Office Information Systems,* **4 (1),** January 1986, pp. 42-63.

Jones, M. and Myers, D. *Hands-on HyperCard.* NY: John Wiley and Sons, 1988.

Katz, B. Text processing with the START natural language system. In: Barrett, E. (Ed.) *Text, ConText and HyperText.* Cambridge, MA: MIT Press, 1988.

Kay, A. and Goldberg, A. personal dynamic media. *IEEE Computer,* **10 (3),** March 1977, pp. 31-41.

Kibby, M. and Mayes, J. Towards intelligent hypertext. In: McAleese, R. (Ed.) *Hypertext theory into practice,* pp. 164-172. Oxford: Intellect Books, 1989.

Kinnell, S. Comparing HyperCard and Guide. *Database,* **11 (3),** June 1988, pp. 49-54.

Kinnell, S. An online interface within a hypertext system: Project Jefferson's electronic notebook. *Online,* **13 (4),** July 1989, pp. 33-38.

Kinnell, S. Hypertext on the PC: Guide, Version 2.0. *Database,* **12 (4),** August 1989, pp. 62-64.

Kitza, W. *Inside HyperCard.* NY: Addison-Wesley, 1988.

Klein, J. and Cooper, D. Cognitive maps of decision-makers in a complex game. *Journal of the Operational Research Society,* **33 (1),** January 1982 pp. 63-72.

Knopik, T. and Ryser, S. AI-methods for structuring hypertext-information. *Proceedings of Hypertext II,* University of York, June 29-30 1989.

Knuth, D. Literate programming. *The Computer Journal,* **27 (2),** 1984, pp. 97-111.

Koh, T. and Chua, T. On the design of a frame-based hypermedia system. *Proceedings of Hypertext II,* University of York, June 29-30 1989.

Koved, L. and Shneiderman, B. Embedded menus: selecting items in context. *Communications of the ACM,* **29 (4),** April 1986, 312-318.

Lambert, S. and Ropieqet, S., (Eds.) *CD ROM, The New Papyrus* (Microsoft Press), Bellevue, Washington, 1986

Landauer, T. Tasks, text and functionality (symposium remarks). *Proceedings of Hypertext II,* University of York, June 29-30 1989.

Lasky, R. How Super is SuperCard? *BYTE,* **14 (10),** October 1989, pp. 217-218, 220.

Levine, L. Corporate culture, technical documentation, and organization diagnosis. In: Barrett, E. (Ed.) *Text, ConText and HyperText.* Cambridge, MA: MIT Press, 1988.

Lewis, B. and Hodges, J. Shared books: collaborative publication management for an office information system. In: Allen, R. (Ed.) *Proceedings of the Conference on Office Information Systems,* March 23-25 1988, Palo Alto, California. *ACM SIGOIS Bulletin,* **9 (2-3),** April and July 1988, pp. 197-204.

Lichtenstein, S., Fischoff, B. and Phillips, L. Calibration of probabilities: the state of the art to 1980. In: Kahneman, D., Slovic, P. and Tversky, A. (Eds.) *Judgement Under Uncertainty: Heuristics and Biases.* Cambridge University Press, 1982, pp. 306-334.

Lippincott, R. Beyond Hype. *BYTE,* **15 (2)**, February 1990, pp. 215-218.

McAleese, R. The graphical representation of knowledge as an interface to knowledge based systems. In: Bullinger, H. and Shackel, B. (Eds.) *Human-Computer Interaction — INTERACT'87,* pp. 1089-1093, Elsevier Science Publishers (North-Holland), 1987.

McAleese, R. (Ed.) *Hypertext theory into practice.* Oxford: Intellect Books, (1989).

McAleese, R. Navigation and browsing. In: McAleese, R. (Ed.) *Hypertext theory into practice,* pp. 6-44. Oxford: Intellect Books (1989).

McCracken, D. and Akscyn, R. Experiences with the ZOG human-computer interface. *International Journal of Man-Machine Studies,* **21 (2),** August 1984, pp. 293-310.

McClelland, B. Hypertext and online... a lot that's familiar. *Online,* **13 (1),** January 1989, pp. 20-25.

McKnight, C., Dillon, A. and Richardson, J. A comparison of linear and hypertext formats in information retrieval. *Proceedings of Hypertext II,* University of York, 29-30 June 1989.

McKnight, C., Richardson, J. and Dillon, A. The construction of hypertext documents and databases. *The Electronic Library,* **6 (5),** October 1988, pp. 338-342.

McKnight, C., Richardson, J. and Dillon, A. The authoring of hypertext documents. In: McAleese, R. (Ed.) *Hypertext theory into practice.* Oxford: Intellect Books (1989).

Marchionini, G. Making the transition from print to electronic encyclopedias: adaptation of mental models. *International Journal of Man-Machine Studies,* **30 (6),** June 1989, pp. 591-618.

Marchionini, G. and Shneiderman, B. Finding facts vs. browsing knowledge in hypertext systems. *IEEE Computer,* **21 (1),** January 1988, pp. 70-80.

Meyrowitz, N. The missing link: why we're all doing hypertext wrong. In: Barrett, E. (Ed.), *The Society of Text.* Cambridge, MA: MIT Press, 1989.

Miller, G. The magical number seven, plus or minus two: some limits on our capacity for processing information. *Psychological Review,* **60,** 1956, pp. 81-97.

Miller, P. *Expert Critiquing Systems: practice based medical consultation by computer.* Springer Verlag, 1987.

Minsky, M. A framework for representing knowledge. In: Winston, P. (Ed.), The psychology of computer vision. NY: McGraw-Hill, 1975.

Monk. A. Getting to known locations in a hypertext. *Proceedings of Hypertext II,* University of York, 29-30 June 1989.

Monk, A. The Personal Browser: a tool for directed navigation in hypertext systems. *Interacting with Computers, The Interdisciplinary Journal of Human-Computer Interaction,* **1 (2),** August 1989, pp. 191-196.

Monk, A., Walsh, P. and Dix, A. A comparison of hypertext, scrolling and folding as mechanisms for program browsing. In: Jones, D. and Winder, R. (Eds.) *People and Computers IV.* Cambridge University Press, pp. 421-435, 1988.

Morrison, A. Hypertext and expert systems — experiences and prospects. *Proceedings of the Fifth International Expert Systems Conference,* 6 June 1989.

Motta, E., Eisenstadt, M., Pitman, K. and West, M. Support for knowledge acquisition in the Knowledge Engineer's Assistant (KEATS). *Expert Systems, 5 (1),* February 1988, pp. 6-27.

Nelson, T. *Literary Machines.* Swathmore, PA: Nelson (1981); (see note).

Nelson, T. Managing immense storage. *BYTE,* **13 (1)** January 1988, pp. 225-238.

Niblett, T. and van Hoff, A. Structured hypertext documents via SGML. *Proceedings of Hypertext II,* University of York, 29-30 June 1989.

Nicolson, R. Towards the third generation: the case of IKBH (Intelligent Knowledge Based Hypermedia) environments. *Proceedings of Hypertext II,* University of York, June 29-30 1989.

Nielson, J. Hypertext Bibliography. *Hypermedia,* **1 (1),** Spring 1989, pp. 74-91.

Nielson, J. and Lyngbaek, U. Two field studies of hypermedia usability. *Proceedings of Hypertext II,* University of York, 29-30 June 1989.

Nieuwenhuysen, P. Criteria for the evaluation of text storage and text retrieval software. *The Electronic Library,* **6 (3),** June 1988, pp. 160-166.

Northwood, J. Links to the past? *Personal Computing (UK),* March 1990, pp.110-112.

Oatley, K. Inference, navigation and cognitive maps. In: In Johnson-Laird, P. and Wason, P. (Eds.) *Thinking: readings in cognitive science.* Cambridge University Press, 1977.

O'Connor, B. Access to moving image documents: background concepts and proposals for surrogates for film and video works. *Journal of Documentation,* **41 (4),** 1985, pp. 209-220.

Oxborrow, E. *Databases and Database Systems.* Chartwell-Bratt, 1986.

Parsaye, K. et al. *Intelligent Databases — Object-oriented, deductive hypermedia technologies.* John Wiley and Sons, 1989.

Poole, L. *HyperTalk.* Microsoft Press, 1988.

Porat, M. Global implications of the information society. *Journal of Communication (University of Pennsylvania Press),* Winter 1978, pp. 70-80.

Potter, W. and Trueblood, R. Traditional, semantic, and hyper-semantic approaches to data-modelling. *IEEE Computer,* **21 (6),** June 1988, pp. 53-66.

Price, J. Creating a style for online help. In: Barrett, E. (Ed.) *Text, ConText and HyperText.* Cambridge, MA: MIT Press, 1988.

Rahtz, S., Carr, L. and Hall, W. Creating multimedia documents: hypertext-processing. *Proceedings of Hypertext II,* University of York, 29-30 June 1989.

Raymond, D. and Tompa, F. Hypertext and the Oxford English Dictionary. *Communications of the ACM,* **31 (7),** July 1988, pp. 871-879.

Rheinhart, A. Desktop manager with hypertext power. *BYTE,* **14 (7),** July 1989, pp. 90, 92.

Rich, E. *Artificial Intelligence.* NY: McGraw-Hill, 1983.

Robinson, P. The four multimedia gospels. *BYTE,* **15 (2),** February 1990, pp. 203-212.

Rubens, P. Online information, hypermedia, and the idea of literacy. In: Barrett, E. (Ed.), *The Society of Text.* Cambridge, MA: MIT Press, 1989.

Rubens, P. and Krull R. Designing online information. In: Barrett, E. (Ed.) *Text, ConText and HyperText.* Cambridge, MA: MIT Press, 1988.

Rumelhart, D. and McClelland, J. (1986). *Brainy Minds: a critical review of Parallel Distributed Processing (Vols. 1 and 2),* Cambridge, MA: MIT Press.

Salton, G. Another look at automatic text-retrieval systems. *Communications of the ACM,* **29 (7),** July 1986, pp. 648-656.

Salton, G. *Automatic Text Processing*. Addison-Wesley, 1989.

Salton, G. and Buckley, C. Term-weighting approaches in automatic text retrieval. *Information Processing and Management*, **24 (5)**, 1988, pp. 513-523.

Savoy, J. The electronic book Ebook3. *International Journal of Man-Machine Studies*, **30 (5)**, May 1989, pp. 505-523.

Schank, R. and Abelson, R. *Scripts, plans, goals and understanding*. Hillsdale, NJ: Erlbaum, 1977.

Seabrook, R. and Shneiderman, B. The user interface in a hypertext multiwindow program browser. *Interacting with Computers, The Interdisciplinary Journal of Human-Computer Interaction*, **1 (3)**, December 1989, pp. 299-337.

Shetler, T. Birth of the BLOB. *BYTE*, **15 (2)**, February 1990, pp. 221-226.

Shirk, H. Technical writers as computer scientists: the challenges of online documentation. In: Barrett, E. (Ed.) *Text, ConText and HyperText*. Cambridge, MA: MIT Press, 1988.

Shneiderman, B. *Designing the User Interface: Strategies for Effective Human Computer Interaction*. Reading, MA: Addison-Wesley, 1987.

Shneiderman, B. Reflections on authoring, editing and managing hypertext. In: Barrett, E. (Ed.), *The Society of Text*. Cambridge, MA: MIT Press, 1989.

Shneiderman, B. and Morariu, J. *The interactive encyclopaedia system (TIES)*. Dept. of Computer Science, University of Maryland, College Park, Maryland, June, 1986.

Siegel, R. and White, T. The development of spatial representations of large-scale environments. In: Reese, H. (Ed.) *Advances in Child Development and Behaviour*, **10,** NY: Academic Press, 1975.

Simpson, A. and McKnight, C. Navigation in hypertext. *Proceedings of Hypertext II*, University of York, June 29-30 1989.

Slatin, J. Hypertext and the teaching of writing. In: Barrett, E. (Ed.) *Text, ConText and HyperText*. Cambridge, MA: MIT Press, 1988.

Sloman, A. Research and development in expert systems. In: Bramer, M. (Ed.) *Proceedings of the Fourth Technical Conference of the British Computer Society Specialist Group on Expert Systems*, University of Warwick, 18-20 December, 1984. Cambridge University Press.

Smart Card storage technologies — Technical Notes (unattributed). *The Electronic Library*, **6 (6),** December 1988, pp. 432-438.

Smith, K. Hypertext — linking to the future. *Online,* **12 (2),** March 1988, pp. 32-40.

Stanton, N. and Stammers, R. Learning styles in a non-linear training environment. *Proceedings of Hypertext II,* University of York, June 29-30 1989.

Stark. H. What do readers do to pop-ups, and pop-ups do to readers? *Proceedings of Hypertext II,* University of York, June 29-30 1989.

Stefanac, S. On beyond HyperCard. *MacWorld (UK),* July 1989, pp. 12-14.

Stefanac, S. SuperCard 1.0. *MacWorld (UK),* October 1989, pp. 125, 129, 133.

Stefik, M., Foster, D., Bobrow, K., Kahn, K., Lanning, S. and Suchman, L. Beyond the chalkboard: using computers to support collaboration and problem solving in meetings. *Communications of the ACM,* **30 (1),** January 1987.

Stepno, B. A HyperCard for the PC. *BYTE,* **14 (9),** September 1989, pp. 189-190, 192.

Storrs, G. The Alvey DHSS Large Demonstrator Project Knowledge ANalysis Tool: KANT. In: McAleese, R. (Ed.), *Hypertext theory into practice.* Oxford: Intellect Books Limited, 1989.

Stotts, P. and Furuta, R. Petri-Net-based hypertext: document structure with browsing semantics. *ACM Transactions on Information Systems,* **7 (1),** January 1989, pp. 3-29.

Sullivan, P. Writers as total desktop publishers: developing a conceptual approach to training. In: Barrett, E. (Ed.) *Text, ConText and HyperText.* Cambridge, MA: MIT Press, 1988.

Tebbutt, D. Screentest: Guide. *Personal Computer World,* June 1988.

Tebbutt, D. Screentest: Web. *Personal Computer World,* October 1989.

Thimbleby, H. Experiences of 'literate programming' using CWEB (a variant of Knuth's WEB). *The Computer Journal,* **29 (3),** pp. 201-211.

Thomas, D. What's in an object. *BYTE,* **14 (3),** March 1989, pp. 231-240.

Thomas, P. and Norman, M. Interacting with hypertext: functional simplicity without conversational competence. *Proceedings of Hypertext II,* University of York, June 29-30 1989.

Thompson, R. and Croft, W. Support for browsing in an intelligent text retrieval system. *International Journal of Man-Machine Studies,* **30 (6),** June 1989. pp. 639-668.

Toffler, A. *The Third Wave.* NY: William Morrow, 1980.

Tompa, F. A data model for flexible hypertext database systems. *ACM Transactions on Information Systems,* **7 (1),** January 1989, pp. 85-100.

Trigg, R. Guided tours and tabletops: tools for communicating in a hypertext environment. *ACM Transactions on Office Systems,* **6 (4),** October 1988, pp. 398-414.

Trigg, R. and Suchman, L. Collaborative writing in NoteCards. In: McAleese, R. (Ed.), *Hypertext theory into practice.* Oxford: Intellect Books Limited, 1989.

Trigg, R., Suchman, L. and Halasz, F. Supporting collaboration in NoteCards. *Proceedings of the Conference on Computer Supported Cooperative Work,* Austin, TX, December 3-5 1986.

Trigg, R. and Weiser, M. TEXTNET: a network-based approach to text handling. *ACM Transactions on Office Information Systems,* **4 (1),** January 1986. pp. 1-23.

Tulving, E. and Thompson, D. Encoding specificity and retrieval processes in episodic memory. *Psychological Review,* **80,** 1973, pp. 352-373.

Van Dam, A. Hypertext '87 keynote address. *Communications of the ACM,* **31 (7),** July 1988, pp. 887-895.

Vicente, K. and Williges, R. Accommodating individual differences in searching a hierarchical file system. *International Journal of Man-Machine Studies,* **29,** 1988, pp. 647-668.

Walker. J. Supporting document development with Concordia. *IEEE Computer,* **21 (1),** January 1988, pp. 48-59.

Walker, M. Framed documents. *Desktop Publishing Today,* **4 (5),** May 1989. pp. 36-37.

Walter, M. IRIS Intermedia: pushing the boundaries of hypertext. The *Seybold Report on Publishing Systems,* **18 (21),** August 1989, pp. 21-32.

Weiss, E. Usability: stereotypes and traps. In: Barrett, E. (Ed.) *Text, ConText and HyperText.* Cambridge, MA: MIT Press, 1988.

Wesley, M. A guide to Guide. *MacUser,* January 1988, pp. 126-132.

Weyer, S. The design of a dynamic book for information search. *International Journal of Man-Machine Studies,* **17 (10),** July 1982, pp. 87-107.

Weyer, S. Questing for the ''Dao'': Dowquest and intelligent text retrieval. *Online,* **13 (5),** September 1989, pp. 39-48.

Weyer, S. and Borning, A. A prototype electronic encyclopaedia. *ACM Transactions on Office Information Systems*, **3 (1)**, January 1985, pp. 63-88.

Wight, T. Annotation — a new metaphor for hypertext. *Proceedings of Hypertext II*, University of York, June 29-30 1989.

Willett, P. Recent trends in hierarchic document clustering: a critical review. *Information Processing and Management*, **24 (5)**, 1988, pp. 577-597.

Williams, G. First Impressions: HyperCard. *BYTE,* **12 (4),** December 1987 pp. 109-117.

Winograd, T. *Understanding Natural Language.* New York: Academic Press, 1972.

Winograd, T. Frame representation and the declarative-procedural controversy. In: Bobrow, D. and Collins, A. (Eds.), *Representation and Understanding,* NY: Academic Press, 1975.

Woodhead, N. Master's Dissertation, Polytechnic of the South Bank, London, 1989 (unpublished).

Woods, W. What's in a link: foundations for semantic networks. In: Bobrow, D. and Collins, A. (Eds), *Representation and Understanding.* NY: Academic Press, 1975.

Wright, P. and Lickorish, A. An empirical study of two navigation systems for two hypertexts. *Proceedings of Hypertext II,* University of York, June 29-30 1989.

Yankelovich, N., Meyrowitz, N., and Van Dam, A. Reading and writing the electronic book. *IEEE Computer,* **18 (10),** October, 1985, pp. 15-30.

Yankelovich, N., Haan, B., Meyrovitz, N. and Drucker, S. Intermedia: the concept and the construction of a seamless information environment. *IEEE Computer,* **21 (1),** January 1988, pp. 81-96.

Younggren, G. Using an object-oriented programming language to create audience-driven hypermedia environments. In: Barrett, E. (Ed.) *Text, ConText and HyperText.* Cambridge, MA: MIT Press, 1988.

Zimmerman, M. Are writers obsolete in the computer industry. In: Barrett, E. (Ed.) *Text, ConText and HyperText.* Cambridge, MA: MIT Press, 1988.

Zimmerman, M. Reconstruction of a profession: new roles for technical writers in the computer industry. In: Barrett, E. (Ed.), *The Society of Text.* Cambridge, MA: MIT Press, 1989.

Index